History of Eastern Europe

A Captivating Guide to a Shortened History of Russia, Ukraine, Hungary, Poland, the Czech Republic, Bulgaria, Slovakia, Moldova, Belarus, and Romania

Free Bonus from Captivating History (Available for a Limited time)

Hi History Lovers!

Now you have a chance to join our exclusive history list so you can get your first history ebook for free as well as discounts and a potential to get more history books for free! Simply visit the link below to join.

Captivatinghistory.com/ebook

Also, make sure to follow us on Facebook, Twitter and Youtube by searching for Captivating History.

Contents

Introduction

When you think of a European country, what comes to mind? Is it France? Germany? England?

How about Slovakia or Romania? The Czech Republic?

Most people know a few details about Eastern European history. But how can that be? Eastern Europeans have made many contributions to popular culture.[1] Many famous scientists, writers, and artists claim Eastern European origin.[2] For example, Andy Warhol was a first-generation American with immigrant parents from modern-day Slovakia.[3] Franz Liszt, the famous pianist of the Romantic period, was born in Hungary.[4]

---

[1] Francis Tapon. "Eastern Europe: Innovation's Hidden Hub." *The Washington Post.* December 28, 2011.

[2] Tomek Jankowski. *Eastern Europe! Everything You Need to Know About the History (and More) of a Region that Shaped Our World and Still Does.* Kindle edition. Williamstown, Massachusetts: New Europe Books, 2013, pg. 10.

[3] Jankowski, *Eastern Europe!*, 2015, pg. 10; "Andy Warhol." *The Andy Warhol Museum.* https://www.warhol.org/andy-warhols-life/

[4] "Franz Liszt." *BIOGRAPHY.* Updated April 27, 2020. Original April 27, 2017. https://www.biography.com/musician/franz-liszt

Science and technology seem to be Eastern Europe's key to success.[5] Gregor Mendel—the founder of genetics—was from the Czech Republic.[6] Tetris comes from Russia, and so does one of the founders of Google.[7] Skype came from Estonia. And did you know that a Hungarian invented the Rubik's Cube?[8] If these inventions came from Eastern Europe, then why don't we know more about it?

Since the ancient period, the region's borders have grown and shrunk, only to grow and shrink again.[9] It was often the buffer zone between expanding empires, its identity in limbo at the whims of its more powerful neighbors. Western countries like England, France, and Germany might dominate Europe, but Eastern Europe has a rich and vibrant history filled with fascinating characters, extraordinary events, and sweeping tides of change.[10]

The reader should know that this is not a full, comprehensive history. We've collected the most fascinating tales from Eastern European history as an introduction to this intriguing subject. We hope you'll do more research on your own. From the Romans and the Byzantines to the fall of the Soviet Union, the history of Eastern Europe reads like a dramatic tale, and it is one that we can't wait to share with you.

[5] Tapon, "Eastern Europe: Innovation's Hidden Hub," 2011.

[6] Jankowski, *Eastern Europe!*, 2015, pg. 301.

[7] Tapon, "Eastern Europe: Innovation's Hidden Hub," 2011.

[8] Jankowski, *Eastern Europe!*, 2015, pg. 10.

[9] Ibid., pg. 13.

[10] Ibid., pg. 10.

Chapter 1 – Where is Eastern Europe?

Many people might have trouble pointing out an Eastern European country on a map. Their idea of Europe is limited to Western Europe, which is home to global powerhouses like Great Britain, France, and Germany. Between Western Europe and Asia lies Eastern Europe—a region with fascinating histories and thriving cultures. So, why is it so difficult to conjure up ideas of Eastern Europe?

The idea of "Eastern Europe" is actually a modern concept.[11] Western Europeans considered themselves more politically and culturally evolved than their neighbors, and they created the term to draw a metaphoric border between the two regions.[12] Although the separation wasn't an official legal or political barrier, the natural comparison between the West and East illustrated the point.[13] It

---

[11] Ibid., pg. 13.

[12] Jankowski, *Eastern Europe!*, Kindle edition, 2015, pg. 10-13; Professor Vejas Gabriel Liulevicius. "The Other Europe: Deep Roots of Diversity." Lecture 1. *The Great Courses: A History of Eastern Europe.* Chantilly, VA: The Teaching Company, 2015.

[13] Liulevicius, "The Other Europe." Lecture 1. *The Great Courses: A History of Eastern Europe*, 2015.

still classified Eastern Europe as the "other," the less sophisticated nations of the continent.[14]

That isn't the only reason Eastern Europe is hard to define. The region has always been a neutral zone between the world's greatest empires. At any point in history, Eastern Europe was surrounded by or occupied by the Roman, Byzantine, Ottoman, Russian, German, and Habsburg empires, just to name a few.[15] These empires were often in conflict, and they aired out their grievances on Eastern European soil. As a result, the region's borders constantly changed throughout most of its history.[16] On several occasions, it tried to break free of the shackles of its powerful neighbors, with varying degrees of success and failure.

Despite Western attempts to lump them into a one-size-fits-all box, the countries of Eastern Europe have unique histories that make up a part of who the Eastern Europeans are. For example, Polish history is different from the Czech experience. Hungarian history is different from Romanian history. Yet, there are several themes throughout the region's history that unite the Eastern European experience as a common one.

---

[14] Jankowski, *Eastern Europe!*, Kindle edition, 2015, pg. 13; Liulevicius, "The Other Europe." Lecture 1. *The Great Courses: A History of Eastern Europe*, 2015.

[15] Liulevicius, "The Other Europe." Lecture 1. *The Great Courses: A History of Eastern Europe*, 2015.

[16] Jankowski, *Eastern Europe!*, 2015, pg. 13.

A physical map of Europe. (Pixnio.com)

Where Exactly is Eastern Europe?

Defining Eastern Europe is not as easy as circling a region on a map.[17] History, economics, and culture are all elements that define a nation, let alone a region. However, considering the map above, Eastern Europe seems easier to locate when compared to the whole of Europe. Generally, Eastern Europe is considered to be the region between Western Europe and Asia. However, Eastern Europe has its own political and geographical limits that play a crucial role in its history.

---

[17] Liulevicius, "The Other Europe." Lecture 1. *The Great Courses: A History of Eastern Europe*, 2015.

According to the map above, the division between Western Europe and Eastern Europe is clearly visible. Western Europe is defined by powerhouses like the United Kingdom, France, Germany, Spain, and Italy. These countries are also much larger than countries one generally finds to the east.

East of Western Europe is a collection of smaller states, with a few larger ones mixed in. This book will attempt to lay out the major differences and similarities that define Eastern Europe, but it is important to know what countries and landmarks are considered "Eastern."

The eastern border of Germany and Italy draws an imaginary line between what is considered Western Europe and Eastern Europe. From north to south, the region is blocked in from Scandinavia to Greece. The Baltic Sea makes up the northwestern limits, while the Adriatic Sea, the Aegean Sea, and the Black Sea make a "U" around the southern limits. Some may think that the eastern border of Eastern Europe may lie at Russia, that Russia is a region unto itself, but this country has had such an impact on Eastern European history that it can't be considered anything but Eastern European.

What about the spaces in between? Eastern Europe is its own region, yet it has subregions within it. Beginning in the north, the Baltic states lie to the east of the Baltic Sea. These include Estonia, Latvia, and Lithuania. Moving to the south are the Central Eastern European states: Poland, Belarus, Ukraine, the Czech Republic, Slovakia, Austria, and Hungary. Poland's borders have changed throughout its history, as it was a battleground for the empires that surrounded it. The Czech Republic and Slovakia came from Czechoslovakia, just as Austria and Hungary were part of the Austro-Hungarian Empire. The Austro-Hungarian Empire, the center of the Habsburg dynasty, would become a major player in Eastern European history.

Central Eastern Europe lies between the Baltic states and Southeastern Europe. Southeastern Europe includes the Balkan Peninsula, which is usually referred to as the Balkans. The southern borders of Austria, Hungary, and Ukraine form the northernmost limits of Southeastern Europe. From north to south, this region includes Moldova, Romania, Serbia, Slovenia, Croatia, Bosnia and Herzegovina, Montenegro, Albania, Kosovo, North Macedonia, Bulgaria, and Greece.

Eastern European Geography

If geography makes a region, then Eastern Europe has it all. The characteristics of the land in Eastern Europe, from vast plains to rugged mountains, have contributed to its history. It brought people groups into the region, and it isolated trade centers to certain areas. The areas of Eastern Europe that are easy to travel became the path where migrations took place. People moved into the area, and while some stayed, others moved on toward Western Europe.

Stretching from the Ural Mountains west to the Atlantic coast of France, the Great Northern European Plain is a vast lowland that is easy to travel. Extending from the Baltic Sea to the Carpathian Mountains, the plain has little in the way of geography. The Great Northern European Plain was a highway for the migration of peoples and ideas, which affected Eastern European development, for better or for worse.[18] The plain is a flat expanse of land with little mountains or hills.[19] There are enough water sources to support mass migrations and a thriving trade economy—or an invading army.

---

[18] Liulevicius, "Formative Migrations: Mongols to Germans." Lecture 2. *The Great Courses: A History of Eastern Europe*, 2015.

[19] Liulevicius, "The Other Europe." Lecture 1. *The Great Courses: A History of Eastern Europe*, 2015; Jankowski, *Eastern Europe!*, 2015, pg. 55-56.

The Carpathian Basin is another plain in Eastern Europe that saw much activity throughout Eastern European history. Located between the Alps and the Carpathian Mountains, it is a green flatland that would support travel animals with protection from the mountains. It became a well-traveled path on the way into Western Europe. Not all migrants using the Carpathian Basin had well-meaning intentions, as nomadic invaders often used this pass while traveling west.

The Balkans are the gateway into Europe from Asia. These lands between the Black Sea and the Adriatic Sea have been in use since the prehistoric era. Named after the Balkan Mountains of Bulgaria, it is a rugged landmass with plenty of mountain passes to support foot traffic. It became a thoroughfare for merchants, bringing Middle Eastern and Asian goods into Europe.

A map of Eastern Europe, 2009. (Public Domain)

From Central Asia to Europe, the Eurasian Steppe was used by nomadic horsemen traveling along the Eurasian landmass.[20] With flatlands without many forests, the steppe was perfect for invading nomads, like the Scythians, Mongols, and Huns, to move into Europe. This flat landmass stretched along the southern edge of the Russian and Siberian borders, including the territories of Kazakhstan and Mongolia, all the way to the western side of the Black Sea.[21] Large groups of people used the steppe all at once, allowing the barbarians to settle in Western Europe by way of Eastern Europe. Since 1000 BCE, the steppe was a migration highway, facilitating the "massive and almost constant westward flow of humanity across Eurasia, scraping and grinding like a vast human glacier past all the great civilizations—China, Central Asia, India, Persia, the Middle East, Byzantium—before finally depositing them abruptly (and violently) at the end of the steppe in Europe, in the Carpathian Basin, the Great Northern European Plain, or the Balkans."[22]

Geography played a vital role in the development of Eastern Europe.[23] It determined who migrated to the area and when they did. While the plains supported movement en masse, Eastern Europe's mountain ranges protected some areas. This determined whether an invasion or a migration would be successful. Eastern Europe's geography also facilitated trade, bringing Eastern luxuries to Western consumers. Most importantly, the flow of knowledge and technology, which generally moved from east to west, moved through the eastern half of Europe first before arriving in Western Europe.

---

[20] Jankowski, *Eastern Europe!*, 2015, pg. 58, 127.

[21] Ibid., pg. 127-129.

[22] Ibid., pg. 129.

[23] Ibid., pg. 89.

Eastern European Diversity and Changing Political Borders

Eastern Europe is one of the most ethnically diverse places in the world, more so than Western European countries. It was a region constantly traveled, with people introducing new religions, cultures, and languages. This ethnic and cultural diversity was both a blessing and a curse.

As the bridge between Europe and Asia, Eastern Europe was the center of conflicts.[24] Too often throughout its history, Eastern Europe was what outsiders said it was.[25] To the neighboring empires fighting over these crucial lands, it was something to tame and control. Today, what is Eastern Europe is the legacy of 1989 and the fall of communism. This was yet another example of world events dictating where the limits of Eastern Europe began and ended.

Why didn't Eastern Europe build strong centralized states as Western Europe did? On the whole, all of Europe—not just the East—didn't develop its statehood as quickly as other empires.[26] Western Europe still had clear-cut borders and spheres of influence long before Eastern Europe. However, Eastern Europe had one thing that the West didn't have—it was home to a greater number of ethnic groups.[27]

---

[24] Liulevicius, "The Other Europe." Lecture 1. *The Great Courses: A History of Eastern Europe*, 2015.

[25] Jankowski, *Eastern Europe!*, 2015, pg. 13.

[26] Ibid., pg. 27.

[27] Jankowski, *Eastern Europe!*, 2015, pg. 5; Liulevicius, "The Other Europe." Lecture 1. *The Great Courses: A History of Eastern Europe*, 2015.

Eastern Europe has a diverse collection of ethnic groups, all of whom made their way into the area at different times throughout its history.[28] We will meet them all over the course of this book. The Slavs, Bulgars, Mongols, Germanic tribes, Magyars, Turks, Jews, and the Roma all made Eastern Europe their home.

Since Western Europe had a less diverse population, it was able to centralize quickly. Eastern Europe's constantly changing jurisdictions never clearly defined who ethnic groups were and how they were different from each other.[29] This made it difficult to centralize, making the region less stable compared to its neighbors. Overall, the nations of Western Europe, while chaotic in their own right, had a much easier time securing self-rule and keeping it than Eastern Europeans.[30]

With the constantly changing borders in Eastern Europe, each individual country went through its own phases of foreign control or independence. This ebb and flow characterizes the region's experience.[31] Since the beginning, the larger states of Eastern Europe have attempted to shore up their own power by subjugating their neighbors. The empires of Europe tried to create their own spheres of influence by controlling other territories physically through methods such as invasion and war or economically through tribute or trade restrictions. The peoples under pressure from larger empires either resisted foreign domination or learned how to coexist with the people who wanted to subjugate them in order to keep their autonomy. At any one time throughout Eastern European history, a state enjoyed its independence before it was conquered by its neighbors. It endured foreign rule until it fought for its independence.

---

[28] Liulevicius, "The Other Europe." Lecture 1. *The Great Courses: A History of Eastern Europe*, 2015.

[29] Jankowski, *Eastern Europe!*, 2015, pg. 15.

[30] Ibid., pg. 90.

[31] Jankowski, *Eastern Europe!*, 2015, pg. 93; Liulevicius, "The Other Europe." Lecture 1. *The Great Courses: A History of Eastern Europe*, 2015.

During the High Middle Ages, there were several successful states in Eastern Europe that ruled themselves without foreign interference. For this reason, the medieval period is considered the golden age of Eastern European nations. By the 17th century, many of the smaller independent states in Eastern Europe fell to their larger neighbors. They were now under foreign control, mostly by external powers, but in some cases, there were Eastern European states conquering other Eastern European states.

Let's look at a few examples. Generally, all Eastern European nations had their own unique experience with self-rule, while the region as a whole experienced foreign interference.[32] For example, Lithuania experienced a long period of independence until the 17th century. After a century of foreign interference, it lost its independence entirely by the mid-18th century. It regained its independence, only to lose it again in the 20th century. Russia has more or less ruled itself since the 17th century, but it was ruled by others for a few hundred years before that. Another great example is that of Transylvania. At first, it was a Roman territory, and then it became part of Hungary. Transylvania became a land engaged in a tug-of-war between the Habsburgs and the Ottomans, with both empires leaving their lasting mark on the area. After World War I, it became part of Romania and then transferred back to Hungarian hands during World War II. Postwar Transylvania returned to Romanian control.

Periods of self-rule in Eastern Europe represent long-disappeared ancient and medieval states that helped form the political borders and cultural identities of today. From the end of the 800s to the early 1200s, ancient Rus was located in the northeast, occupying Ukraine and Belarus, as well as parts of Russia. The name "Russia" comes from this medieval powerhouse. When it fell in the 13th century, its legacy became the countries that

---

[32] Jankowski, *Eastern Europe!*, 2015, pg. 90; Liulevicius, "The Other Europe." Lecture 1. *The Great Courses: A History of Eastern Europe*, 2015.

are there today. At the height of the Middle Ages into the Renaissance, Romania controlled its own destiny as Wallachia.

Weak political organization has defined the experiences of Eastern European nations. In the 20th century alone, every nation experienced war, invasion, rebellion, and independence.[33] Among changing allegiances, people were also forced to accept the changing status of the nation and their own place within it.

Eastern Europe's Diverse Languages

Surprisingly, despite the differences in Eastern Europe's population, the region's many languages all come from one source.[34] The most popular theory is the Kurgan hypothesis, which states the spread of languages took place during the Neolithic Age (ca. 10,000–4,500 BCE).[35] In the 5th millennium BCE, the Kurgan people migrated west into Eastern Europe from Anatolia (in present-day Turkey) and later made their way into Western Europe.

The Kurgans spoke Proto-Indo-European, the ancestor language of the Indo-European language family that is spoken across the world today.[36] As they spread into parts of the Middle East and Europe, their languages changed with their new environment. In fact, there are very few languages spoken by Europeans today that aren't related to the Indo-European language family.[37]

[33] Jankowski, *Eastern Europe!*, 2015, pg. 25; Liulevicius, "The Other Europe." Lecture 1. *The Great Courses: A History of Eastern Europe*, 2015.

[34] Jankowski, *Eastern Europe!*, 2015, pg. 35.

[35] Simon Jenkins. *A Short History of Europe: From Pericles to Putin*. New York: Public Affairs, 2019, pg. 8; Jankowski, *Eastern Europe!*, 2015, pg. 35-36.

[36] Jankowski, *Eastern Europe!*, 2015, pg. 36.

[37] Ibid., pg. 38.

The accepted area where the Kurgans lived before moving into Europe is labeled in dark green on the map. It spreads from north of the Black Sea to the north of the Caspian Sea, making up parts of modern-day Kazakhstan, Russia, Ukraine, Moldova, and Romania. In light green, the map shows the spread of the Indo-European languages that came from the Kurgans. (Credit: Joe Roe, 2016)

Some descendants of the Indo-European language, such as the Slavic languages, the Baltic languages, the Finno-Ugric languages, and Romance languages, are all still spoken in Eastern Europe today.[38] The good news is, if you speak one Slavic language, you can get by in another.[39] The Slavic languages come from the Slavs, an ethnic group that settled in Eastern Europe. There are three main Slavic language groups that are still spoken today: Western Slavic, Southern Slavic, and Eastern Slavic. The differences between Slavic languages break down into geographical areas based on where they are spoken.

---

[38] Ibid., pg. 36-47.

[39] Ibid., pg. 40-41.

The West Slavs (who speak Western Slavic languages) settled in Slovakia, Poland, and the Czech Republic.[40] To the northeast, the East Slavs occupied the territory that became the countries of Belarus, Russia, and Ukraine. These countries, which are descended from the medieval state of Kievan Rus, speak Eastern Slavic languages. Finally, the bulk of the Balkan Peninsula was settled by the South Slavs. The Slavic languages spoken in Slovenia, Croatia, Bosnia and Herzegovina, Montenegro, Serbia, North Macedonia, and Bulgaria are South Slavic languages.

While each language group is distinct, each adopted several influences from its history as a hotly contested area, including many Greek words and phrases.[41] The Slavic language group uses two different alphabets: the Latin alphabet and the Cyrillic alphabet. Cyrillic is an alphabet that only Slavic languages use, so you won't use it when speaking English or Spanish!

The Baltic languages are a little different.[42] They used to be spoken across the Baltic region, but today, only Latvian and Lithuanian are considered Baltic languages. These two languages are most likely the closest to the original language spoken by the Proto-Indo-Europeans.

Did you know that Romanian is actually a Romance language, just like French and Italian?[43] Romanian actually has Latin and Slavic elements.[44] The Dacians, who descended from the Illyrians and Thracians who lived in the Balkans before the Romans arrived, added Slavic contributions to the Romanian language,

---

[40] Jankowski, *Eastern Europe!*, 2015, pg. 41-42; Liulevicius, "Formative Migrations: Mongols to Germans." Lecture 2. *The Great Courses: A History of Eastern Europe*, 2015.

[41] Jankowski, *Eastern Europe!*, 2015, pg. 41-42.

[42] Ibid., pg. 43.

[43] Jankowski, *Eastern Europe!*, 2015, pg. 37, 41; Liulevicius, "The Other Europe." Lecture 1. *The Great Courses: A History of Eastern Europe*, 2015.

[44] Jankowski, *Eastern Europe!*, 2015, pg. 44.

making it just as much a Western European language as an Eastern European one.

The Finno-Ugric language family holds just as much weight in Eastern Europe as the Slavic and Baltic languages. It is actually two language families that merged with migrations from the Russian Ural Mountains into Central Europe between the Baltic and the Black Seas.

Of course, we can't forget the contributions of the Semitic languages: Yiddish and Hebrew.[45] Yiddish itself has Slavic elements. Ladino, spoken by Sephardic Jews, remains a spoken language in modern-day Bulgaria. The Ottoman Empire allowed European Jews safe passage as they left the Iberian Peninsula during the Reconquista. They became major players in commerce in the Balkans.

While Eastern Europe hosts a multitude of languages, it isn't as easy as saying that Russian is spoken in Russia or that Czech is only spoken in the Czech Republic. The constant shifting political borders and growing and shrinking states that have plagued Eastern Europe since the beginning of its history led to languages being spoken outside of their original states. After World War II, Eastern European states attempted to eliminate all ethnicities that were considered "outsiders" to their new state boundaries. Despite the multiple languages that exist throughout Eastern Europe, each nation is not as multilingual as it could have been.

Religion

One predominant layer to the conflict that defines Eastern European history is the battle over religion.[46] Christianity, Judaism, and Islam all attempted to coexist at one time or another. Eastern

---

[45] Jankowski, *Eastern Europe!*, 2015, pg. 47; Liulevicius, "The Other Europe." Lecture 1. *The Great Courses: A History of Eastern Europe*, 2015.

[46] Jankowski, *Eastern Europe!*, 2015, pg. 66-68; Liulevicius, "The Other Europe." Lecture 1. *The Great Courses: A History of Eastern Europe*, 2015.

Europe became a battleground for the conflicting forces between Western Christianity and Eastern Orthodox Christianity.

In many Eastern European countries, the introduction of Christianity marks an important milestone in its statehood.[47] Some don't consider themselves truly united as a nation before its people were converted. This shows the power that the church wielded over Europe and the importance that Eastern Europeans placed on their religious lives.

Eastern Europe was the target of a mass Christianization effort, which was led by priests from both the Western Church and Eastern Orthodoxy. Conversion was a religious effort as well as a political one. Religious officials convinced kings to convert to Christianity so the rest of the population would follow. Far too often throughout history, Eastern European rulers earned political legitimacy through their affiliation with the church.[48] Many of the early kings of Eastern Europe were sainted, demonstrating the connection between politics and religion.

Missionaries often came to blows with Eastern European heads of state over the matter of religion.[49] Those kings who were hesitant to convert or flat-out refused altogether were threatened with invasion and war. Each Christian sect— the East and the West—had its own kingdom that supported its cause. Since Constantinople was the center of the Byzantine Empire and Eastern Orthodoxy, it provided its armies to support its religious cause. In the West, the Franks were the representatives of Western Christianity.

Later in the medieval period, Eastern Europe would become one of the centers of conflict during the Protestant Reformation.[50] Before there was Martin Luther, there was Jan Hus. Long before

---

[47] Jankowski, *Eastern Europe!*, 2015, pg. 70.

[48] Liulevicius, "Formative Migrations: Mongols to Germans." Lecture 2. *The Great Courses: A History of Eastern Europe*, 2015.

[49] Jankowski, *Eastern Europe!*, 2015, pg. 70.

[50] Ibid., pg. 71-72.

Luther defied the church, Hus was spreading English reformer John Wycliffe's teachings in the modern Czech Republic. The church burned him for heresy in 1415.

Even though the region is seen as the domain of Christianity, Protestantism successfully spread throughout Eastern Europe. From the 16th to the 17th century, Hungary, Latvia, Estonia, Slovakia, and Poland all practiced or at least introduced some form of Protestantism.

There were other religious influences on the area too.[51] Although there is little left of them in the historical record, the first inhabitants of Eastern Europe practiced paganism—another word for the worship of pre-Christian practices. Catholic and Orthodox missionaries traveled deep within Eastern Europe, influencing local culture and spreading their own. Jews arrived in record numbers, finding safe spaces within the confines of Eastern Europe.[52] As many were merchants by trade, they found success and even thrived in the commercial cities of Eastern Europe. And, of course, there was also Islam, which reached the far corners of Eastern Europe after coming in from the Middle East and Asia.[53]

---

[51] Jankowski, *Eastern Europe!*, 2015, pg. 68; Liulevicius, "The Other Europe." Lecture 1. *The Great Courses: A History of Eastern Europe*, 2015.

[52] Jankowski, *Eastern Europe!*, 2015, pg. 47; Liulevicius, "The Other Europe." Lecture 1. *The Great Courses: A History of Eastern Europe*, 2015.

[53] Jankowski, *Eastern Europe!*, 2015, pg. 79; Liulevicius, "The Other Europe." Lecture 1. *The Great Courses: A History of Eastern Europe*, 2015.

The Importance of Trade in Eastern European History

Trade made Eastern Europe a dynamic actor in the history of the Eurasian landmass.[54] It was the method that allowed a wide variety of people groups to move in and out of Eastern Europe.[55] Various trade routes interconnected lands between Europe and Asia; where one ended, another began.[56] One particular trade route in Eastern Europe that was well-traveled in the ancient period was the Amber Road, which brought amber from the Baltic down to the Mediterranean Sea.

The success of trade routes was at the whim of external factors. Trade routes were popular in one era, but they could die out in another. This could be due to changes in transportation, demand for certain goods, or instability in the region. For example, the Silk Road connected each side of Eurasia through a series of connected routes that spanned from China to Western Europe. The use of these routes ebbed and flowed for thousands of years. Although the Mongol invasion of the 13th century was brutal, lands under new Mongol rule reactivated trading systems that had been long dormant.

More movement through Eastern Europe from the Crusades also stimulated near-extinct trade routes. Crusaders returned home to Western Europe with tales of trade routes that connected Europe with the riches of the East. Even more trade opportunities, such as the Indian Ocean trade route that connected eastern Africa to Southeast Asia by sea, began to stimulate a truly global trade market.

---

[54] Jankowski, *Eastern Europe!*, 2015, pg. 106.

[55] Jankowski, *Eastern Europe!*, 2015, pg. 106; Jenkins, *Short History of Europe*, 2019, pg. 8.

[56] Jankowski, *Eastern Europe!*, 2015, pg. 106, 113.

Another major presence in Eastern Europe trade routes was the Muslim Arab empires.[57] The people of Eastern Europe were connected to the Muslim Arab empires through trade. In modern-day Russia, in the river basins of the Dnieper and the Volga, Slavs and Arabs were frequent trading partners.

When the Vikings moved into the Baltic Sea region, they commandeered Eastern European trade. There was now a trading system that connected Europe to Asia, running right through Eastern Europe. This was the dominant trade route across Eurasia for hundreds of years.

In the 13th century, the Italians figured out that the region between the Mediterranean and the Black Sea, which moved right through Eastern Europe, gave Western Europe easier contact with Asian traders. Within two centuries, the Ottoman Empire cut off European contact with the East. As a result, the Europeans relied on the Indian Ocean trade to restore contact with Asian goods. This left Eastern Europe without its vital trade contacts that ran right through the region.

The combination and diversity of Eastern Europe's geography, history, religion, and language make the history of the region unique.[58] But one question still remains: what countries make up this region?

Generally, the states that lie between the Baltic Sea and the Adriatic Sea (excluding Greece) are considered to be Eastern Europe. Russia is the largest country in the region (not to mention the world), stretching along the whole Eurasian landmass. It has much more in common with Eastern Europe than it does with its other neighbors of Western Europe and Asia.

---

[57] Ibid., pg. 107.

[58] Liulevicius, "The Other Europe." Lecture 1. *The Great Courses: A History of Eastern Europe*, 2015.

Moving from west to east, the eastern borders of Germany, Austria, and Italy will be the starting point. Alongside these countries of Western Europe, down to the Adriatic Sea, are Poland, the Czech Republic, Slovakia, Hungary, Slovenia, and Croatia, which all share common experiences that would make them part of Eastern Europe. Moving inland, one can find Belarus, Ukraine, Moldova, Romania, and Bulgaria, which make up the bulk of the landmass that is Eastern Europe.

This history will also include the smaller but no less important states that separate Europe from Asia. To the north, the Baltic states—Estonia, Latvia, and Lithuania—border Russia and the Baltic Sea, making them the northernmost point of Eastern Europe. To the south, between Slovenia and Hungary to the north, Romania and Bulgaria to the east, and the Adriatic Sea to the west, lies a smattering of small states that all have similar experiences. These nations are Croatia, Bosnia and Herzegovina, Montenegro, Serbia, Kosovo, Albania, and North Macedonia. Although these countries are more familiar for the chaos that occurred at the close of the 20th century, they also were crucial to the development of the region.

In this book, we will dive into the history of Eastern Europe from the beginning, tracing its victories and conflicts until the present day. We will begin in the ancient period, where the great classical civilizations of Greece and Rome discovered what Eastern Europe had to offer.

Chapter 2 – The Ancient World in Eastern Europe (6500 BCE to 475 CE)

From the ancient to the early medieval period, Eastern Europe was flooded with outsiders.[59] This constant flow of peoples from the east crossing the Great Northern European Plain would change the history of Eastern Europe. These new arrivals would settle and form states and, in some cases, grand empires that dominated the region. New peoples also brought with them new religions, which would make Eastern Europe a melting pot of religions, peoples, and ideas. This would have a significant effect on how Eastern Europe would develop in later centuries.

---

[59] Liulevicius, "Formative Migrations: Mongols to Germans." Lecture 2. *The Great Courses: A History of Eastern Europe*, 2015.

The Prehistoric Age

In the prehistoric period, there was no such thing as "Eastern Europe," mostly because Europe, as we understand it to be today, didn't exist yet.[60] However, the region proved to be a critical crossroads for the first developments of civilization.

Prehistory is roughly divided into three major periods: the Stone Age (c. 3.4 million years ago–3000 BCE), the Bronze Age (c. 3300 BCE–1200 BCE), and the Iron Age (1200 BCE–400 CE), although the Iron Age lasted longer in some areas.[61] These phases were named for the innovative method of crafting tools, weapons, and utensils of the time (stone, bronze, and iron, respectively). The movement of peoples that characterized the prehistoric period would bring all of these technologies to Eastern Europe.[62]

During the Stone Age, the Agricultural Revolution, when prehistoric peoples stopped hunting and gathering and became farmers, reached the Balkans by 6500 BCE. Over the next millennium, it spread throughout Eastern Europe. When agricultural technology arrived in the Balkans, it spread to Eastern Europe along the Carpathian Basin. DNA evidence shows that migrants from the first civilizations of the Near East—places like Mesopotamia and the Nile River Valley—moved west along the steppe, entering Eastern Europe through the Danube gorges that cut through the mountains.[63] This area was rich in natural resources, making it the ideal setting for travelers to settle and spread out. Eventually, these migrants, along with their new

---

[60] Jankowski, *Eastern Europe!*, 2015, pg. 83-84.

[61] "Archaeological Timescale." *Encyclopedia Britannica*. Revised and updated June 2, 2008.

[62] Jankowski, *Eastern Europe!*, 2015, pg. 83.

[63] National Science Foundation & University of Wisconsin-Madison, "Isotopic data show farming arrived in Europe with migrants." *Proceedings of the National Academy of Sciences*, Feb 11, 2013.

methods of food production, overtook the hunter-gatherer communities of Eastern Europe.

This beginning episode shows the importance of the region.[64] Even though Western Europe considers itself the home of civilization, everything it needed to become that home came to it through Eastern Europe. It was the path of languages and technology, but more importantly, it offers a land-based theory—instead of a seaborne one—on how the Agricultural Revolution spread through Eurasia.[65]

Due to the movements of people coming into Eastern Europe and later Western Europe, various peoples traded.[66] Artifacts moved from the north, from the Baltic Sea down to the Mediterranean. One example of how technology spread throughout Eastern Europe was the spread of the use of metal tools. The Copper Age was the bridge between the Stone Age and the Bronze Age.[67] During this short period of about five hundred years, people started developing the first uses of smelting that would usher in the Bronze Age. The earliest evidence of the use of metal tools in Eastern Europe lies in present-day Bulgaria. From about 3500 BCE to 3000 BCE, this technology spread from Bulgaria to the rest of Europe.

This period in the 4th millennium BCE brought more people into Europe.[68] As more people started trading their bronze tools and utensils, coastal trading towns appeared. Most of Europe was covered in thick, dense forests, so people started trading on the sea.

---

[64] Jankowski, *Eastern Europe!*, 2015, pg. 84.

[65] National Science Foundation, "Isotopic Data," 2013.

[66] Jenkins, *Short History of Europe*, 2019, pg. 8.

[67] Jankowski, *Eastern Europe!*, 2015, pg. 84.

[68] Jenkins, *Short History of Europe*, 2019, pg. 8.

However, that didn't rule out land travel. In the 3rd millennium BCE, more people from the steppe moved into Europe.

Ancient Civilizations in Eastern Europe

Due to Western Europe's dominance of the European landmass, most people believe that civilizations in the western half of the continent started with the Greeks.[69] Archaeological evidence shows that this is not the case. A 2012 discovery in Bulgaria proves that this area was settled over one thousand years before the Minoan and Mycenaean civilizations.

The Greeks

Surprisingly, the lands of Eastern Europe were not on the radar of the earliest Greeks; they were only vaguely aware of the region.[70] However, with the spread of civilizations during the Classical period, more and more people started to have contact with Eastern Europe. With more contact with Eastern Europe came the knowledge of the region's resources.

Eastern Europe would become one of the trading hubs of the ancient world.[71] It included good terrain and several navigable trade routes, which were also used for travel. At the height of the ancient period, the Greeks and the Romans used these routes to make inroads in the area.

For the most part, the classical civilizations eyed Eastern Europe for expansion. There was no such thing as a division between Eastern Europe and Western Europe. The ancient civilizations were happy to conquer any area that would add to their power. Considering Eastern Europe's convenient location along ancient

---

[69] Jankowski, *Eastern Europe!*, 2015, pg. 85.

[70] Liulevicius, "Formative Migrations: Mongols to Germans." Lecture 2. *The Great Courses: A History of Eastern Europe*, 2015.

[71] Jankowski, *Eastern Europe!*, 2015, pg. 97; Jenkins, *Short History of Europe*, 2019, pg. 8-10.

trade routes, the earliest civilizations saw it in their best interest to control this region.

A map of the Aegean Sea and the surrounding area. In the 1st millennium BCE, a series of invaders, like the Dorians who eventually conquered the Mycenaeans, moved into mainland Greece, drawing the local populations into walled-in cities on the coast. These city-states would become known as the Greek poleis. (Credit: Eric Gaba, 2007)

The first civilization of Greeks might actually have roots in Eastern Europe. According to several studies, although they are far from conclusive, an Indo-European people originating from the Black Sea region moved south, occupying the Balkans. By the time they reached Greece, the tribes had united to create the first official Greek civilization—the Myceneans.

The traditional narrative claims that the Mycenaeans conquered their Minoan neighbors around 1450 BCE, becoming the most powerful Mediterranean civilization in the second half of the 2nd millennium BCE. However, the Minoans were already in decline by the time the Mycenaeans defeated them. Deforestation on the island of Crete affected the Minoan trade in bronze. On the nearby island of Thera (modern-day Santorini, Greece), a volcano erupted in circa 1630 BCE. This catastrophe's environmental and economic effects weakened the Minoan civilization, making them an easy target for Mycenaean attacks. After the Minoans declined, the Mycenaeans later settled the rest of Greece and into Anatolia.

Greece's location to the south made Eastern Europe the perfect place to begin founding colonies. Here, they could harvest the area's natural resources to produce food and commodities for the state. However, the Greeks found the climate unsuitable for growing crops. Still, the Greeks traded with Eastern Europeans. In the Balkans, the Greeks encountered the Illyrians. Modern-day Albanians descend from this ancient people group.

The ebb and flow of Greek civilization throughout the 2nd millennium and 1st millennium BCE had long-term implications for the region of Eastern Europe. The Mycenaeans eventually fell, conquered by the Dorians. The next two hundred years, until 900 BCE, is considered the "Dark Age" of Greek civilization.

Centuries went by before what is considered the height of Greek civilization, which saw the rise of city-states like Athens dominate the Mediterranean. As the Dorians invaded the mainland, Greek communities retreated, finding safety in walled-in cities on the coast. Over the next century, until 800 BCE, these cities grew in population and power. Settlements started to expand, reaching north in the direction of the Black Sea.

The Greek city-states developed sophisticated forms of government; each settlement practiced self-rule with highly segregated social classes.[72] A typical Greek polis had designated areas for business, worship, and entertainment, such as the marketplace (the agora), the religious center (the acropolis), the theater, and the gymnasium (for athletic training).

Throughout the 7th and 6th centuries BCE, Greek city-states started to learn not only how to strengthen their own power but also how they fit together to create a uniquely Greek experience. Differing opinions on how much power a ruler or a social class should have jolted political organizations. Cities governed by assemblies and councils shifted to autocracies governed by tyrants and oligarchies, where the power rested with a small, influential group of people.

In Athens, a visionary ruler would change the nature of government to something much more familiar to us today. In the late 6th century BCE, a politician named Cleisthenes revolted against the ruling tyrant in Athens. After a few years of struggle, he took control of the government. In 508 BCE, Cleisthenes came up with a radical idea: all Athenian citizens should participate in governing the city.

Although democracy looks much different today, the direct democracy of ancient Athens was a turning point in political history.[73] It introduced the idea that the population, albeit only the males, should take an interest in how they are governed. This method of government, particularly ideas of self-government, would be short-lived in Greece, but it would endure to the modern age. However, democracy remained elusive to Eastern Europe until the modern age.

---

[72] Jenkins, *Short History of Europe*, 2019, pg. 11.

[73] Ibid., pg. 13.

Throughout its history, many of the modern countries of Eastern Europe would change hands, falling victim to the stronger powers in the region. In some cases, they *were* the strongest power in the region, at least temporarily. In its postwar recovery in the 20th century, Eastern European nations were also plagued by the power struggle of the Cold War. In some countries, true democracy and self-rule are a new introduction, a novelty that its citizens are exploring.

The Persian Threat

Also at the beginning of the 6th century BCE, a power from the east would define the Greek experience for the next century.[74] The Persians were the descendants of the ancient Iranians, another Indo-European people who migrated into the modern-day Middle East. The ancient Iranians rarely had control over their own destiny in the 1st millennium BCE; until the late 600s BCE, other larger ancient empires strong-armed them into submission.

The ancient Iranians founded the Median Empire in the 7th century BCE, but they hadn't reached Eastern Europe yet. The Median Empire only conquered as far west as Turkey. However, in the 6th century BCE, the Medes were defeated by a rebellion in one of their territories.

The winner of this rebellion was from Parsa, from which the name "Persian" comes. Cyrus the Great united the Persian Empire for the first time, and he expanded much farther than the Medes ever did. By invading the outposts on the Aegean Sea in 546 BCE, the Persians, led by Cyrus the Great (r. 559–530 BCE), occupied most of the Middle East. During his reign, the westernmost part of the Persian Empire controlled the southern coast of the Black Sea in modern-day Turkey and the Bosporus, where modern-day Istanbul resides today.

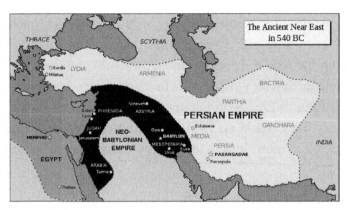

The reaches of the Persian Empire in 540 BCE, around the time the Persians reached the outskirts of Greece. (Public Domain)

The Persians stretched their empire even farther, reaching its most extensive landholdings by 500 BCE. They conquered the Danube Delta region, moving into southernmost Eastern Europe. The Persian Empire stretched as far west as the present-day eastern borders of Eastern Europe. Occupying the Danube Basin, the Persian Empire reached around the southwestern borders of the Black Sea, from the Danube River south to the Aegean Sea. His empire included parts of modern-day Ukraine, Romania, Bulgaria, North Macedonia, and Greece.

---

[74] Jankowski, *Eastern Europe!*, 2015, pg. 98-99; Jenkins, *Short History of Europe*, 2019, pg. 13.

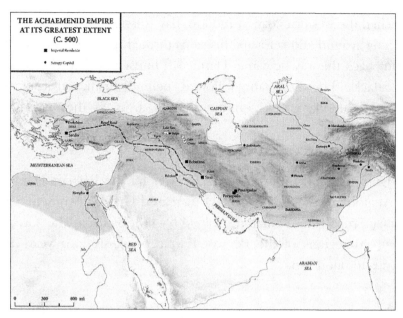

THE ACHAEMENID EMPIRE
AT ITS GREATEST EXTENT
(C. 500)

■ Imperial Residence

● Satrapy Capital

The landholdings of the Achaemenid Empire in 500 BCE are highlighted in red. (Credit: Mossmaps, 2018)

The Persians controlled the Balkans, and its trade and communication networks brought peoples, goods, and information through Eastern Europe. They understood the value of the trade routes and the geographical importance of the region, so the Persians and their successor empires occupied Eastern Europe in the ancient period and fought others for it. The Persian lands in Eastern Europe were an information highway; the Greeks and the Romans borrowed from the information found here extensively.

Cyrus the Great's descendant, Darius I, also found himself within Eastern Europe's borders, according to ancient sources.[75] In 514 BCE, he attacked the Scythians, who were wreaking havoc on the northernmost edge of the Persian Empire. He brought hundreds of thousands of soldiers across the Bosporus, marching up the western coast of Eastern Europe. When the Persians reached Ukraine, the Scythians retreated east. Darius most likely

---

[75] Jankowski, *Eastern Europe!*, 2015, pg. 100-101; Jenkins, *Short History of Europe,* 2019, pg. 13.

reached the western edge of modern-day Russia before he gave up, turning around and retracing his steps through Eastern Europe. By going back the way he came, Darius left himself and his men open to attack. The Scythians followed behind them, engaging in surprise guerilla attacks on the Persian army as they retreated home.

The Greco-Persian Wars (499-449 BCE)

Unfortunately, the trouble wasn't over for the Persians. Unrest in Anatolia (present-day Turkey) increased Greek discontent with Persian rule. The Ionian Revolt (499–493 BCE) in the Greek-occupied regions of the Persian Empire took six long years for Darius to put down.

A map showing the Greek settlements in the Persian Empire by the end of the 6ᵗʰ century BCE. The italicized names along the Aegean Sea and the Mediterranean Sea are the Greek settlements along the western edge of the empire. (Credit: MinisterforBadTimes, 2009)

The Ionian Revolt was the first true conflict between the Greeks and the Persians, but it wouldn't be the last. When Darius finally returned Ionia to his control, he left behind the violence of the past, attempting to come to peace terms that both the Persians and the Ionians could agree on. Instead of punishing the Ionians, which would have led to even more discontent, Darius launched a punitive strike against Athens for supporting the rebellion.

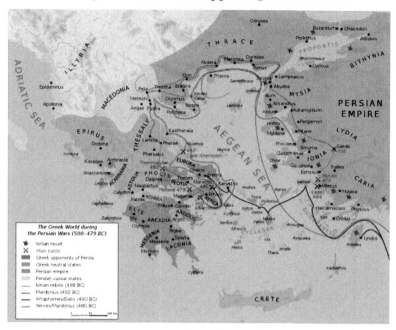

The military movements from the Ionian Revolt to the Persian defeat at Marathon. Under Xerxes, the Persian invasion of Greece moved along the eastern seaboard of the Aegean Sea, reaching parts of modern-day Eastern Europe as far north as North Macedonia. (Credit: Leptictidium/Bibi Saint-Pol, updated 2020)

The Greeks crushed the Persians at the Battle of Marathon in 490 BCE, ending the first Persian invasion of Greece. Darius died in 486 BCE, and his son Xerxes took over where his father left off. He launched the Second Persian Invasion in 480 BCE to conquer all of Greece. Xerxes assembled one of the largest armies of the ancient world, leading a two-pronged attack by land and sea.

A map showing Xerxes's attempted invasion of Greece in 480 BCE. He launched a two-pronged attack by land and sea, rounding the Aegean Sea. He traveled through the lands of modern-day Turkey to modern-day Greece. (Credit: Brian Boru, 2018)

Since the Greek city-states were challenged by the Persians, they allied with each other to protect their lands, even though many of them were in conflict or at war themselves.[76] Together, the allied Greek city-states, led by the most powerful states of Athens and Sparta, defeated the Persian fleet at Salamis in 480.[77] The next year,

---

[76] Jankowski, *Eastern Europe!*, 2015, pg. 97.

[77] Jenkins, *Short History of Europe*, 2019, pg. 13.

the Greeks defeated the Persians again on land at the Battle of Plataea.

The Greeks were massively outnumbered, yet they won major victories over the Persians. If the Persians had won, Eastern European history would have been much different. Xerxes would have undoubtedly moved inland from Greece, securing the lucrative trade routes and the natural resources of the interior.

The Peloponnesian Wars (460-404 BCE)

The peace among the Greek city-states would not last. For the rest of the 5th century BCE, Greece would tear itself apart in the Peloponnesian Wars.[78] After the end of the Second Invasion of Greece, Athens and her allies, the Delian League, went on the warpath, pushing the Persians back and making them hand over their territories. As Athens turned itself into an empire, tensions rose with Sparta, the other most powerful Greek city-state.

For decades, intermittent periods of peace, tension, and warfare strained the relationships between the Greek city-states. The first conflict lasted from 460 to 445 BCE, which ended with a peace treaty between Athens and Sparta. The peace only lasted six years before war broke out again.

The next phase of the Peloponnesian War lasted for twenty-seven years, from 431 to 404 BCE, with a six-year peace between hostilities. At the end of the conflict, Sparta obtained the help of the Persians, who wanted to retaliate against Athens for their humiliating defeat. Sparta eventually defeated Athens and the Delian League.

At the end of the Peloponnesian Wars, Athens lost its influence in favor of Sparta. Peace in the rest of the Greek city-states broke down, and they experienced decades of conflict that crushed their

---

[78] Jankowski, *Eastern Europe!*, 2015, pg. 97-98; Jenkins, *Short History of Europe*, 2019, pg. 16; "The Peloponnesian War." *National Geographic.*
https://www.nationalgeographic.org/encyclopedia/peloponnesian-war/

infrastructure, population, and economy. Greece's Golden Age was over, allowing the rise of another power from the north.

Macedon and Alexander the Great (359-323 BCE)

The Greek city-states were exhausted after decades of war and bloodshed, and they were ripe for domination at the end of the 5th century BCE.[79] In 359 BCE, Philip II became the king of Macedon, a military kingdom to the north of Greece. Philip saw imperialism as the key to power; he wanted to strengthen Macedon by conquering other lands.[80] He started with his weakened Greek neighbors.

Philip II's hardened warriors took Greece by storm.[81] He brought the area under his control through battle or diplomacy, uniting the Greek states under his rule. In 338 BCE, Philip's victory over a Greek coalition at the Battle of Chaeronea finally cemented his control over the Greek city-states.

Philip II created a coalition of Greek states under his control to accomplish his next goal: conquering the Persians. Before he could make a move, he was assassinated in 336 BCE. Philip's son, Alexander, was another leader gifted in military command. A lover of Greek culture, his exploits would ensure the survival of Greek culture after the fall of classical Greece.

Alexander saw an opportunity when his father died, and he continued Philip's assault on the Persians. The Macedonians invaded, conquered, and assimilated lands from Greece to the Middle East to India over the next thirteen years. King Darius III of Persia suffered humiliating defeats at the hands of Alexander.

---

[79] Jenkins, *Short History of Europe*, 2019, pg. 16-17.

[80] Jankowski, *Eastern Europe!*, 2015, pg. 97.

[81] Jenkins, *Short History of Europe*, 2019, pg. 16-18; Jankowski, *Eastern Europe!*, 2015, pg. 98; "Philip II, king of Macedonia." *Encyclopedia Britannica.* https://www.britannica.com/biography/Philip-II-king-of-Macedonia; "Alexander the Great, king of Macedonia." *Encyclopedia Britannica.* "Macedonia." *HISTORY.*

Alexander defeated the Persians in 330 BCE, adding Persian lands to his Macedonian Empire.

A map of the Macedonian Empire, 334-323 BCE. (Credit: Generic Mapping Tools, 2006)

Alexander the Great's empire was the largest ever seen before. It controlled the eastern edge of Eastern Europe, where the modern-day countries of North Macedonia and Bulgaria are today south to North Africa. It included Asia Minor and went eastward all the way to the Himalayas. Alexander still pushed farther, reaching the Indus River in modern-day India. The unforgiving terrain and his disgruntled soldiers forced him to turn back.

Alexander spent 326 to 324 BCE reorganizing the government of his extensive empire. His exhausted army resented Alexander's equal treatment of Persians and his policy of assimilation with lands he conquered. To calm his men, he decided to return home. He moved backward through his empire, heading back in the direction of Macedon, stopping in Susa and then Babylon. After wintering in Babylon, Alexander came down with a fever and died in 323 BCE.[82]

---

[82] Jenkins, *Short History of Europe*, 2019, pg. 16-18; Jankowski, *Eastern Europe!*, 2015, pg. 98; "Philip II, king of Macedonia." *Encyclopedia Britannica*; "Alexander the Great, king of Macedonia." *Encyclopedia Britannica*. "Macedonia." *HISTORY*.; Donald L. Wasson. "Wars of the Diadochi." *World History Encyclopedia*.

Alexander the Great's empire wouldn't last long. He hadn't named an heir, so his generals squabbled over regions of the empire in the Wars of the Diadochi. For over thirty years, Alexander's generals fought over territory, splitting his lands up into smaller territories for themselves. While Alexander's generals secured their lands, three generals emerged in a lengthy struggle to become Alexander's successor: Antigonus Monophthalmus I, Ptolemy I Soter, and Seleucus I Nicator.

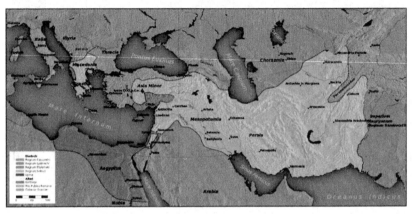

A map of the successor states of Alexander the Great's Macedonian Empire. The states controlled by Alexander's generals Cassander and Lysimachus made up the majority of the Macedonian landholdings in Eastern Europe. They would later become controlled by the Antigonid dynasty. (Credit: Luigi Chiesa, Captain_Blood, 2014)

These generals established their own dynasties: the Antigonid Empire in Macedonia, the more well-known Ptolemaic dynasty in Egypt, and the Seleucid Empire in western Asia. Until the late 1st century BCE, these dynasties spread the Greek language, knowledge, science, law, politics, and culture in the former Macedonian Empire.[83] After the fall of classical Greece, Greek culture continued in its former domain. This process was known as Hellenization, and this period was called the Hellenistic Age.

[83] Donald L. Wasson. "Wars of the Diadochi." *World History Encyclopedia*, Jankowski, *Eastern Europe!*, 2015, pg.98; Jenkins, *Short History of Europe*, 2019, pg. 17-18.

In Eastern Europe, parts of Bulgaria, Serbia, Kosovo, Albania, North Macedonia, and Greece experienced Hellenization. These three dynasties would continue for several centuries until the rise of the Romans. The borders of Alexander's empire were not solid, and they constantly ebbed and flowed over the next three hundred years. After the Wars of the Diadochi, the successor states were gradually reduced to little more than territories. The last of the successor states, Ptolemaic Egypt, fell to the Romans at the end of the 1st century BCE, ending Greek influence over the lands from Eastern Europe to the Middle East.

The Romans

As the successor states started to decline, a new power from the west was just beginning.[84] By the 1st century BCE, a small city-state on the Italian Peninsula had become a full-fledged empire. Instead of following the Greek model of creating a wide region of states joined by language, culture, and politics, the Romans would preserve Greek culture while implementing their own militaristic society across Eurasia.

A Small City-State Dominates the Mediterranean

As the influence of the Macedonian Empire declined and was sectioned off into successor states, it allowed for the rise of another power. Rome filled the void. After fulfilling their goal of expanding outside of the Italian Peninsula, the Romans maintained a steady presence in Eastern Europe and points beyond for hundreds of years.[85] Rome's reliance on warfare to grow its territory made it the dominant power of the ancient world.[86]

---

[84] Jankowski, *Eastern Europe!*, 2015, pg.97; Jenkins, *Short History of Europe*, 2019, pg. 22; Joshua J. Mark. "Ancient Rome." *World History Encyclopedia.* Published September 2, 2009. https://www.worldhistory.org/Rome/.

[85] Liulevicius, "Formative Migrations: Mongols to Germans." Lecture 2. *The Great Courses: A History of Eastern Europe*, 2015.

[86] Jankowski, *Eastern Europe!*, 2015, pg.101; Jenkins, *Short History of Europe*, 2019, pg. 23; Joshua J. Mark. "Ancient Rome." *World History Encyclopedia.*

In the 8th century BCE, Rome was founded as a small city-state, and it was ruled by a line of Etruscan kings. In 509 BCE, these kings were deposed, and Rome became a republican city-state. Until Julius Caesar seized power, Rome ruled itself as a republic. During this period, Rome would spread out, gaining command of the Italian Peninsula and the lands beyond. It was the Roman Republic that conquered the lands that the Roman Empire would inherit in the 1st century BCE.

From the 5th century to the 3rd century BCE, Rome spread out past the Italian Peninsula.[87] Roman colonies were Roman territories. They paid taxes and followed Roman laws, and in exchange, the colonies were protected by Rome. Any attack on the colony was an attack on Rome itself.

On the southeastern side of the Mediterranean, Rome's main rival was Carthage, located in modern-day Tunisia, North Africa. Carthage commanded the Mediterranean trade. Rome went to war with Carthage three times throughout the 3rd and 2nd centuries BCE. After the fall of Carthage, Rome replaced it as the main power in the Mediterranean.

After removing the threat of Carthage, the Romans set their sights east, quickly conquering Greece. The Romans wanted to control the trade from Asia, and they knew that holding the lands of Eastern Europe was the best way to do it. The Romans launched a campaign of conquer and assimilate until the end of the 1st century BCE, bringing the Balkans under their control.

Here, the last of Alexander the Great's empire was hanging on by a thread. As the Romans conquered Greece and Eastern Europe and moved east into western Asia, they would become the next preservers of Greek culture. Just as the Macedonians had spread Greek culture throughout their lands, the Romans would do the same. Members of the upper classes read Greek literature,

---

[87] Jankowski, *Eastern Europe!*, 2015, pg.103; Joshua J. Mark. "Ancient Rome." *World History Encyclopedia.*

spoke the Greek language, and collected Greek works of art. They emulated Greek architecture and design in their homes. In fact, the Romans would emulate the Greeks in almost everything. They adopted Roman names for the Greek gods and employed Greek artistic styles in their own art and sculptures. The Greeks became the inspiration for much of Roman law and politics, but the Romans would take it to a new level.

A Republic in Trouble: The First Triumvirate and the Rise of Julius Caesar

In the 1st century BCE, the republic weakened.[88] As Rome had grown over the past six centuries, it led to corruption among the upper classes and exploitation of the lower classes and slaves.[89] A push for land reforms in the 2nd century BCE ended violently. While some public land was taken from the upper classes and given to the lower classes, it wasn't enough. The conflict between the two factions would define the next stage of the Roman government: the Optimates, who represented the interests of the upper class, and the Populares, who advocated for the lower class.

In the meantime, Rome had descended into a civil war between two generals: Lucius Cornelius Sulla and Gaius Marius.[90] Sulla was victorious, and Marius's family, of which Julius Caesar was a part, found themselves in a poor position.[91] Caesar lost his wealth and titles, and he was forced to join the army. He worked his way up and achieved modest political power.[92] Although he was a Populare, Caesar was a member of the upper class, and he had

---

[88] Jenkins, *Short History of Europe*, 2019, pg. 23

[89] Joshua J. Mark. "Ancient Rome." *World History Encyclopedia.*

[90] Andrews, Evan. "6 Civil Wars That Transformed Ancient Rome." *HISTORY.* Published August 28, 2015. https://www.history.com/news/6-civil-wars-that-transformed-ancient-rome

[91] "Julius Caesar." *HISTORY.* Published November 4, 2019. https://www.history.com/topics/ancient-history/julius-caesar

[92] "Julius Caesar." *HISTORY.*; "The Triumvirate." Episode 1. *Roman Empire: Julius Caesar - Master of Rome.* Netflix documentary. 2019.

other powerful Populare friends: Marcus Licinius Crassus and Gnaeus Pompeius Magnus (better known as Pompey).[93] In 60 BCE, the three men ruled Rome as the First Triumvirate. Together, they were unstoppable, with Crassus's wealth and Pompey's and Caesar's popularity with the people.

This method of government would only last seven years. In 58 BCE, Caesar was granted governorship of Gaul, parts of modern-day northern Italy and southern France.[94] Until 50 BCE, Caesar stabilized the area, defeating the Gallic tribes and occupying more land to the northwest. Along with Caesar in Gaul was a young soldier named Mark Antony. By the end of the campaign, Roman Gaul included lands in modern-day France and Germany west of the Rhine River. Caesar's campaign extended Rome's dominions to modern-day England to the north and east to the Rhine River Valley.

Caesar's success in the Gallic Wars made him incredibly popular at home, as Roman society valued military success as much as status and wealth.[95] Back in Rome, Crassus, the wealthiest member of the Triumvirate, hated how well-liked Pompey and Caesar were among the people.[96] He sought the military glory that

[93] Joshua J. Mark. "Ancient Rome." *World History Encyclopedia*, "The Triumvirate." Episode 1. *Roman Empire: Julius Caesar - Master of Rome*. Netflix documentary. 2019. "The Great Conqueror." Episode 2. *Roman Empire: Julius Caesar - Master of Rome*. Netflix documentary, 2019.

[94] Joshua J. Mark. "Ancient Rome." *World History Encyclopedia*, "The Great Conqueror." Episode 2. *Roman Empire: Julius Caesar - Master of Rome*. Netflix documentary, 2019; Jenkins, *Short History of Europe*, 2019, pg. 23-24.

[95] Joshua J. Mark. "Ancient Rome." *World History Encyclopedia*; Donald L. Wasson. "First Triumvirate." *World History Encyclopedia*. Published March 20, 2016. https://www.worldhistory.org/First_Triumvirate/; "Crossing the Rubicon." Episode 3. *Roman Empire: Julius Caesar - Master of Rome*. Netflix documentary, 2019.

[96] Joshua J. Mark. "Ancient Rome." *World History Encyclopedia*.; "The Great Conqueror." Episode 2. *Roman Empire: Julius Caesar - Master of Rome*. Netflix documentary, 2019; Mark Cartwright. "Marcus Licinius Crassus." *World History Encyclopedia*. Published November 5, 2013. https://www.worldhistory.org/Marcus_Licinius_Crassus/

made his co-consuls so popular and decided to wage a campaign against the Parthian Empire to the east.

The Parthian Empire Challenges Rome from the East

Just as the Persians had challenged the Greeks, Parthia would become a thorn in the side of the Romans as they pushed east.[97] The Parthians contested Roman hegemony in areas just past the borders of Eastern Europe, like Turkey, Armenia, and Iraq. These were areas that required movement through Eastern Europe to reach. The Parthians were a formidable enemy. They mastered the horse for travel and battle, and they could shoot a bow and arrow while riding, which made them particularly effective at blitz attacks. [98] The Parthians could also hunt down their targets and get away quickly when they were the targets.

When Persia fell to Alexander the Great, its lands were incorporated into his great empire.[99] Seleucus I Nicator, one of Alexander's generals, gained control of the former Persian lands during the Wars of the Diadochi, forming the Seleucid Empire. The Seleucids kept most of the Persian organization intact, including the government.[100] Parthia, which was located east of the Caspian Sea, was a satrap of the Seleucid Empire for nearly one hundred years. By the mid-3rd century BCE, the Seleucid Empire was in trouble. Internal divisions destabilized the government, and war with nearby Ptolemaic Egypt—another subdivision of Alexander's empire—used all its resources. In 247 BCE, the governor of Parthia, Andragoras, took advantage of the diversion. He rebelled against Seleucid authority, proclaiming Parthia an independent state.

---

[97] Jankowski, *Eastern Europe!*, 2015, pg.100.

[98] Patrick Scott Smith. "Parthia (Empire)." *World History Encyclopedia*. Published July 22, 2019. https://www.worldhistory.org/Parthia_(Empire)/

[99] Donald L. Wasson. "Wars of the Diadochi." *World History Encyclopedia*, Patrick Scott Smith. "Parthia (Empire)." *World History Encyclopedia*.

[100] Patrick Scott Smith. "Parthia (Empire)." *World History Encyclopedia*.

Andragoras made a fatal error, though. By separating from the Seleucid Empire, Parthia lost the empire's protection. A Scythian tribe, the Parni, set their sights on Parthia. The Parni were East Iranian nomads that traveled west along the steppe. They were incredibly mobile and masters of horseback riding, archery, and blitz attacks. The Parni were experts at stealthy invasions, and they were even better at escaping their enemies.

In 238 BCE, the chief of the Parni, Arsaces, invaded Parthia and killed the governor. With Andragoras dead, Arsaces took over the territory, making himself the first king of Parthia. He established all the telltale symbols of an ancient power; he established a succession, and he consolidated power into his hands. Throughout his reign, Arsaces managed to hold the Seleucids back from retaking Parthia.

Over the next century, wars continued between the Parthians and the Seleucids. During that time, it would expand in all directions: east, west, and south. In 209 BCE, the Seleucid Empire would eventually get Parthia back, but it would only be temporary. King Antiochus III was lenient with the new Parthian king, Arsaces II. Instead of deposing or killing him, Antiochus allowed Arsaces to keep his position. However, Parthia returned to a satrapy of the empire. By 191 BCE, the Parthian nobility grew frustrated with the weak Arsaces and usurped the throne, putting another king on the throne in his place.

Conflicts with Rome in the early 2nd century BCE permanently weakened the Seleucids. At the end of the Roman-Seleucid War in 188 BCE, Rome gained control of the Greek city-states, making it the dominant power in the Mediterranean. This continued the Roman push to the east, which would bring them into contact with the Parthians.

By 129 BCE, Parthia had taken the Median Empire and Mesopotamia, putting them further in the Romans' line of sight. That year, King Antiochus VII Sidetes was killed in a battle with the Parthians. He would be the last powerful Seleucid king, and his death marked the beginning of the empire's end. Within five years, the most powerful king of Parthia would rise—Mithridates II. He is considered Parthia's greatest king, as he oversaw the largest expansion of the empire. Through his efforts, Parthia stretched to the northeast, ever closer to Rome. The swath of land that stretched from east of the Mediterranean Sea to China was all controlled by Parthia. Mithridates II was the king that made Parthia into a major world power.

In the 1st century BCE, Parthia would find its footing against the might of Rome. As Rome pushed east, it took Mesopotamia from the Parthians, who, at the time, were ruled by Phraates III (r. 70–57 BCE). A brief dynastic struggle between Phraates's sons (who had murdered him) broke out, with Orodes II emerging victorious. He retook the Seleucian capital on the Tigris River, which was a major military and psychological victory for the Parthians.

The extensive lands that were part of the Parthian Empire allowed it to control trade from Europe to Asia. The Parthians were merchants as much as warriors, and they grew rich on the movement of food and luxury items from Europe to Asia and back again. When they weren't at war or expanding their territory, they introduced Eastern goods to the West and shuttled Western goods all the way to Asia.

Land borders of Rome and Parthia at the time of the Battle of Carrhae in 53 BCE. (Credit: Cplakidasm, 2021)

By the time Crassus arrived with his army in 53 BCE, he was facing one of the most powerful states of the ancient period.[101] At the Battle of Carrhae, the Romans were no match for ten thousand Parthian warriors on horseback.[102] Their expert archers decimated Crassus's army. During the peace negotiations, the Parthians murdered Crassus; according to Cassius Dio, the Parthians poured

[101] Patrick Scott Smith. "Parthia (Empire)." *World History Encyclopedia,* "The Great Conqueror." Episode 2. *Roman Empire: Julius Caesar - Master of Rome.* Netflix documentary, 2019

[102] Patrick Scott Smith. "Parthia (Empire)." *World History Encyclopedia,* Joshua J. Mark. "Ancient Rome." *World History Encyclopedia,* Mark Cartwright. "Marcus Licinius Crassus." *World History Encyclopedia,* "The Great Conqueror." Episode 2. *Roman Empire: Julius Caesar - Master of Rome.* Netflix documentary, 2019.

melted gold down Crassus's throat—a humiliating end to the richest man in Rome.[103]

Caesar as Dictator: The Fall of the Roman Republic

After Crassus died, the First Triumvirate devolved into a rivalry between Pompey, who began siding with the Optimates, and Caesar, who remained loyal to the Populare cause.[104] Without a third member, the other two men couldn't check their own power and ambition. Caesar was still in Gaul, but Pompey made a power grab, trying to force Caesar to return to Rome for a trial. Instead of returning in peace, Caesar returned with an escort of soldiers. And when he crossed the Rubicon into Italy, it was seen as an act of war. Pompey and his supporters didn't have time to make enough preparations for a defense of the city, so they left Rome.

In 48 BCE, Caesar and Pompey met at the decisive Battle of Pharsalus in Greece.[105] Caesar was victorious, and Pompey retreated to Egypt.[106] Although Pompey believed he would find sanctuary (and help) there, he was murdered as soon as he arrived. This left Caesar as the undisputed ruler of Rome.

---

[103] Even after the fall of Rome, the descendants of the Persians troubled the descendants of the Romans. In 224 CE, the Parthian Empire fell, making way for the Sassanid Empire. The Sassanids and the Byzantine Empire—the former Eastern Roman Empire—fought over lands east of the Mediterranean and south of the Black Sea. Jankowski, *Eastern Europe!*, 2015, pg.100-101; "The Great Conqueror." Episode 2. *Roman Empire: Julius Caesar - Master of Rome.* Netflix documentary, 2019; Patrick Scott Smith. "Parthia (Empire)." *World History Encyclopedia*; Joshua J. Mark. "Ancient Rome." *World History Encyclopedia*; Mark Cartwright. "Marcus Licinius Crassus." *World History Encyclopedia.*

[104] "Crossing the Rubicon." Episode 3. *Roman Empire: Julius Caesar - Master of Rome.* Netflix documentary, 2019; Joshua J. Mark. "Ancient Rome." *World History Encyclopedia.*

[105] "Crossing the Rubicon." Episode 3. *Roman Empire: Julius Caesar - Master of Rome.* Netflix documentary, 2019; "Queen of the Nile." Episode 4. *Roman Empire: Julius Caesar - Master of Rome.* Netflix documentary, 2019; Joshua J. Mark. "Ancient Rome." *World History Encyclopedia.*

When Julius Caesar returned to Rome, he strong-armed the Senate to make him dictator for ten years. This placed an extraordinary amount of power in his hands—power he used to pass reforms that were equal parts self-serving and beneficial to the Roman people.[107] Many senators feared he would eliminate the governing body.[108] Caesar's assassination in March 44 BCE left the foundering Roman Republic in turmoil.[109]

Caesar's death was essentially the end of the Roman Republic, although you could argue that its demise began much earlier than that.[110] The Roman Republic only lasted four centuries, and it officially ended in 27 BCE. The end of Caesar marked the rise of another Roman personality, one who would turn Rome into an empire: his nephew, Octavian.

Augustus: The First Roman Emperor

Since Caesar had no legitimate children, he adopted Octavian and made him his heir.[111] Rome experimented with another triumvirate when Octavian joined forces with Mark Antony and another general, Lepidus. The Second Triumvirate, which was formed in 43 BCE, used the power of their alliance to murder

---

[106] "Queen of the Nile." Episode 4. *Roman Empire: Julius Caesar - Master of Rome.* Netflix documentary, 2019; Joshua J. Mark. "*Ancient* Rome." *World History Encyclopedia.*

[107] "The Ides of March." Episode 5. *Roman Empire: Julius Caesar - Master of Rome.* Netflix documentary, 2019; Joshua J. Mark. "Ancient Rome." *World History Encyclopedia.*

[108] "Queen of the Nile." Episode 4. *Roman Empire: Julius Caesar - Master of Rome.* Netflix documentary, 2019; Joshua J. Mark. "Ancient Rome." *World History Encyclopedia.*

[109] Jenkins, *Short History of Europe*, 2019, pg. 24; "The Ides of March." Episode 5. *Roman Empire: Julius Caesar - Master of Rome.* Netflix documentary, 2019.

[110] Jankowski, *Eastern Europe!*, 2015, pg.101; Joshua J. Mark. "Ancient Rome." *World History Encyclopedia.*

[111] Joshua J. Mark. "Ancient Rome." *World History Encyclopedia.*

---

their enemies.[112] The Triumvirate also went after Caesar's assassins, defeating the last of the conspirators at the Battle of Philippi in 42 BCE.

Octavian sought control of Rome as his birthright as Julius Caesar's heir.[113] The Triumvirate assigned sections of the empire to each member to check their influence.[114] As Caesar's heir, Octavian took Rome, and Antony controlled the east. Octavian and Antony originally gave Lepidus Spain and Africa, but he was soon deposed, breaking the Triumvirate.[115] The real power and struggles of the empire lay between Octavian and Mark Antony.

Antony retreated to the east to cement his power base.[116] He defended his borders against Parthian incursions and secured the east under his control.[117] His personal and political alliance with the queen of Egypt, Cleopatra, turned Rome against him.[118] On top of that, Octavian humiliated Antony in public as he tried to restore the influence that had been taken from him with Antony's alliance with Egypt.[119] [120] The Triumvirate broke down, and Antony and Octavian declared war. In 31 BCE, Octavian defeated Mark Antony and Cleopatra at the Battle of Actium. They killed

---

[112] Joshua J. Mark. "Ancient Rome." *World History Encyclopedia*; Joshua J. Mark. "Augustus." *World History Encyclopedia*. Published May 4, 2018. https://www.worldhistory.org/augustus/

[113] Jankowski, *Eastern Europe!*, 2015, pg.101.

[114] Joshua J. Mark. "Ancient Rome." *World History Encyclopedia*.

[115] Joshua J. Mark. "Ancient Rome." *World History Encyclopedia*; Joshua J. Mark. "Augustus." *World History Encyclopedia*.

[116] Joshua J. Mark. "Ancient Rome." *World History Encyclopedia*.

[117] Jenkins, *Short History of Europe*, 2019, pg. 24.

[118] Joshua J. Mark. "Ancient Rome." *World History Encyclopedia*.

[119] Joshua J. Mark. "Ancient Rome." *World History Encyclopedia*; Joshua J. Mark. "Augustus." *World History Encyclopedia*.

[120] Joshua J. Mark. "Ancient Rome." *World History Encyclopedia*.

themselves when Octavian invaded Alexandria, as they refused to be taken hostage and shipped back to Rome in humiliation.[121]

Lorenzo A. Castro, The Battle of Actium, September 2, 31 BC, 1672. (Public Domain)

According to historian Simon Jenkins, "If any man deserved the title of founder of modern Europe, it is Octavian (Caesar Augustus)."[122] With Mark Antony's death, Octavian became the most powerful man in Rome.[123] In 27 BCE, the Senate gave Octavian unlimited powers that were very similar to the rights Julius Caesar demanded years before.[124] How did Augustus do what Caesar did but succeed?[125] Caesar was well-loved by the people, but politicians saw him as a threat. However, Augustus managed to toe the line between both, keeping everyone happy.

---

[121] Jenkins, *Short History of Europe*, 2019, pg. 26; Joshua J. Mark. "Ancient Rome." *World History Encyclopedia.*

[122] Jenkins, *Short History of Europe*, 2019, pg. 26.

[123] Joshua J. Mark. "Ancient Rome." *World History Encyclopedia.*

[124] Joshua J. Mark. "Ancient Rome." *World History Encyclopedia*; Joshua J. Mark. "Augustus." *World History Encyclopedia.*

[125] Joshua J. Mark. "Augustus." *World History Encyclopedia.*

Instead of greedily forcing the Senate into bending to his will, Octavian knew how to play the Roman politicians. Although he initially rejected them, he took unlimited powers and a new title, Augustus, publicly stating that it was only to help recover the might of the Roman Republic. [126] Instead, beginning with his reign in 27 BCE, Rome was no longer a republic; it was an empire.

This is perhaps the best-known image of Augustus (formerly known as Octavian). The sculptor is unknown, but Augustus of Prima Porta is named after where it was excavated. (Public Domain)

[126] Jankowski, *Eastern Europe!*, 2015, pg.101; Joshua J. Mark. "Augustus." *World History Encyclopedia.*

Octavian was also successful on the battlefield—a quintessentially Roman attribute.[127] One of the first victories Augustus made was taking the land of Illyricum and turning it into a Roman province.[128] Modern-day Albanians trace their lineage to these Illyrians. Augustus only suffered one defeat of note: the Battle of the Teutoburg Forest in the year 9 CE.[129] The battle was fought in Saxony, the eastern region of modern-day Germany that borders the Czech Republic and Poland. Augustus's general Varus was betrayed by Arminius, who was a member of the Germanic auxiliary troops. Arminius learned Roman military tactics, so he knew how to exploit the weaknesses in the army's defenses. He led a coalition of Germanic tribes in a victory so overwhelming that the Romans abandoned their designs on conquering Germania for over 150 years.

The loss at the Battle of the Teutoburg Forest is important for another reason.[130] The river became a natural barrier between Roman Gaul and the Germanic tribes. The lands east of the Rhine River became the conventional Roman frontier, the extent of Roman-controlled lands in Western Europe. Instead, the lands that were considered "Roman Germania"—Germania Superior and Germania Inferior—were west of the river, along the northeastern edge of Roman Gaul.

---

[127] Jenkins, *Short History of Europe*, 2019, pg. 26-28.

[128] Liulevicius, "Formative Migrations: Mongols to Germans." Lecture 2. *The Great Courses: A History of Eastern Europe*, 2015

[129] Jenkins, *Short History of Europe*, 2019, pg. 26.

[130] Jenkins, *Short History of Europe*, 2019, pg. 28.

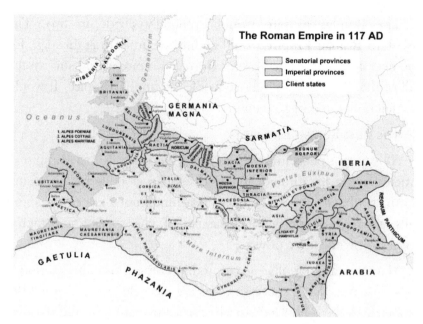

The Battle of Teutoburg Forest defined the Rhine River as the border of Roman lands in Western Europe. This map of the Roman provinces held in the 2nd century shows that the lands named "Germania Superior" and "Germania Inferior" are at the northeastern limit of Roman territory. The Germanic tribes that lived on the eastern side of the Rhine River were free from Roman control. (Public Domain)

Eastern Europe was no-man's-land; it was a place so rugged and dangerous that even the Romans couldn't penetrate it. The notion of Eastern Europe as we know it today became a sort of punishment, as Rome sent those who challenged its authority there. The well-known poet Ovid wrote racy poetry that directly contradicted Augustus's policy of morality. The emperor punished Ovid by sending him to the Black Sea.

The reforms that Augustus put in place would form the structure of the Roman Empire for centuries to come. He reigned over a Rome that rebirthed itself into an empire for four decades. What he left behind would grow, stretching far beyond the Black Sea.

The Roman Empire would eventually divide in two. The Western Roman Empire would endure, at times drag through, for the next 450 years. The Eastern Roman Empire would survive the fall of the West and be reborn as the Byzantine Empire. It would not fall until the mid-15th century.

The First Roman Emperors

All was not peaceful and serene in the early Roman Empire.[131] Augustus and his immediate successors never bothered to secure the path of succession. This led to a tumultuous era of rises and falls, where an emperor was assassinated, chaos ruled, and then a successor would seize power.

Many names familiar to us today come from this period.[132] Tiberius, Augustus's successor, was a good soldier who served the emperor well.[133] He led successful campaigns on the eastern frontier in Pannonia (modern-day Austria, Hungary, Serbia, Croatia, Slovenia, and Bosnia-Herzegovina) and Germania. Tiberius defeated Arminius, the victor of the Battle of Teutoburg Forest.

However, he was a horrible emperor. The pattern of eliminating enemies through assassination began with Tiberius, and it would last throughout the 1st century.[134] He had his rival for the throne murdered at the beginning of his reign. Tiberius most likely eliminated his nephew Germanicus because he was too popular among the Roman people. He also stationed the Praetorian Guard nearby to ensure the Senate's good behavior. Tiberius adopted

---

[131] Jenkins, *Short History of Europe*, 2019, pg. 28-29.

[132] Ibid., pg. 29.

[133] Jenkins, *Short History of Europe*, 2019, pg. 29; "Tiberius." *Encyclopedia Britannica*. https://www.britannica.com/biography/Tiberius

[134] "Tiberius." *Encyclopedia Britannica*.

Germanicus's son, Caligula, who then unleashed his own reign of terror.[135]

The 2nd century was much calmer and less chaotic, as Roman emperors learned how to rule effectively.[136] The Flavian and the Nerva-Antonine emperors brought relative peace and prosperity to Rome. Trajan, perhaps one of the best Roman emperors, expanded the empire to its furthest extent, conquering (among other territories) Dacia in modern-day eastern Hungary to Romania and Moldova to northern Bulgaria.[137] Trajan was a conqueror and a builder, and he began a public works campaign that would be continued by his successor, Hadrian.

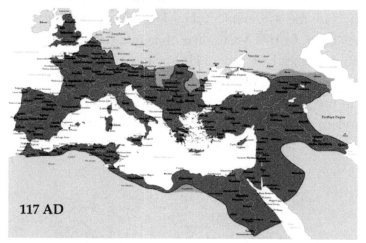

117 AD

A map of the Roman Empire at its furthest extent during the reign of Trajan in the year 117. Trajan conquered lands in Eastern Europe, making them part of the Roman Empire. By the 2nd century, Eastern Europe lay in the center of the Romans' vast landholdings, reaching as far north as Dacia and Pannonia, which includes parts of the modern-day borders of Romania, Hungary, Austria, Croatia, Serbia, Slovenia, and Bosnia and Herzegovina. (Credit: Tataryn, 2012)

[135] "Caligula." *Encyclopedia Britannica.* https://www.britannica.com/biography/Caligula-Roman-emperor

[136] Jenkins, *Short History of Europe*, 2019, pg. 30.

[137] Jankowski, *Eastern Europe!*, 2015, pg. 119; Jenkins, *Short History of Europe*, 2019, pg. 30-31; "Trajan." *Encyclopedia Britannica.* https://www.britannica.com/biography/Trajan

However, Hadrian would retreat from the borders Trajan had laid. He was less expansive, choosing to improve the infrastructure and society of the empire instead of grabbing more land.

During the reign of Marcus Aurelius, the calm sophistication of Rome started to crumble.[138] When the Parthians conquered Roman Syria, Marcus's co-emperor Varus led a successful campaign to reclaim the territory in 161. However, the returning troops infected the capital and the surrounding areas with the plague. This coincided with an invasion by Germanic tribes that shook Rome's confidence.

Marcus Aurelius and Varus went to the Danube to reinforce the border, but the Germanic tribes looped around, attacking the Adriatic coast. In 169, Varus died of natural causes, leaving Marcus to push the tribes back alone. He spent the next six years securing the Danube frontier, placating the Germanic tribes by letting them settle in two new provinces: Marcomanni and Sarmatia (located in the modern-day Czech Republic, Hungary, and Slovakia).

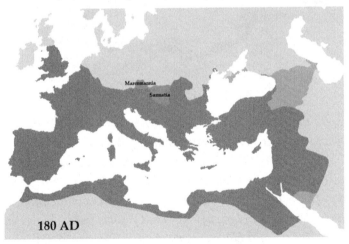

A map of the Roman Empire in 180 after the death of Marcus Aurelius. During his reign, he established two new provinces for the resettling of invading Germanic tribes: Marcomanni and Sarmatia. (Public Domain)

---

[138] "Marcus Aurelius." *Encyclopedia Britannica.*
https://www.britannica.com/biography/Marcus-Aurelius-Roman-emperor

---

The Disintegration of the Roman Empire

Although Marcus Aurelius is considered one of the better Roman emperors, his reign includes the beginnings of a dark chapter in Roman history: the Christian persecutions. By the end of the 2nd century, Christians were a distinct sect of Judaism, but they were not well-liked. The Romans saw them as a threat to paganism, which was the chosen form of worship in Rome.[139] Even though Marcus Aurelius persecuted Christians, he was not as steadfast in his beliefs as later emperors.

Aurelius's real objection was not that Christians were a monotheistic religion but that they refused to toe the line. The key to Roman supremacy was the idea that the emperors were gods and that they should be regarded as such. However, Christians refused to do that, stating that there was only one God.

After Marcus Aurelius died, the Roman Empire started to disintegrate.[140] The last years of the 2nd century leading into the 3rd century were characterized by barbarian invasions, an extensive empire without the means to govern it properly, and a shaky line of succession. The Roman emperors, starting with Marcus Aurelius's son and heir, Commodus, lost the respect of their own bureaucracy.[141] The governors of Rome's colonies started acting like emperors of their own territories.

At the turn of the 3rd century, Roman Emperor Septimius Severus strengthened Rome's eastern borders. He secured the borders on all sides, but his reign was the beginning of the shift to the East. The Roman Empire was about to enter the "Crisis of the Third Century," which was a fifty-year period in which political instability, plague, and barbarian invasions shook Rome to its core.

---

[139] Jenkins, *Short History of Europe*, 2019, pg. 31; "Marcus Aurelius." *Encyclopedia Britannica.*

[140] Jenkins, *Short History of Europe*, 2019, pg. 31-32.

[141] Ibid., pg. 32.

In 284, Diocletian brought the empire out of the Crisis of the Third Century. Diocletian was born in Dalmatia (in modern-day Croatia, Serbia, Bosnia and Herzegovina, Montenegro, Kosovo, and Albania) along the eastern edge of the Adriatic Sea, and he was a strong ruler who pushed several invaders out of Roman jurisdiction, including Germanic and Slavic tribes.[142] He established a strong infrastructure and bureaucracy, strengthening Roman borders.

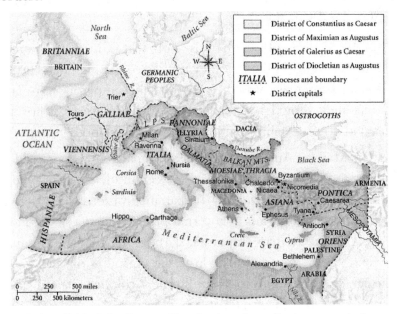

Diocletian divided the Roman Empire into four districts, appointing each territory to its own ruler. There were two emperors and two co-emperors under Diocletian's system, which was known as the Tetrarchy. (Credit: Coppermine Photo Gallery, 2008)

Diocletian continued what Septimius Severus had started; he officially split Rome into the Western Roman Empire and the Eastern Roman Empire. His idea was to make the borders smaller; the empires would be equal states with separate rulers, which would make administration easier. Having succeeded in bringing

---

[142] Ibid., pg. 34.

stability back to Rome, Diocletian passed the throne to his successor, living the last seven years of his life in peace in Dalmatia.

Although Diocletian had divided the empire to make it stronger, he actually tore it apart.[143] With the division came rivalry and power plays; it was a constant game of who was more powerful?[144] Many other changes occurred. Christianity arose in the East, while Rome held on to its pagan beliefs. The invading barbarians introduced Romans to a culture that was so unlike their own.

Constantine and the Eastern Roman Empire

The rise of the Eastern Roman Empire was secured during the reign of Constantine, who inherited the throne of the Western Roman Empire. He united both the East and West under his rule by 324. Constantine felt a great affinity for the Eastern lands, where he studied rulership under Diocletian. Constantine wanted to build a great city in the East, one that would rival all others. Its name? Constantinople.

Constantine shifted power to the East, reigning both empires from Constantinople. His decision to make the city the capital of both empires may have been pragmatic.[145] It was a trading center, and it was closer to the Danube, which had become harder and harder to secure. Its location on the Bosporus Strait provided natural protective barriers. However, his decision may well have been due to the fact that Christianity had taken root in the East more so than the West.

---

[143] Ibid., pg. 34-35.

[144] Ibid., pg. 35.

[145] Ibid., pg. 37.

The school of Raphael interpreted this scene as The Baptism of Constantine, which was completed in 1517. (Public Domain)

Constantine is famous for his deathbed conversion to Christianity, allowing the religion to spread throughout the empire.[146] The truth is, he planned the spread of Christianity long before his death. In 313, he signed a decree proscribing religious freedom across the Roman Empire. He also allowed Christianity to make its home in Constantinople.

This wouldn't be enough for the cracks already rising in Christianity to reverse themselves.[147] As early as the 4th century, there was disagreement over doctrine. A subsect, Arian Christianity, did not believe in the Trinity as other Christians did. This spelled trouble for the new religion that Constantine swore to protect. Before his city could become a Christian mecca, he called the Council of Nicaea in 325 to resolve the differences in doctrine.

Even by the time of the Council of Nicaea, Christianity had already made its home in the Eastern Roman Empire. Almost 60 percent of Christian bishops practiced there, and only about 2

---

[146] Ibid., pg. 35.

[147] Ibid., pg. 36.

percent of the bishops who attended the Council of Nicaea represented the Western Roman Empire. Even though Constantine promised to observe the meeting, he put pressure on the proceedings for what he saw as a favorable outcome. Under the Nicene Creed, anyone who followed Arian Christianity, which believed that the supreme being, God, was superior to the mortal Jesus, became a heretic.

In 326, Constantine did something that would torment the Roman Empire for the rest of its existence. He traveled to Rome, claiming that Constantinople would be the capital of the Roman Empire.[148] Rome would play a secondary role from here on out. Constantine also tried to enforce Christianity while he was there, which upset those who still clung to the old ways and revered the old temples. To show how serious he was about making this upstart religion the dominant one across the empire, he ordered two churches constructed. They would later become known as Archbasilica St. John Lateran and St. Peter's Basilica.

Now that he had thrown his weight around, Constantine had to make Constantinople the beacon of the empire he made it out to be. When it was completed in 330, it had all the features of a great Roman city: protective walls, breathtaking palaces, a forum, and other public spaces. The riches of the empire that passed through Constantinople went to lavishly decorate the city.

---

[148] Ibid., pg. 37.

The Column of Constantine was built in 330 to mark the foundation of Constantinople as the new capital of the Roman Empire. (Credit: Dmitry A. Mottl, 2018.)

Constantine died in 337, seven years after his great city was complete. While he had pushed and supported Christianity throughout his reign, he never really got around to officially converting. He did that on his deathbed. It seems strange that the emperor of Rome would have promoted something that was so fundamentally broken. He took great pains to unite his empire, but he replaced paganism with a fragmented church. Instead of abolishing Arianism, the Nicene Creed just ignored it; it spread to the West, making its home there. Arguments over doctrine turned into sectionalism.

There were now many different sects of Christianity, and none of them could agree on anything. However, maybe Constantine knew what he was doing. Within thirty years of his death, Roman emperors became Roman *Christian* emperors. Any attempts to crush the opposition in Christianity just made the subsects stronger.[149] While Constantine prided his city of Constantinople as being the center of his grand empire, it was tearing itself apart from the inside on matters of religion.

The Birth of Christianity

The Christian faith was an offshoot of Judaism.[150] In the Roman Empire, the Jews did not try to spread their religion. For this reason, the Romans did not see the Jews as a challenge to their pagan religion. The Jews were still persecuted, depending on the emperor, but they were relatively left alone.

The Overextended Roman Empire

The following century was when Rome would come into its own as a multi-continental empire.[151] Under Trajan, Rome extended from Western Europe to the Middle East to North Africa. During Trajan's reign, the Romans expanded to the eastern border of Eastern Europe, establishing the province of Dacia.[152] The Roman influence over the province remains today. Today, Roman Dacia lies in Romania. The Dacians are the ancestors of the Romanians. The Romans then left behind their language and culture, giving Romania unique characteristics among its neighbors.

---

[149] Ibid., pg. 38.

[150] Ibid., pg. 29.

[151] Jankowski, *Eastern Europe!*, 2015, pg.102.

[152] Liulevicius, "Formative Migrations: Mongols to Germans." Lecture 2. *The Great Courses: A History of Eastern Europe*, 2015.

Dacia and the Vlachs: The Roman Legacy in Eastern Europe

When the Romans arrived in Eastern Europe, they immediately took command of the people living there.[153] What made Rome so great and long-lasting is that they practiced assimilation, not massacre. They granted the people of Eastern Europe full citizenship and all of the protections that came with that citizenship. The Romans carved out provinces in the Balkans, one of which was known as "Dacia."

The people who inhabited Dacia are mysterious to modern-day historians, but they were most likely related to the tribes who inhabited two other territories in the Roman Balkans: Thrace and Illyricum. The earliest evidence of a Dacian state comes in the 1st century BCE. It would have been a contemporary of Rome under the dictatorship of Julius Caesar (although the Romans would not have seen it that way.)

For two centuries, the Dacians occupied the area northeast of the Black Sea. In the meantime, Rome emerged from the chaos of the 1st century CE, forming an empire that was a global force in the ancient world. At the turn of the 2nd century CE, under the leadership of the soldier-emperor Trajan, Rome defeated the Dacians, absorbing their state into the Roman Empire as the province "Dacia." It was only one of many victories Rome would enjoy during this period, which was the time of the greatest expansion of the empire after the reign of Augustus.

As we will see later, the Roman collapse of the 5th century caused widespread panic and disorder across Europe.[154] Former Roman provinces were forgotten, left to the stampede of barbarian invaders from across the steppe. These former Roman citizens were slaughtered or assimilated. Some left the area if they could, retreating to the southern Balkans. They stayed there, as the mountainous landscape offered some protection against the

---

[153] Jankowski, *Eastern Europe!*, 2015, pg.119.

[154] Ibid., pg.121.

raiding, looting, and general chaos of Eastern Europe in the 5th century and beyond.

After centuries of living in the same area, the tribes that retreated from the post-Roman Balkans formed their own distinct ethnic groups. These groups split geographically by the middle of the medieval period. The ancestors of the Albanians rose in the west of the southern Balkans, and the Vlachs rose in the east.

The Vlachs were pastoral nomads, and they can still be found today from Serbia to Greece. They especially stuck down roots in Bulgaria. Unlike other tribes that formed their own identities and settled in the Balkans, the Vlachs were 100 percent committed to their Roman past, and they considered themselves the descendants of Roman culture.

Roman Trade and the Amber Road

As Roman contacts expanded across Europe into the modern-day limits of Eastern Europe, they brought economic stability to the region.[155] Trade from the Mediterranean to the East moved back and forth across Roman lands, enriching farmers, craftsmen, and merchants. The Romans instituted building projects across the empire, employing masons, builders, and architects. With economic success came progress. The Romans installed aqueducts that provided running water to its citizens, as well as better roads to connect the vast edges of its empire and deploy troops to quell unrest. There was even a mail service!

---

[155] Jenkins, *Short History of Europe*, 2019, pg. 28.

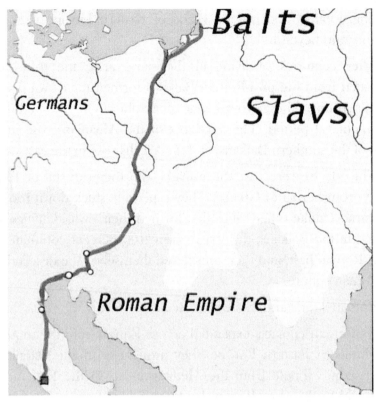

The trading route of the Amber Road. It stretched from the Baltic all the way south into Italy. (Credit: Bearas, 2011)

The Romans had a very important reason for maintaining their connections with Eastern Europe as long as they did.[156] They wanted access to the Amber Road. This trade network, named after its highly desirable amber stones, reached as far south as the Mediterranean Sea. Amber, which is fossilized pine sap, came from the forests of the Baltic region, and it was a luxury item. Thought to have healing properties, amber stone was a favorite among the elite and royalty of ancient civilizations.

---

[156] Jankowski, *Eastern Europe!*, 2015, pg.113; Liulevicius, "Formative Migrations: Mongols to Germans." Lecture 2. *The Great Courses: A History of Eastern Europe*, 2015.

Rome maintained its hold on Eastern Europe in more ways than one.[157] It was not just a land that they had conquered; Eastern Europe was a crucial part of the Roman machine. Over twenty men who would become Roman emperors came from the Balkan region. The trade that came through the Balkans was critically important for the empire's survival. Provinces like Noricum, Dalmatia, and Macedonia stretched down the eastern coast of the Adriatic Sea. Moving east, Moesia, Thrace, and Dacia gave the Romans unbroken control of the Mediterranean, Adriatic, Aegean, and Black Seas.

The Roman Empire maintained a consistent presence in the Balkans for hundreds of years.[158] However, Rome would not be able to hold on to this crucial trade area.[159] The vast Roman Empire had become hard to control. It was forced to evacuate its Balkan provinces, moving its eastern borders closer to home.

The Celts

The Celts also make an appearance in Eastern Europe. They arrived in the region in 800 BCE.[160] The Celtic tribes were more associated with Western Europe (and their conflicts with the Romans), but many of them settled along the eastern borders of Eastern Europe. Overall, the Celtic tribes spanned from Britain and Spain to Bulgaria and Turkey! They left their footprint on the culture of this area. The names of several rivers, cities, and regions in Eastern Europe were inspired by their ancient Celt names.

Like so many peoples before and after them, the Celts' homes in Eastern Europe were not permanent. Pushed out by two opposing forces—invading Germanic tribes and the expanding

---

[157] Jankowski, *Eastern Europe!*, 2015, pg.104.

[158] Ibid., pg.102.

[159] Jankowski, *Eastern Europe!*, 2015, pg.104; Liulevicius, "Formative Migrations: Mongols to Germans." Lecture 2. *The Great Courses: A History of Eastern Europe*, 2015.

[160] Jankowski, *Eastern Europe!*, 2015, pg. 87-88.

Roman Empire—the Celts left Eastern Europe. Celtic tribes then occupied Western Europe, where their conflicts with the Romans became legendary.

The Fall of the Western Roman Empire

The relative peace and prosperity that characterized Rome from the 1st and 2nd centuries CE gave way to chaos and instability.[161] In 285 CE, the Roman Empire split in half, becoming the Western Roman Empire and the Eastern Roman Empire. It would only reunite under one ruler twice until the fall of the Roman Empire. Constantine and Theodosius, who were both 4th-century emperors, maintained control over both halves of the Roman Empire by ruling from the Balkans. The Balkans were centrally located between both empires, allowing the emperor to rule most effectively.

The disintegration of the Roman Empire was a lengthy process, which included a breakdown of law and order.[162] Politically, the Western Roman Empire was decentralized, with a stronger East and a weaker West.[163] Beginning in the 3rd century, the slow trickle of barbarian tribes entering Roman territory turned into waves, and the constant onslaught of peoples pushing against the Roman borders further weakened the empire (this will be talked about in more detail in the next chapter).[164]

The Roman Empire eventually fell near the end of the 5th century.[165] However, the "fall of Rome" is actually a misnomer, as the Eastern Roman Empire continued on for nearly one thousand more years as the Byzantine Empire. The truest definition of the "fall of Rome" is that the Western Roman Empire disintegrated.

---

[161] Ibid., pg.102.

[162] Ibid., pg.112.

[163] Joshua J. Mark. "Ancient Rome." *World History Encyclopedia.*

[164] Jankowski, *Eastern Europe!*, 2015, pg.104.

[165] Ibid., pg.102, 114.

The fragile stability holding Europe together disappeared.[166] Roman citizens who lived in modern-day Eastern Europe found themselves living in no-man's-land, with no law and order and little help from the empire that was supposed to protect them.[167] There was no police force to protect Roman citizens from attack and theft.[168] There was no trade and no communication networks. Without food or supplies, people starved or died of disease or violence. As a result, the infrastructure in former Roman lands fell apart, and getting around became increasingly difficult.[169]

The Byzantines would survive the chaos of the 5th century, and they became a major player in the development of Eastern Europe until the fall of Constantinople in 1453.[170] The Byzantine Empire secured the Danube region, defending their territories against the barbarian invasions. After the fall of Rome, the Byzantines returned peace to the region, but Eastern Europe would no longer have Roman masters.[171]

---

[166] Ibid., pg.109-110.

[167] Ibid., pg.104.

[168] Ibid., pg.112.

[169] Ibid., pg.109-112.

[170] Ibid., pg.102, 114.

[171] Ibid., pg.104.

Chapter 3 – The Migration Period (300–800 CE)

Between the period 500 and 800 CE, a series of new peoples would move into the lands that make up Eastern Europe today.[172] Known colloquially as the "barbarian invasions," the Migration Period brought peoples who would establish the first states of Eastern Europe.[173] This collection of little states all competed for dominance.[174] The Early Middle Ages in Eastern Europe already included the beginnings of the states of the Czech Republic, Russia, Bulgaria, Ukraine, and Belarus.[175] These smaller states would make way for the larger empires that would form beginning in the 8th century CE.

---

[172] Jankowski, *Eastern Europe!*, 2015, pg. 113.

[173] Ibid., pg.109.

[174] Ibid., pg.27-28.

[175] Ibid., pg.16.

The Barbarian Invasions

The Germanic Tribes

While Rome was in decline, a wave of new peoples settled in the lands of Eastern Europe.[176] Along the Eurasian Steppe and the Great Northern European Plain came the most familiar demographic from the barbarian invasions—the Germanic tribes.[177] These migrations would continue until after the fall of Rome.[178] Along the Great Northern European Plain, waves of Germanic tribes crossed into Roman-held territory in Eastern Europe. They reached the Balkans first, with many using Eastern Europe as a stopping point before infiltrating today's Western Europe.[179] However, many Germanic tribes stayed and settled the area.

---

[176] Liulevicius, "Formative Migrations: Mongols to Germans." Lecture 2. *The Great Courses: A History of Eastern Europe*, 2015.

[177] Jankowski, *Eastern Europe!*, 2015, pg.113.

[178] Jankowski, *Eastern Europe!*, 2015, pg.109; Liulevicius, "Formative Migrations: Mongols to Germans." Lecture 2. *The Great Courses: A History of Eastern Europe*, 2015.

[179] Jankowski, *Eastern Europe!*, 2015, pg.113; Liulevicius, "Formative Migrations: Mongols to Germans." Lecture 2. *The Great Courses: A History of Eastern Europe*, 2015.

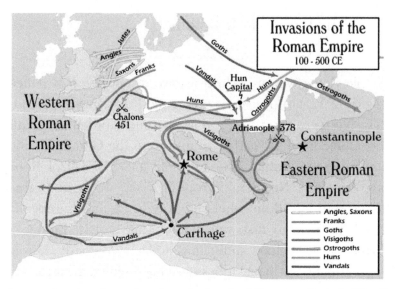

A map showing the paths taken during the Migration Period. (Credit: MapMaster, 2006)

The Germanic tribes were not the only outsiders from the east to make their way into the region. The Carpathian Basin fell to invaders from the steppe.[180] They were primarily equestrians; they had learned how to domesticate the horse thousands of years ago.[181] The peoples of the Eurasian Steppe used horses for food, as well as for travel and defense.

There was a strict system of social organization among the peoples of the steppe.[182] This meant that leaders could arrange an invasion and launch strategic attacks, wiping out a settlement more quickly than other tribes of Europe had seen before. Everyone had a place, and everyone had a role to play. This included women. Archaeological evidence shows that in graves among the steppe peoples, women were buried with weapons and armor designed specifically for them. However, female soldiers tended to stick to

---

[180] Jankowski, *Eastern Europe!*, 2015, pg.114.

[181] Ibid., pg.127-128.

[182] Ibid., pg.128-129.

land combat, while men learned to fight and shoot arrows while riding.

The Germanic Visigoths

When it came to the Visigothic tribes being pushed out of Eastern Europe, their king, Alaric I, wasn't going to go quietly.[183] He had learned military tactics from the Romans, and he and his army had come to their defense more than once. The Visigoths had helped put down rebellions, and he and his army were not properly rewarded.

More than anything, he wanted a safe place for him and his people without the threat of the Huns or any other marauders. By the late 4th century, the Huns had reached the farthest areas of Eastern Europe. They invaded the Danube River Basin, alarming officials in Constantinople. The Huns were even worse than the Parthians, as they were skilled cavalry warriors who specialized in sieges. The Huns moved into Eastern Europe, in some cases intermarrying with the peoples they conquered. However, their brutal form of invasion pushed many Germanic tribes out, forcing them deeper into Eastern and Western Europe.

Alaric felt like he could find a home in the Roman West, but he quickly found himself and his tribe unwelcome. To prove that he meant business, Alaric conquered Roman-held Athens in 395. He moved even farther west, arriving in Italy in 401. He approached the new emperor of the Western Roman Empire, Theodosius's son Honorius, with an offer. Alaric wanted his own position in the Roman army with compensation for himself and his men.

Honorius didn't take Alaric seriously, and he laughed at the offer. In 410, he would regret those words. Alaric and his Visigoths sacked Rome for the very first time. Despite the reputation the Germanic tribes had for raping and pillaging, the Visigoths really just stole whatever they could find of value. They generally left people, homes, and infrastructure alone.

Along with the Visigoths, the Vandals and the Burgundians also moved away from Eastern Europe into Roman territory in Western Europe. Germanic tribes were invading elsewhere too, but Honorius was bogged down on the Continent, and he refused to send troops to defend Britannia.[184] The West prepared for the worst.

It's not as if the Eastern Roman Empire wanted to help. They had their own problems, as religion was still fracturing the empire. Arianism was still around since it had never been fully eliminated by the Nicene Creed.

In 431, Theodosius II called another council to straighten matters of doctrine out again.[185] There was another Christian subsect that was shaking things up. Nestorianism questioned that Christ was eternal because he died as a man. The Council of Ephesus eliminated Nestorianism and forcefully denounced any other doctrine than their own that had been outlined in the Nicene Creed. The council also straightened out other details, like when Holy Week would be. Twenty years later, Pope Leo I tried to bring both sides together at the Council of Chalcedon. It didn't work; Christianity was permanently fractured.

The Huns

Less than fifty years after Constantinople was founded, the Huns reached the Danube River.[186] These warriors on horseback were related to the Scythian tribe, and to the Romans, they spoke a strange language and made strange sounds. They would turn out to be Constantinople's greatest challenge yet.

---

[183] Jenkins, *Short History of Europe*, 2019, pg. 38-39.

[184] Ibid., pg. 39-40.

[185] Ibid., pg. 40-41.

[186] Ibid., pg. 38-39.

The Huns were something that the Romans had never seen before, despite their struggles in the East. They could shoot arrows on horseback, and they were one with their horses. The Huns rode hundreds of miles a month; some said one thousand! More importantly and unfortunately for the Romans, the Huns knew how to siege a city and starve the population into submission. The sounds of galloping horses terrified all who heard it since the Huns took every town they could find.

The Huns weren't alone. Other nomadic tribes from the East followed them across the steppe, looking for places to settle. Like the Huns, they exacted tribute from those cities that wanted to be left alone.

While the historical memory of the Huns is one of terror and conquest, biological evidence says otherwise. The Huns didn't just tear through Europe and leave. They stayed and settled alongside the Gothic tribes they encountered, leading to many marriages and offspring. While they were indeed terrifying, they didn't come and leave as swiftly as legend says they did. The Hun "invasion" wasn't an invasion at all.

Eventually, their nomadic nature caught up to them. The Huns started to claim territory, and the Germanic tribes that had settled in Eastern Europe fled to the west. There was only one problem: the Romans held Western Europe. The Romans were inundated with unwelcomed visitors, as the Burgundians, Ostrogoths, Vandals, and Visigoths all migrated west, intruding on Roman territory. Between the Huns and the Germanic tribes fleeing west, many governors, especially in the frontier lands, chose to hole up inside their cities.

In 434, Attila became the king of the Huns.[187] He was terrifying in looks and in action. He attacked Constantinople in 443 and 447. But as terrifying as he was in person, Attila was no different than any other nomadic tribesman. For instance, he could be bribed

---

[187] Ibid., pg. 41.

into going away. Constantinople and other Eastern European cities found that they could pay Attila and the Huns, and they would leave their cities untouched. So, the Eastern Roman emperor paid him to go away. Western Roman Emperor Marcian (r. 467–472) refused to play ball anymore, and he stopped all tribute to the Huns.

In 451, the Romans had had enough of Attila's economic terrorism. They joined forces with the Visigoths against the might of the Huns. General Flavius Aetius and the king of the Visigoths, Theodoric I, met the Huns at the Battle of the Catalaunian Plains. Aetius's and Theodoric's armies of Roman and Germanic soldiers destroyed the Huns, forcing them to retreat.

They pulled back and moved into Italy. Pope Leo persuaded Attila to go back east, and the king of the Huns settled his warriors in modern-day Hungary. Two years later, Attila the Hun, the scourge of Europe, was dead. Although legend states that he was assassinated by his new Gothic wife, it is much more likely that he died of internal bleeding.

After the defeat of the Huns, they were replaced in the Carpathian Basin by other Germanic invaders.[188] The Ostrogoths occupied the northern Balkans and the Carpathian Basin, where they remained until they were defeated by the Byzantines in 562.

The Huns and the other barbarian invasions proved that Roman lands were susceptible to invasion and defeat.[189] As the people fled the invading barbarians, people sought shelter in cities and fortified settlements that dotted the Eurasian landmass. These cities became units unto themselves, setting a precedent for the first kingdoms that would soon dominate Europe.

The fall of the Roman Empire is generally timed in 476. The previous year, a Roman general named Orestes led a coup, placing his son on the throne as Romulus Augustulus. The teen didn't last

---

[188] Jankowski, *Eastern Europe!*, 2015, pg. 114.

[189] Jenkins, *Short History of Europe*, 2019, pg. 41-42.

long on the throne. In 476, a Roman-Germanic general, Odoacer, deposed Romulus, taking control of Italy. The Western Roman Empire was no more.

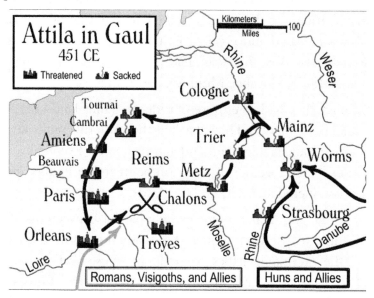

A map showing the advance of the Huns into Eastern and Western Europe. They moved in from the Eurasian Steppe to the Danube River Basin, traveling northeast along the Rhine River. They split into two advances, traveling west into modern-day France. (Credit: Goldsztajn, 2009)

The Turkic Peoples: The Avars, Bulgars, and Khazars

Eastern Europe was also a target for invading Central Asian nomads.[190] After the Ostrogoths were defeated, a new tribe moved in. They were the Avars, and they added yet another layer of ethnic diversity to Eastern Europe. This collection of Turkic tribes were horse riders, so the flat terrain of the Carpathian Basin was perfect

---

[190] Jankowski, *Eastern Europe!*, 2015, pg.114; Liulevicius, "Formative Migrations: Mongols to Germans." Lecture 2. *The Great Courses: A History of Eastern Europe*, 2015.

for them.[191] There was only one problem—that area wasn't exactly empty.

After the Byzantines conquered the Ostrogoths, another Germanic tribe—the Lombards—settled in the Carpathian Basin. The Avars defeated and pushed out the Lombards, gaining access to the basin. By 578, the Avars had built an empire that included lands in Bulgaria, Slovakia, Moldova, and Romania.

Although they had an empire of wide-stretching lands, the Avars were raiders by nature. They attacked the western Franks and the southern Bulgars, taking their land and resources. Eventually, these two forces joined together. A coalition between the Franks and the Bulgars conquered and defeated the Avars.

For a time, the Avar Empire set up a barrier between the steppe and Europe. Its presence limited the steady flow of invaders while forcing the Germanic tribes to settle in Western Europe. The defeat of the Avar Empire opened up Eastern Europe for settlement by other peoples.

Also among the first imports were another Turkic people from Central and West Asia: the Bulgars.[192] Like the Germanic tribes, the Bulgars actually appeared before the fall of Rome.[193] They occupied the Ural Mountains, moving south into the area of modern-day southwestern Russia between the Caspian and the Black Seas in the 2nd century.

The Bulgars splintered off into groups as they migrated west into Eastern Europe. One such group gained control of the northern coast of the Black Sea by the 7th century. Onogur (Great Bulgaria) spread from the Danube River to the Sea of Azov in today's Ukraine, Moldova, Romania, and Bulgaria.

---

[191] Jankowski, *Eastern Europe!*, 2015, pg.114.

[192] Jankowski, *Eastern Europe!*, 2015, pg.118; Liulevicius, "Formative Migrations: Mongols to Germans." Lecture 2. *The Great Courses: A History of Eastern Europe*, 2015.

[193] Jankowski, *Eastern Europe!*, 2015, pg.109, 118.

This Bulgar state didn't last. It befell the fate of so many of the early states of Eastern Europe: it was conquered by another people. The Khazars overtook the Bulgars in 670 CE. The survivors of Great Bulgaria spread out, separating into distinct groups. One, the Volga Bulgars, relocated to where the Volga River branches off into the Kama River in western Russia. Forming their own successful state, the Volga Bulgars occupied this area until the Mongols arrived in 1241.

Another group of the Bulgars moved to present-day Moldova. They found themselves in conflict with the Byzantines. In the late 7th century, after years of war between the two states, the Byzantines gave up. They left the Bulgars to build their own state to the south, along the Danube River region that separates modern-day Bulgaria and Romania.

When the Bulgars arrived, they realized they weren't alone.[194] The Slavs had moved in, making their home in the territory promised to the Bulgars.[195] After just concluding a war with the Byzantines, the Bulgars decided on a peaceful route. They allowed the Slavs to stay, and the two groups cooperated with each other in the new government. By the late 8th century, the Bulgars and the Slavs had intermingled into one ethnic group. The Bulgarians were now Slavs, and the Slavs were now Bulgarians. The Bulgarians were well known for their militarism, especially their horseback riding skills. In fact, the Bulgars were just as terrifying on horseback as the Huns were. The Bulgars' former enemies, the Byzantines, called on them to protect Constantinople from attack by Arab forces in 718.

---

[194] Ibid., pg.119.

[195] Jankowski, *Eastern Europe!*, 2015, pg.119; Liulevicius, "Formative Migrations: Mongols to Germans." Lecture 2. *The Great Courses: A History of Eastern Europe*, 2015.

When the Khazars made their way into Eastern Europe, they possessed highly-developed notions of statecraft, allowing them to build a lasting empire for centuries.[196] Since the beginning of the 6th century CE, the Khazars were part of an expansive territory known as the Göktürk Empire. It reached from northern China to the edge of the Balkans along the eastern border of the Black Sea.

The Göktürk state was too expansive to last long. A century and a half later, it disintegrated; the Göktürks abandoned their western lands and concentrated their power in Asia. The western Göktürk Empire was picked off between the two major powers that flanked it: the Bulgarian Empire and the Khazars.

By the last decades of the 7th century, the Bulgars were also booted out, leaving the Khazars to spread into Eastern Europe. The Khazar Khanate occupied western Asia, the northern Caucasus, and the easternmost reaches of Eastern Europe. It included access to the Aral Sea, the Caspian Sea, and the Black Sea. At its westernmost point, the Khazars reached present-day Moldova.

The Khazars were fiercely protective of their lands, and they maintained their position between Eastern Europe and the Arab empires to the southeast for hundreds of years. The empire formed a barrier between the Christian Byzantine Empire, the Slavic reaches in Eastern Europe, and the Arab Muslim Umayyads (and later the Abbasids).

The Khazars knew how to run a multicultural state, and their influence is seen among the medieval states of Eastern Europe. Over time, the tensions between the Khazars and the Arabs cooled, and the Abbasids became valued trading partners with the Khazars. This allowed Arab merchants to reach deep into Europe by way of Eastern Europe. The Khazars were also not religious fanatics, and they embraced Judaism in the 8th century CE. Based on findings among Khazar graves, this conversion seems to only

---

[196] Jankowski, *Eastern Europe!*, 2015, pg.109, 121.

have reached the elite. Many historians believe that the Khazars took their role as the peacekeepers of the region very seriously, and they refused to side with either Christian Europe or the Islamic Abbasids. Allowing the spread of Judaism was a way to keep both the Christians and the Muslims in check on either side of their lands.

The First Slavic States

From the 5th century to the 7th century, Eastern Europe became the point of destination for another group of peoples: the Slavs.[197] These tribes entered Eastern Europe together, eventually forming the most extensive ethnolinguistic family in Europe.[198] Eventually, the Slavs separated, settling in different regions of Eastern Europe. This created the different Slav language families (West Slav, East Slav, and South Slav) mentioned in Chapter 1.

In the 6th century CE, the Slavs conquered the area between Aquileia, Italy, to Constantinople.[199] The Slavic occupation of the Balkans connected the Italian Peninsula to the desirable Asian trade routes. The Slavs who settled in the southern Balkans to the east of the Black Sea were assimilated into Greek culture. However, to the north, the Slavs outnumber any other population, and their language and culture dominate Eastern Europe.

While it is not exactly known from where the Slavs come, research places the earliest Slavs in the expanse of land from the Czech Republic to western Russia.[200] What was left of the Avars moved east into Byzantine lands. When the Slavs arrived, the Byzantines hired the Avars to attack the Slavs and push them out.

---

[197] Liulevicius, "Formative Migrations: Mongols to Germans." Lecture 2. *The Great Courses: A History of Eastern Europe*, 2015; Cristian Violatti. "Slavs." *World History Encyclopedia*. Published September 10, 2014. https://www.worldhistory.org/Slavs/

[198] Liulevicius, "Formative Migrations: Mongols to Germans." Lecture 2. *The Great Courses: A History of Eastern Europe*, 2015.

[199] Jankowski, *Eastern Europe!*, 2015, pg.114.

[200] Jankowski, *Eastern Europe!*, 2015, pg.114-115; Cristian Violatti. "Slavs." *World History Encyclopedia*.

Instead of fighting each other, the Avars and the Slavs made an alliance with each other. Then, they started attacking Byzantine outposts!

The partnership between the Avars and the Slavs allowed the Slavs to move farther into Eastern Europe.[201] These Slavic invasions would last until the end of the 7th century. The tribes moved into lands flanked by the Mediterranean Sea to the south and the Baltic Sea to the north, settling far west into modern-day Germany. It is interesting that most of these travelers were Slavic, but many could have been from other tribes and backgrounds that joined and were assimilated into Slavic culture.

There is too much unknown about the early Slavic states to make a definitive statement about them.[202] Some 6th-century sources record a small Slavic state run by the Antes, a small group of Slavs shrouded in mystery. Considered the first example of organization within the Slavic tribes, the Antes set up this small state in the Dniester and Dnieper River valleys. This state didn't last long, for the Antes don't appear in the historical record after the early 7th century.

In the early 600s, the Avars still dominated the Carpathian Basin, and they dominated the local Slavic tribes there. Eventually, the Slavic tribes decided that self-rule was a better idea, and they rebelled against the Avars. The Slavs freed themselves from Avar rule in 623, electing their own leader. Interestingly enough, he wasn't Slavic at all! The new ruler of the Slavs was Samo, a Frankish merchant. The Franks were of Germanic descent, living in what is today France and Germany. The Frankish Empire was centered in what the ancient sources refer to as "Roman Gaul," which was made famous during Julius Caesar's attempts to crush the tribes living there.

---

[201] Jankowski, *Eastern Europe!*, 2015, pg.109, 115.

[202] Ibid., pg.117.

Samo's new state was located in the present-day borders of the Czech Republic and Slovakia, but he wouldn't hold on to it. Samo successfully defended the state against an attack by the Franks in 631, reaching the height of his power. However, Samo's death in the 660s brought an end to his empire.

When Samo's state fell, many Slavs relocated east of the Alps. They formed another early Slavic state, Carinthia, centered in Slovenia and stretching into Austria and Italy. Not much is known about this state either, except that the people who live in Slovenia believe they are descended from these Slavs. After Carinthia was conquered by the Franks, it disintegrated.

A common element of the earliest Slavic states is that they were under constant threat. However, new arrivals were on the move across the steppe, and they would find themselves in control of a whole region of Slavs.

The Umayyads and the Abbasids

In the 7th century CE, the Arab influence in Eastern Europe bore fruit.[203] The Prophet Muhammad united the clans that occupied the area, creating a powerful army to support his rule of the Arabian Peninsula. For the next thirty years, Muhammad and his successors, the Four Caliphs, spread out, carving out a Muslim Arab Empire that controlled lands from the peninsula as far north as the southern Caucasus Mountains on the eastern Black Sea.

In the 650s, Islam split in half due to the competing Shiite and Sunni sects. In 661, the Umayyad dynasty inherited Muhammad's Muslim Arab Empire. Until the fall of the Umayyads in 750, they continued to conquer lands for Islam. At the height of their power, the Umayyads spread east and west, controlling lands from Western Europe to North Africa to the Middle East. Eastern Europe was in the purview of the Umayyads, and they attacked the

---

[203] Ibid., pg.104.

area surrounding the Black Sea with the intent to conquer more than once.

To the very south of Eastern Europe was the coast of the Mediterranean Sea, which was a favorite haunt of Arab pirates. They would sack cities along the coast, stealing goods and people to sell into slavery.[204]

The inheritors of the former Persian Empire—the Muslim Arabs of the 7th century to the Seljuk Turks of the 10th century—knew the importance of the borders of Eastern Europe.[205] They constantly fought the Byzantines for control of the territory.

In 750, the Abbasid dynasty defeated the Umayyad Empire, forming their own critically important Arab empire.[206] Ruling from the Middle East, the Abbasids formed centers of learning, preserving ancient Western texts. They were traders, connecting the riches of Asia with Western Europe. During the Crusades, Western Europeans were exposed to the riches of the East, and they wanted more. Abbasid traders traveled north from the Mediterranean through the Black Sea to the major rivers of modern-day Russia to satisfy the European demand for spices and silk. The Abbasids were the last of the great Muslim Arab empires, controlling their lands until the Mongols conquered them in the 13th century.

The Northern States along the Baltic Sea

Although they are the most widespread tribe, the Slavs were not the only imports to Eastern Europe.[207] East of the Baltic Sea, the Finnic tribes and the Baltic tribes staked their claim in Eastern Europe. About 3000 BCE, the Finns spread from the Ural Mountains into Siberia, Russia, Estonia, and, of course, Finland.

---

[204] Ibid., pg.104-105.

[205] Ibid., pg.101.

[206] Ibid., pg.105.

[207] Ibid., pg.123.

They mostly remained out of sight, preferring the heavily forested areas to the north over the wide-open spaces of the Eurasian Steppe.[208]

The Finns weathered the Roman occupation of Eastern Europe. However, by 800 CE, the Slavic tribes were settling throughout the region, so the Finns moved even farther north. Despite their attempts to remain in the shadows, the Finns were well-adapted to running their own states, and they helped found Kievan Rus.

Around the same time the Finnic tribes were spreading out, so were another people: the Baltic tribes. Like the Finns, they preferred to keep to themselves. Hundreds of years passed, with the Baltic tribes occupying the wooded areas to the east of the Baltic Sea. However, they faced the double threat of the Germanic invasions and the Slavic invasions during the Roman period.

The Baltic tribes retreated south, keeping to the river valleys in modern-day Poland, Latvia, and Belarus. They used these river valleys to become skilled merchants and commanded a well-organized system east of the sea. The Vikings saw the potential of the region, and they frequently harassed the Baltic tribes and tried to push them out of the trading business.

Beginning in the late 12th century, after nearly one hundred years of outside attacks on the Baltic region, the Crusades had gone sour. Christian missionary knights abandoned the Holy Land for a time. They saw the pagan tribes of the Finns and the Baltics as fair game; after all, the Crusades were a mission to convert everyone, not just the Islamic empires. In 1193, after permission was granted by Pope Celestine III, Crusaders went on a "slash-and-burn" campaign. They attacked settlements and trade routes. Even though the Crusaders destroyed everything in their path, the tribes still held on to their traditions and beliefs much longer than the

---

[208] Ibid., pg.124.

Crusaders thought they would.[209] When the Baltic tribes faced decimation, they united to officially challenge the Crusaders' warpath through their territory. They would eventually form the community that is now the ancestors of the Lithuanians.

[209] Ibid., pg.125.

Chapter 4 – The Rise of Medieval Empires and Spheres of Control (800–1242 CE)

As new states formed during the Migration Period, Eastern Europe coalesced into four major spheres.[210] They were controlled by the Byzantines, the Franks, the Khazars, and the Bulgarians. Most people who lived in Eastern Europe were either under the direct control of these empires or at least under their influence. They spread their concept of religion, government, economy, and social hierarchies throughout their territories. The influence of Rome was strong, and it permeated through its former lands, influencing the new states of Europe.[211] Stronger, more sophisticated states started appearing in this period, leading to over four hundred years of relative peace.[212] However, there would be one polarizing event that took place during this period: the spread of Christianity.[213]

---

[210] Ibid., pg.131.

[211] Jenkins, *Short History of Europe*, 2019, pg. 44.

[212] Jankowski, *Eastern Europe!*, 2015, pg.131.

[213] Liulevicius, "Formative Migrations: Mongols to Germans." Lecture 2. *The Great Courses: A History of Eastern Europe*, 2015.

The Pope and the King of the Franks: The Beginnings of the Holy Roman Empire

The Franks were one of the many Germanic tribes that made their way into Europe during the Roman period.[214] The Franks moved through Eastern Europe, heading toward modern-day Western Europe. In 11 BCE, they occupied Roman Gaul (today's France and western Germany).

The Frankish tribes organized into confederations under a strong leader. The Romans allowed them to stay in Gaul, hiring them as *foederati*–allies who would fight for the Romans when their territories were under attack. As the Roman Empire was waning, the Franks helped defend Roman borders. When the Huns came storming through Europe, the Franks helped push them back. They were instrumental in defeating the Huns at the decisive Battle of Châlons in 453 CE.

---

[214] Jankowski, *Eastern Europe!*, 2015, pg.134.

A map of the Frankish tribes in Roman Gaul, c. 3ʳᵈ century CE. (Credit: Odejea, 2009)

After the fall of Rome, the Franks settled in their territories in former Roman Gaul. Their confederations sectioned off, forming their own states. In 481, Clovis became the king of the Franks. His father had founded the Merovingian line of kings, and Clovis united the Frankish tribes under their rule.[215] He conquered parts of modern-day France and Germany, expanding the Frankish lands and making the Merovingians a major force in Western Europe.[216] His descendants would wield even more power.

---

[215] Jenkins, *Short History of Europe*, 2019, pg. 43; Jankowski, *Eastern Europe!*, 2015, pg.134-135.

[216] Jenkins, *Short History of Europe*, 2019, pg. 43.

Clovis set a precedent without even knowing it. He had been raised pagan, but his wife, Clotilde, was a Christian. She believed it would be a good idea for him to convert. In time, the Franks became a Christian people, and they allied with the Church of Rome. The Franks and their descendants, the French, would remain close allies with Rome for the next several centuries.

While consolidating his rule, Clovis also understood the importance of building strong alliances. The Ostrogothic leader Theodoric the Great, who lived in today's limits of the Balkans, understood that too, although he was affiliated with a different church. Since Theodoric was a close ally of Eastern Roman Emperor Zeno, he did the emperor's bidding. Zeno wanted Italy back, and he sent Theodoric to get it. How could he achieve that, though? Allegedly, Theodoric murdered Odoacer at a dinner in 493.

Theodoric also found allies on the other side of Europe, such as Clovis and the Franks. After Theodoric conquered Italy, Clovis and Theodoric formed an alliance as neighbors. Clovis gave Theodoric his sister in marriage, and their children would later marry into the royal families of other Germanic tribes. These allies, who are considered the "founding fathers of medieval Europe," died fifteen years apart; their efforts set the stage for state-building in the Middle Ages.[217]

Meanwhile, the Avars moved into the Carpathian Basin, forcing the Lombards to leave by the end of the 6th century CE.[218] The Lombards relocated to northern Italy; here, they found a place where they could really dig in their roots. Five years after reaching the shores of Italy, the Lombards were inching dangerously close to Rome in 572.[219]

---

[217] Ibid., pg. 44.

[218] Jankowski, *Eastern Europe!*, 2015, pg.134.

[219] Jenkins, *Short History of Europe*, 2019, pg. 48.

Rome was in a bad state after its fall. Plague, political instability, and now the threat of invasion drove the city's prefect, Gregorius Anicius, to leave public service and establish a monastery. In 579, the pope persuaded him to go east and ask the Byzantines for help. It didn't work, and Gregorius returned empty-handed. Within ten years, Gregorius would become the pope himself. He was elected to the office in 590.

The Lombards still occupied the region. Gregorius, taking the name Pope Gregory I, now had to deal with the Lombards himself. His experience as a prefect and a man of God helped him out. He paid the Lombards off, keeping Rome safe for the moment. Known as Gregory the Great, he eliminated pagan temples and started sending missionaries from Rome to convert others to Christianity.

Over the next two centuries, the Lombards stood their ground, constantly threatening Rome's security.[220] As if that wasn't bad enough, the Umayyad Arabs led surprise raid attacks on the Italian coastline. The Umayyad threat was very real for Christian nations, even though they were religiously tolerant and weren't interested in forced conversion. The Umayyads just wanted land, obeisance, and tribute.[221]

Rome was the center of the Catholic Church, which had stepped into the power vacuum left open by the fall of the Roman Empire.[222] Technically, the Church of Rome was secondary to the Eastern Orthodox Church in Byzantium.[223] However, the Byzantines refused to assist Rome with its invasion.[224] They were dealing with their own Arab invasions in Byzantium.

---

[220] Jankowski, *Eastern Europe!*, 2015, pg.134.

[221] Jenkins, *Short History of Europe*, 2019, pg. 50-52.

[222] Jankowski, *Eastern Europe!*, 2015, pg.134.

[223] Jankowski, *Eastern Europe!*, 2015, pg.134; Jenkins, *Short History of Europe*, 2019, pg. 48.

[224] Jankowski, *Eastern Europe!*, 2015, pg.134.

If either the Lombards or the Umayyads reached Rome, they could control the church—or destroy it. The Roman Church didn't need that; it was already fractured enough as it was.[225] The monastic movement, where the faithful retreated to live an ascetic life in monasteries in a peaceful protest to church policies, had spread to the West from the East. Monasteries were popping up all over Western Europe, with monks removing themselves from the purview of the church. With monasteries accommodating more and more monks, they further fractured the power that the church was struggling to build.

Pope Stephen II (in off. 752-757) was desperate for protection, so he went north to visit the new king of the Franks.[226] The Merovingians had led the Franks for about three hundred years, but their power waxed and waned in the last century of their rule. Pepin the Short deposed them for good in 751.[227] Pepin had already managed to hold on to power for three years when he received a visit from Pope Stephen II in 754.[228] As it stood, the two men needed each other. The church needed powerful friends, and allying with it added legitimacy to anyone's reign. Thus, Pepin saw the potential in an alliance with the church.[229]

Pepin and Stephen came to an agreement. If the Franks helped Stephen defeat his and the church's enemies, namely the Arabs and the Lombards, then he would support Pepin's rule. Despite how ill-gotten Pepin's position was, the pope would overlook the usurpation. That year, the pope crowned Pepin as "King of the Franks" and "Patrician of the Romans," which were titles that he craved.

---

[225] Jenkins, *Short History of Europe*, 2019, pg. 43-44.

[226] Jankowski, *Eastern Europe!*, 2015, pg.134.

[227] Ibid., pg.134-135.

[228] Ibid., pg.135.

[229] Jankowski, *Eastern Europe!*, 2015, pg.134-135; Jenkins, *Short History of Europe*, 2019, pg. 52-53.

This agreement allowed the Franks to become the spokespeople of the church. They became the worldly champions of the Roman Catholic Church, invading and conquering lands and sending missionaries into areas that had not converted yet. As a result of this meeting between the king of the Franks and the pope of Rome, the Franks brought Christianity to Western and Eastern Europe.

To their credit, the Franks upheld their end of the deal. They used their military might to push the Lombards away from Rome, and they eventually ended Rome's reliance and subordination to Byzantium and the Eastern Orthodox Church. The Lombards abandoned their landholdings surrounding Rome, evacuating the lands that would become known as the Papal States. Pepin granted control of these lands to Pope Stephen, but that was a big no-no for Constantinople. The Byzantines claimed the lands as the supreme power of Christianity, and they said the lands weren't Pepin's to give. That led to the Donation of Constantine, which is probably the most infamous forged document in history. This dubious document, supposedly signed by Constantine, states that he gifted the same lands that Pepin just drove the Lombards out of as a donation to the Roman Church.

The Franks had felt closely allied to Rome, but they grew closer due to their success against the Lombards. Of course, the Franks used their relationship with the Church of Rome to spread Christianity throughout their lands and conquer new territories.

In 768, Pepin the Short died, and his sons, Carloman and Charles, inherited his lands. Of course, as brothers do, they fought over who had more land and who was more powerful. Three years later, Carloman died, and Charles confiscated his brother's lands from his sons. The lands of Pepin the Short were joined together again.

Pepin's son Charles continued the Frankish alliance with the church. Although he carried himself like a king, he was a hardened soldier.[230] He spent the last years of the 8th century conquering land after land as he headed toward the east, using the support of the church to do it.[231] He did what Rome could not: he brought the Germanic tribes past the Elbe River under his rule.[232] Charles particularly targeted the Slavs, forcing them to relocate to the eastern side of the Elbe River.[233]

Charles is most familiar by the Anglicized version of his French name: Charlemagne. In 800, Pope Leo III bestowed a new title on Charlemagne: Holy Roman Emperor.[234] The new title was just as political as it was symbolic. It gave the Franks the religious authority they needed to spread Christianity throughout the lands they controlled, but it also served as a symbol that Charles and the Franks were the inheritors of the Western Roman Empire that fell over three hundred years prior. Thanks to both the Church of Rome and the Franks' imperialistic efforts, the Eastern Orthodox Church had no choice but to recognize the growing power of the West.

The Christianization of Eastern Europe

The new title also served the pope well.[235] He needed a closer ally than Byzantium, and the Franks had a history of doing what they said they would do. The Holy Roman Empire would last until 1806, although its territories would shift throughout the years. In fact, historians debate over whether the Holy Roman Empire truly

---

[230] Jenkins, *Short History of Europe*, 2019, pg. 53-54.

[231] Jankowski, *Eastern Europe!*, 2015, pg.135.

[232] Jenkins, *Short History of Europe*, 2019, pg. 54.

[233] Jankowski, *Eastern Europe!*, 2015, pg.135.

[234] Jankowski, *Eastern Europe!*, 2015, pg.135; Jenkins, *Short History of Europe*, 2019, pg. 54.

[235] Jenkins, *Short History of Europe*, 2019, pg. 55.

---

began at this stage, as Charlemagne's empire didn't even last until the end of the century. Other scholars attribute the start of the Holy Roman Empire to Otto I; he revived Charlemagne's empire in 962, and the empire would survive for over eight centuries.

In either case, the Holy Roman Empire was a collection of German-speaking lands under the emperor's control. However, the real power was in the title. The church proved its power over secular matters by granting or withholding the honor, which means the popes basically used the title to get emperors to do what they wanted.

In turn, the Holy Roman Emperor became the hand of the church in the secular world. The power of the East had dwindled, and Charlemagne and his empire were the real power behind Christianity now.

Charlemagne's efforts were just the beginning.[236] He considered it his mission to Christianize the whole of Europe. He pushed past the Elbe River, settling the southern border of modern-day Austria. He cleared the Slavs out of today's Croatia and Slovenia on the northeastern coast of the Adriatic Sea. Even farther east, he formed an alliance with the Bulgarians, and they fought and defeated the Avars by 810 CE.

The first Holy Roman emperor's influence expanded past his border, and it was carried even farther east by missionaries and diplomats. The Byzantines had a problem with this threat against Orthodox Christianity, but Charlemagne's empire didn't last long enough for them to make any serious moves against the Franks.

The Carolingian dynasty would realize that one's rule was only as strong as one's successor.[237] Just as Pepin's sons had fought over lands, Charlemagne's heirs would do the same. In 814, after Charlemagne died, his only surviving son Louis the Pious inherited

---

[236] Jankowski, *Eastern Europe!*, 2015, pg.135-136.

[237] Jankowski, *Eastern Europe!*, 2015, pg.136; Jenkins, *Short History of Europe*, 2019, pg. 55-56.

the entirety of the Carolingian Empire. The 830s were defined by a civil war between Louis's sons that would spill over after Louis's death. After their father died, they spent three years entrenched in a civil war against each other, which resulted in the Treaty of Verdun in 843. It officially divided the Carolingian lands, creating the modern-day boundaries of France and Germany. The treaty created three separate states that were divided among Louis the Pious's surviving sons: Charles the Bald, Louis the German, and Lothar I.[238] Charles the Bald inherited lands in modern-day France, while Louis the German assumed leadership over modern-day Germany. Lothar I took the lands in the middle, from the Loire and Rhone Rivers in the west and the Rhine River in the east. This territory was named after him. The middle Frankish state of Lotharingia was the only one of the three kingdoms to come with the title of Holy Roman emperor.

Lotharingia never did consolidate itself. The Frankish tradition of splitting inheritances equally further broke it into smaller territories. Although it wasn't an impressive state, trade made Lotharingia a hot commodity. It boasted the burgeoning trade cities of Antwerp, Ghent, Genoa, and Milan.

---

[238] Jenkins, *Short History of Europe*, 2019, pg. 55-56; "Lothar I." Encyclopedia Britannica. https://www.britannica.com/biography/Lothar-I

Europe in 814. (Public Domain)

The spread of Charlemagne's empire brought with it the spread of Latin Christianity.[239] This put the Franks in direct conflict with the Byzantines and Orthodox Christianity. As both the Frankish Empire and the Byzantine Empire fought each other for supremacy, which equated to how many countries and peoples they could convert, they drew a line in the sand between which Christianity was the "right" one. These conflicts between Latin and Orthodox Christians continued for hundreds of years until the Great Schism of 1077. Rome and Byzantium each excommunicated the other, formally separating the Christian churches.

As Latin Christianity spread from the west and Orthodox Christianity spread from the east during the medieval period, the two spheres of influence crashed in the middle—in the heart of Eastern Europe. Christian missionaries from France to Poland

---

[239] Liulevicius, "Formative Migrations: Mongols to Germans." Lecture 2. *The Great Courses: A History of Eastern Europe*, 2015.

traveled east and west (respectively), Christianizing any pagan tribes they could find.[240]

The defining era of the medieval period was the Crusades.[241] While this time period of religious wars is generally lumped together and classified as a series of holy wars against the Muslim rulers of the Holy Land, the Crusades were actually a mission to Christianize all of Europe. The Northern Crusades of the 12th century wanted to convert the Slavic populations of the Baltic states to Christian nations.[242]

The People's Crusade, which saw the faithful stomp across Eastern Europe to get to the Holy Land. It took place during the First Crusade. (Public Domain)

[240] Jankowski, *Eastern Europe!*, 2015, pg.135.

[241] Liulevicius, "Formative Migrations: Mongols to Germans." Lecture 2. *The Great Courses: A History of Eastern Europe*, 2015.

[242] Jankowski, *Eastern Europe!*, 2015, pg.135-136; Liulevicius, "Formative Migrations: Mongols to Germans." Lecture 2. *The Great Courses: A History of Eastern Europe*, 2015.

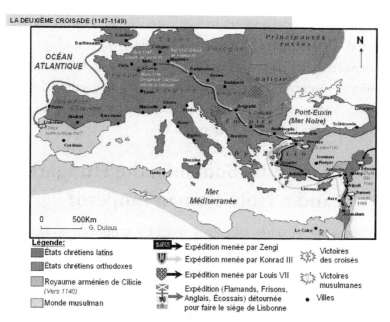

*This French map shows the paths of the Second Crusade (1147-1150).
The expeditions of Conrad III of Germany and Louis VII of France
marched across Eastern Europe to reach the Holy Land. On this map,
Conrad's path is marked in yellow arrows, and Louis's path is marked in
blue arrows. (Credit: Gulhem06, 2011)*

In 1147, the Kingdom of Denmark led a crusade against
Estonia. At the same time, the Germanic Teutonic Knights
invaded Lithuania. The Lithuanian campaign was a resounding
defeat for the Crusaders, but they had more success against the
ancient Prussians, who occupied modern-day Poland and
Kaliningrad. Just like in the Holy Land, victorious Crusader
knights remained in the lands they Christianized to make sure the
population didn't revert back to their old religions in their absence.
While most Baltic and Slavic tribes assimilated with the Christian
power that conquered them, some survived and resisted this
external pressure.

While the medieval period saw the mass conversion of states
and territories, there was also a political element to
Christianization, as there was a direct link between church and
state. The church offered legitimacy to a Christian ruler, so these

rulers pushed conversion in their lands. Newly converted states associated themselves with the representatives of the church who had converted them, namely either the Frankish Empire or the Byzantine Empire. The spread of Christianity also created a mass of satellite states for the Franks and the Byzantines, adding to the religious tensions throughout Europe.

Greater Moravia, Bohemia, the Hungarians, and a Holy Roman Emperor

Just beyond the reaches of Charlemagne's empire, another great power was growing to challenge the West's spread into Eastern Europe.[243] By the end of the 8th century, Nitra, a city pressed between the expanding Carolingian Empire from the west and the Avars from the east, became an important political and cultural center for the Slavs who settled in modern-day western Slovakia. To the northeast, in the modern-day Czech Republic, the leader of the Moravian Slavs, Mojmir, conquered Nitra and incorporated western Slovakia into his own lands. Mojmir's new empire was called Greater Moravia.[244]

The Moravians would become major political players in 9th-century Eastern Europe. According to scholar Tomek Jankowski, "Moravia established institutions and traditions of government, church and diplomacy—and resistance to German control—that served as a model for successive Eastern European states over the next two centuries."[245]

Mojmir's successor, Rastislav, who took power in the 840s CE, was more of a diplomat. Even though he wanted to form a good relationship with the Franks, he saw the powerful Frankish Empire

[243] Jankowski, *Eastern Europe!*, 2015, pg.137.

[244] Jankowski, *Eastern Europe!*, 2015, pg.137; Liulevicius, "Formative Migrations: Mongols to Germans." Lecture 2. *The Great Courses: A History of Eastern Europe*, 2015.

[245] Jankowski, *Eastern Europe!*, 2015, pg.137-138.

as a danger, even though they were the official spokespeople of Western Christianity. Rastislav didn't have a problem with conversion; he just did not want to be converted by the Franks, as he saw that as a one-way ticket to Moravia becoming a satellite state of the Frankish Empire. So, Rastislav did the next best thing. He imported Byzantine missionaries to Moravia in 862.[246]

These missionaries were two Greek brothers named Cyril and Methodius.[247] They spoke Slavic, so they could communicate with the Slavic population in Moravia. Cyril and Methodius set to translating religious texts into Slavic languages, using them in their conversion work. First, though, they needed an alphabet. They created one of their own, which would become Old Church Slavonic. These Slavonic texts spread throughout Eastern Europe, and missionaries successfully used them in Slavic states to convert residents to Christianity.[248] Eventually, Old Church Slavonic would become the Eastern Orthodox Church's official language.[249]

Five years after they arrived, the brothers were successfully converting Moravian Slavs to Eastern Orthodox Christianity, which conflicted with Roman Catholic missionaries' aspirations in the area.[250] The Franks threw their weight around, forcing the pope to call Cyril and Methodius to Rome. The brothers arrived in 867, where they found the new pope, Adrian II, more flexible. Adrian allowed them to return to their work and use their translated religious texts. Unfortunately, Cyril died, leaving his brother to return to Moravia to pick up their missionary work alone.

---

[246] Jankowski, *Eastern Europe!*, 2015, pg.137-138; Liulevicius, "Formative Migrations: Mongols to Germans." Lecture 2. *The Great Courses: A History of Eastern Europe*, 2015.

[247] Cyril's birth name was actually Constantine; he changed his name to Cyril before he died around 867.

[248] Jankowski, *Eastern Europe!*, 2015, pg.139.

[249] Liulevicius, "Formative Migrations: Mongols to Germans." Lecture 2. *The Great Courses: A History of Eastern Europe*, 2015.

[250] Jankowski, *Eastern Europe!*, 2015, pg.137-138.

Methodius remained in Moravia until the Franks finally forced him out in 885. Methodius and his followers went to Bulgaria, founding churches and training missionaries there. These new schools were instrumental in converting Kievan Rus to Christianity.

In the meantime, the Franks had had enough of Rastislav's machinations and removed him from the throne. His nephew, Svatopluk, kept Moravia independent of Frankish influence while building positive relations with them. However, there was a more threatening enemy—one that he didn't even consider.

During his reign, Svatopluk expanded Moravian landholdings. This earned him many enemies, and warfare plagued his reign.[251] He used Magyar auxiliary soldiers to defeat his enemies. The Magyars, the peoples from whom the Hungarians are descended, came from the Ural Mountains in modern-day Russia.[252] Around 4000 BC, the Magyars moved south, reaching the Volga River. In the 700s CE, the Khazar Empire conquered the Magyars, who would remain under Khazar rule for about one hundred years.

By 830 CE, rebellion and instability drove the Magyars away from the Volga, and they settled in present-day Ukraine. Despite the struggle to find a stable home, the Magyars had a gift that was well known throughout the medieval period. They were the best steppe warriors of the age, and others wanted to exploit that.

The Magyars found their most enthusiastic client in Svatopluk. With Magyar help, he grew Greater Moravia's landholdings to include modern-day southern Poland, Slovakia, the Czech Republic, as well as parts of Hungary, Slovenia, and Austria.[253] In the late 9th century, Svatopluk conquered Bohemia in the present-

[251] Ibid., pg.144.

[252] Jankowski, *Eastern Europe!*, 2015, pg.144; Liulevicius, "The Other Europe." Lecture 1. *The Great Courses: A History of Eastern Europe*, 2015.

[253] Jankowski, *Eastern Europe!*, 2015, pg.137; Liulevicius, "Formative Migrations: Mongols to Germans." Lecture 2. *The Great Courses: A History of Eastern Europe*, 2015.

day western Czech Republic.[254] Bohemia would become the farthest western reaches of Greater Moravia, but the Moravians would only control it during Svatopluk's lifetime.

During their war missions, the Magyars learned the geography of the region.[255] In the last years of the 9th century, the Magyars were pushed out of modern-day Ukraine by their rivals, the Pechenegs and the Bulgarians. In the meantime, Svatopluk had died, and the local elite in Bohemia rebelled and declared independence.[256] The Bohemians chose their own rulers, the Přemysl clan, which controlled Bohemia until the early 14th century.

The loss of Bohemia further weakened Greater Moravia, giving the Magyars the perfect opportunity to strike.[257] The Magyars knew the geography of Eastern Europe, and they knew which lands would be the easiest to take. The Magyars descended on the Pannonian Plain, the stretch of land just inside the arc of the Carpathian Mountains.[258] Using this land as a center of operations, the Magyars spread out, attacking settlements all across Eastern Europe. The locals were so terrified of the Magyars that they gave them a name, one that was inspired by the fear of a previous invading tribe. The Magyars were called "Hungarians," a phrase that quickly brought the Huns to mind.

The Magyar chief Árpád founded a new state, Hungary, around the year 895. The Magyar occupation separated the Slavic inhabitants. They separated the South Slavs from their neighbors, the East Slavs and West Slavs. By 907, Árpád and the Magyars, now the Hungarians, crushed Greater Moravia. Hungary wasn't

---

[254] Jankowski, *Eastern Europe!*, 2015, pg.138.

[255] Ibid., pg.144.

[256] Ibid., pg.138.

[257] Ibid., pg.144.

[258] Jankowski, *Eastern Europe!*, pg.144; Liulevicius, "Formative Migrations: Mongols to Germans." Lecture 2. *The Great Courses: A History of Eastern Europe*, 2015.

enough for the Magyars, and they still raided the surrounding areas for supplies and food, as well as for fun.[259]

Let's not forget about Bohemia. Like Greater Moravia, the first Přemyslid rulers of Bohemia had to worry about outside influences.[260] The nearby Germanic states of powerful Eastern Francia (the eastern lands of Charlemagne's Carolingian Empire) put pressure on the Bohemians. Under Vaclav I (r. 925–929), Bohemia became a vassal state of the Franks.[261] It had to make tribute payments, but it was allowed to keep its own autonomy.

Many members of the Bohemian nobility didn't like this subordination, but Vaclav was more worried about ending the religious warfare in his country. He was a Christian, and he encouraged the spread of Christianity throughout Bohemia. In 929, Vaclav was murdered while he was on his way to mass; he was ambushed by his enemies, who were led by his brother, Boleslav the Cruel. Vaclav is reportedly the inspiration for the Christmas carol "Good King Wenceslas."

Boleslav (also spelled as Boleslaus) resisted German control throughout his reign. Otto I, the new king of East Francia, had had enough and declared war on Bohemia. The two powers fought for nearly fifteen years before Bohemia sued for peace and submitted to German authority.[262] Bohemia became part of the Ottonian Empire for about a century and a half until it was acknowledged as an independent kingdom.[263]

---

[259] Jankowski, *Eastern Europe!*, 2015, pg.145; Liulevicius, "Formative Migrations: Mongols to Germans." Lecture 2. *The Great Courses: A History of Eastern Europe*, 2015.

[260] Jankowski, *Eastern Europe!*, 2015, pg.138.

[261] Ibid.; "Wenceslas I." *Encyclopedia Britannica*.
https://www.britannica.com/biography/Wenceslas-I-prince-of-Bohemia

[262] "Boleslav I." *Encyclopedia Britannica*. https://www.britannica.com/biography/Boleslav-I

[263] Jankowski, *Eastern Europe!*, 2015, pg.138.

By the mid-10th century, East Francia Empire had transitioned into the Kingdom of Germany.[264] In 955, King Otto I took on the Magyars in a bitter showdown in modern-day Augsburg. Otto didn't expect to win the battle, but his forces decimated the Magyar defenses. His victorious army immediately saluted him as "Emperor" Otto—a raise in rank from a mere king.

Otto's new title was renewed eight years later in an official ceremony in Rome. For his role in defending Christian lands against pagan invasions and continuing the legacy of the Franks, the pope crowned Otto as the Holy Roman emperor.

Although the Magyars were defeated, they were not annihilated. They retreated back to their lands in modern-day Hungary, their shattered confidence in tow. The Magyar leaders soon realized that the Christian states of Europe were winning. The only way that Hungary would succeed was by becoming a Christian state. The Hungarians stopped raiding and opened up their lands to Christian missionaries. Hungary officially became Christianized when its king, Saint Stephen, was baptized in 1001.[265] The Hungarians eventually built an extensive empire that included modern-day Hungary, Croatia, Slovakia, and Transylvania.[266]

The Bulgarian Empire

In 810 CE, Bulgaria was a client state of the Byzantine Empire.[267] Its ruler, Krum, fought Byzantine control throughout his reign. That year, the Franks needed help defeating the Avar Empire. The Bulgarians went to war and helped the Franks defeat the Avars.

---

[264] Ibid., pg.145.

[265] Jankowski, *Eastern Europe!*, 2015, pg.146; Liulevicius, "Formative Migrations: Mongols to Germans." Lecture 2. *The Great Courses: A History of Eastern Europe*, 2015.

[266] Liulevicius, "Formative Migrations: Mongols to Germans." Lecture 2. *The Great Courses: A History of Eastern Europe*, 2015.

[267] Jankowski, *Eastern Europe!*, 2015, pg.139.

Krum believed he was owed a gift of gratitude, as he had conquered the corner of the Carpathian Basin where Hungary, Serbia, and Romania meet today.

Krum was tired of Byzantine control, and he made the risky move of invading Byzantine territory. For years, he seized cities and territories, adding them to his empire. With every victory, Krum and his successors shored up Bulgarian power, eventually forming the First Bulgarian Empire. About a century after Krum seized the Carpathian Basin, one of his successors, Simeon I, stormed into Constantinople and strong-armed the emperor into granting him a title: "Caesar of all Bulgarians and Romans." The symbolism was clear—Byzantine control over Bulgaria was over, at least for now.

During the 10th century, Bulgaria controlled the Balkans, becoming a significant political player in Europe equal to the Franks and Byzantines. After sustaining a devastating attack from Kievan Rus in 969, the First Bulgarian Empire fell in 1018.

The Byzantines got their revenge for their previous humiliation. Emperor Basil II defeated the Bulgarians in battle, taking over fifteen thousand prisoners of war.[268] He spitefully had all the prisoners' eyes cut out. The Bulgarians then returned to Byzantine rule for two hundred years.

Two brothers led a rebellion, overthrowing Byzantine control and founding the Second Bulgarian Empire, which would rule itself for many centuries.[269] Byzantium had its own problems, like the disastrous Fourth Crusade, so it never attacked or tried to regain control of Bulgaria. At its most extensive point, the Second Bulgarian Empire moved past Bulgaria's modern-day borders, extending to Albania and including parts of Serbia to the north.

---

[268] Ibid., pg.139-140.

[269] Ibid., pg.140.

Kievan Rus

Unlike how Western European history portrays them, the Vikings were not all about raids and razing towns. They were also quite business savvy! While the Vikings focused on pillaging in Western Europe, they were keen on controlling the lucrative trade routes that filtered through Eastern Europe.

The middle of the 7th century saw Vikings from Sweden moving south of Scandinavia.[270] These Vikings called themselves the Varangians, but the Finnic peoples they encountered referred to them as the "Ruotsi." The lucrative potential of the Baltic region was too good of an opportunity to pass up, and the raiding Vikings conquered the area, taking the trade routes for themselves.[271]

As the Varangians continued trekking south, they occupied the river basins of the Dnieper, Don, and Volga Rivers from eastern Ukraine to western Russia.[272] Building upon their own networks, the Vikings established trading relationships that stretched from the Baltic to Asia.[273] For hundreds of years, Eastern Europe was a thoroughfare for goods, spices, and luxuries from Eastern lands. The Varangians controlled the trade in modern-day Eastern Europe and founded states that would unite as Kievan Rus.[274]

While luxury items like furs and precious metals were exchanged along the Varangian trade routes, they mostly dealt with slaves. There was a huge market for Slavic slaves; according to Tomek Jankowski, "before the Atlantic slave trade that plundered Africa in the 15th -19th centuries, by far the largest slave network in the world centered on the trade of Slavic peoples as slaves."[275] The

---

[270] Ibid., pg.142.

[271] Ibid., pg.106.

[272] Ibid., pg.142.

[273] Ibid., pg.106.

[274] Ibid., pg.142.

[275] Jankowski, *Eastern Europe!*, 2015, pg.142.

trade in Slavic peoples was so widespread that the word "Slav" is the root of the word "slave" in most European languages.

The years between the 700s and 1100s were the height of the Slavic slave trade.[276] While the trade included Varangians, merchants from Italy, Byzantium, and the Frankish Empire also traded in slaves. In most cases, these Slavs, who were, for the most part, prisoners of war, were sent east to the Arab world, where they were sold again. However, as more Slavic states converted to Christianity, Slavs stopped becoming targets of the slave trade.

The Varangians established many city-states along their trade routes over the centuries. They encountered Finns and Slavs, and the three groups all fought over the area. To end the warfare, Varangians combined the states around modern-day Novgorod, Russia, electing the Viking Rurik to be its first ruler.

By the 880s, the federation spread out; it now included modern-day Kyiv (also known as Kiev). This union of states became known as Kievan Rus. This would be the ancestor of present-day Russia, Belarus, and Ukraine.[277] Even though the leadership of Kievan Rus was initially Varangian, the Vikings completely assimilated into the population by the 950s.[278] Kievan Rus became a powerful Eastern Slavic state.

In the 10th century, the Rus fought with the Khazars over access to the Volga River.[279] The Rus defeated the Khazars around the year 965; the loss crippled the Khazars, and they never recovered. The Khazars disappeared soon after that, most likely by the end of the century.

---

[276] Ibid., pg.143.

[277] *Ibid., pg.144.*

[278] *Ibid., pg.143.*

[279] "Khazars." *The Jewish Virtual Library.* https://www.jewishvirtuallibrary.org/khazars

After the Rus defeated the Khazars, the rulers of Kievan Rus created a viable culture that lasted until the 12th century.[280] The Byzantines sent priests from Bulgaria into Rus to convert the area to Christianity, although it should be noted that the Western Church also sent its delegates to the area.[281] Missionaries were allowed to spread Byzantine Christianity within the realm, and scholars applied the Cyrillic alphabet, which had been adopted from their neighbor Bulgaria, to write religious texts and law codes.[282] Even with improvements in law, religion, and education, Kievan Rus was so dependent on trade that its fate intertwined with its trade neighbors, the Abbasids and the Byzantines. When these powers declined, Kievan Rus declined. By the 1220s, Kievan Rus lost the power it had commanded less than two centuries before.[283]

---

[280] Jankowski, *Eastern Europe!*, 2015, pg.143.

[281] Ibid., pg.42.

[282] Ibid., pg.143.

[283] Ibid., pg.144.

Legend:
- Boundaries of Kievan Rus' in 1015
- State boundaries in 1113
- Lands dependent on Kievan Rus' and under colonization
- Boundaries of main lands/principalities according to Yaroslav the Wise's partition (1054)
- Boundaries of some appanage principalities

Kievan Rus'
in 11th century (1015-1113)

Kievan Rus at its height in the 12ʰ century. (Credit: Koryakov Yuri/Hellerick, 2009)

Slovenia and Croatia

In the early 800s, the Franks dominated the Dalmatian coast, which lies on the northeast Adriatic Sea in modern-day Croatia.[284] Under Duke Ljudevit, the Slavs resisted the Franks in 818. This rebellion failed, and the area would be controlled by the Eastern Franks (later the Germans) for the next millennium. Present-day Slovenia descends from these rebellious Slavs under Ljudevit.

---

[284] Ibid., pg.147.

However, Slovenia wouldn't organize into a territory for more than one thousand years. In 1918, Slovenia was finally organized into a country as part of Yugoslavia.

Even though the Slavic rebellion of 818 failed, the Franks were having a hard time maintaining control over the Dalmatian coast. And as the Franks lost control throughout the 9th century, small Slavic states along the coast of the Adriatic rose in their place. Although they were Slavic states, they were Christianized—a legacy from their time under Frankish control. In 845, this collection of Christian Slavic states joined together under one leader, Trpimir, to form modern-day Croatia.

Understanding the limits of their defeat, the Franks officially recognized Croatia rather than fight for it. Less than one hundred years later, in 925, the Croatian state was recognized as a full Christian kingdom. The Kingdom of Croatia was established, and it included the lands the Croatians had added to their state in the meantime. To the west, it reached the Istrian Peninsula in the northern Adriatic, where the borders of modern-day Slovenia and Croatia meet. To the east, it reached the Drava River, a tributary of the Danube River in modern-day eastern Croatia.

Unfortunately, this united Croatia only lasted three years.[285] In 928, Croatia became a weak centralized state, and it was easily picked off by its ambitious neighbors. Croatia weakened further until it was torn apart by civil war in 1089. Croatia was absorbed into Hungary in 1102, but it was allowed to rule itself relatively intact. However, Croatia's history and politics were very much aligned with Hungary for hundreds of years.

---

[285] Ibid., pg.148.

Serbia

Although it started as a smattering of small states, Serbia would go through an ebb and flow throughout the medieval period to become the most powerful state in the Balkans.[286] The first tribes arrived by the mid-600s. They settled in the Balkans, where they stayed for about two hundred years. Serbia organized into an official state in the mid-9th century through the machinations of the Byzantines. The Byzantines convinced a prominent Serbian prince named Vlastimir that a united Serbian state would check the growth of the First Bulgarian Empire. Vlastimir established the first dynasty of Serbia, but the state would grow under his great-grandson, Časlav.

During Časlav's reign, he pulled Serbia away from Bulgarian influence, allowing the spread of Byzantine culture. Časlav brought in Byzantine artists, architects, and authors, and he introduced Christianity. He also expanded Serbia's borders, but it is unknown to what extent. Unfortunately, Časlav was the last of his dynasty. When he died around 960, all of his hard work fell apart.

---

[286] Ibid., pg.148-149.

A map of the suggested extent of Serbian lands under Časlav. As you can see, the Bulgarian Empire stretched from the Black Sea to the Adriatic, dominating the region. However, there is little reliable source material on how much the Serbians expanded past their original borders. (Public Domain)

Serbia disintegrated into three main principalities: Duklja, Raška, and Zahumlje. Of these three states, Duklja took the lead, dominating the other two states until the late 11th century. Later instability in Duklja allowed the rise of Raška as the dominant state. Raška started reuniting the rest of the Serbian states until Stefan Nemanja founded the Nemanjić dynasty in 1166. Throughout the rest of his reign, he finished bringing Serbia back together. When Stefan Nemanja abdicated in 1196, he had expanded Serbia south toward Macedonia and north toward present-day Bosnia and Herzegovina.[287]

---

[287] Ibid., pg.149-150.

Under Stefan Nemanja's son, Saint Sava, Serbia was officially converted to Orthodox Christianity.[288] The Nemanjić dynasty continued to secure its power, and Serbia reached its height in the 13th century. In 1217, it became the Kingdom of Serbia.

The Piast Dynasty Unites Poland

In the medieval period, the present-day borders of Poland were divided in two. The southern edge was controlled by Bohemia. The Western Slavic Lechitic tribes known as the Polanie occupied the flatlands between the tribes on the Baltic Sea and Bohemian-controlled lands.

In the 940s, the Polanie loosely organized into the first state of Poland. This is a loose definition of the word "state," as it was really just an organization of tribes that united under one leader. Under the first ruling family, the Piast dynasty, Poland transformed from an organization of tribes into a centralized duchy. The Piast family would lead Poland more or less for the next four hundred years until the late 14th century.[289]

Mieszko I, who ruled in the late 10th century, was largely responsible for this transition by introducing Christianity to his territory. He married a Bohemian princess who was a Christian—a fact that may or may not have played a role in his conversion. After their marriage, Mieszko converted to Christianity himself. He officially declared Christianity as the state religion and appealed to the pope in Rome to recognize Poland as a Christian state. The more likely reason for Mieszko's conversion may have been political; by joining Christian Europe, Mieszko ensured that the German Holy Roman emperor, Otto I, would leave his lands alone.

---

[288] Ibid., pg.150.

[289] Ibid., pg.150-151.

Poland grew even larger and more powerful under Mieszko's son, Boleslaw the Brave.[290] Boleslaw conquered territory in all directions, expanding Polish borders into neighboring lands for most of his reign. In 1025, Poland was recognized as a kingdom, and Boleslaw became the first king of Poland. By then, he had extended his borders west into modern-day Germany and the Czech Republic.

A map showing the political borders of Europe in the year 1000. (Credit: Mandramunjak, 2014)

Under the Piast dynasty, Poland continued to spread out, taking territories from neighboring lands like Bohemia and spending decade after decade building its own power. However, the unity of Poland under Piast rule didn't last. One of Boleslaw the Brave's descendants, Boleslaw III, reigned from 1107 to 1138.[291] Comparatively, he wielded more power than any of the early Piast kings, as he ruled over the Kingdom of Poland at its height. Unfortunately, he made a fateful decision that would affect Poland for hundreds of years.[292] He had five sons, and he gave them each

---

[290] Ibid., pg.151.

[291] Ibid., pg.151-152.

[292] Ibid., pg.152.

an equal part of the kingdom as their inheritance. When Boleslaw died in 1138, Poland descended into civil war.

Polish expansion during the reign of Boleslaw. (Public Domain)

The German Crusaders: The Livonian Brotherhood and the Teutonic Knights

While the larger empires of Croatia, Serbia, and Poland were forming in Eastern Europe, the Crusades were tearing apart the Holy Land. Crusader armies from Christian nations across Europe flocked to Jerusalem, determined to win back this holy city from Muslim occupation. By the 13th century, it was clear the Crusades were not going well for the Christian knights. They turned their attention to the pagan Baltic states, intent on enforcing Christianity there instead. In particular, German crusaders flooded into Poland in two main groups.

German missionaries founded the Livonian Brotherhood in 1202 to enforce conversion to Christianity among the Finnic and Baltic tribes living in present-day Estonia and Latvia.[293] Local tribes successfully resisted the missionaries, so the priests founded the Livonian Brotherhood to enforce their will. The "Brothers of the Sword," another name for the Livonian Brotherhood, arrived in Poland, crossing into the northern Baltic states. They terrorized the local Baltic and Finnic tribes into submission. Tired of the brutality that came with the occupation of German missionaries and knights, several Baltic tribes formed a coalition and defeated the Livonian Brotherhood at the Battle of Saule in 1236. The Livonian Brotherhood scattered and joined another group of German crusader knights known as the Teutonic Knights. The newly-named Livonian Order still had its own organization, but it remained under the purview of the Teutonic Order.[294]

Like the Livonian Brotherhood, the Teutonic Knights soon found themselves on the losing side of the Crusades.[295] They returned to Europe in 1211, looking for work. The king of Hungary hired the Teutonic Knights to protect his lands in Transylvania from attack by the Cumans. The Cumans, a Turkic confederation of steppe tribes, founded their own state that included territories from present-day Romania and Bulgaria to Kazakhstan. They had been settled in Eastern Europe since the 11th century, and they were plunderers who terrorized Byzantine, Rus, Bulgarian, and Hungarian cities. In the early 1200s, the Cumans set their sights on Transylvania.

[293] Ibid., pg.154.

[294] Mark Cartwright. "Teutonic Knight." *World History Encyclopedia.* Published July 11, 2018. https://www.worldhistory.org/Teutonic_Knight/

[295] Jankowski, *Eastern Europe!*, 2015, pg.155.

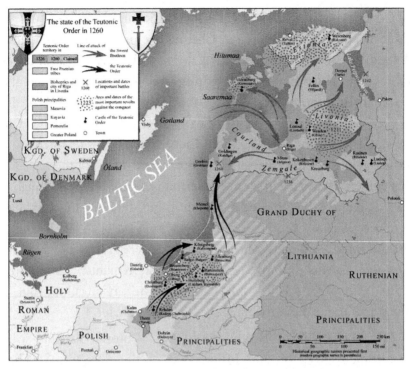

The German Crusader states of the Teutonic Order, 1260. (Credit: S. Bollmann, 2010)

The Teutonic Knights worked for the Hungarians for nearly fifteen years before they got greedy and attempted to turn Transylvania into their own Crusader state. The Hungarians pushed out the knights, but they weren't unemployed for long.

In 1225, Konrad, the duke of Mazovia—a region in central-northeastern Poland—called on the Teutonic Knights.[296] He hired the knights to protect the northern border of Poland from invading Baltic tribes. These tribes, the Brusi, occupied parts of the northern border and the province of Kaliningrad.[297]

The Brusi were unequipped to battle the Teutonic Knights, and they were quickly pushed back and defeated. However, they did lend their name to a new state. The knights started founding states

---

[296] Ibid., pg.155, 198.

[297] Ibid., pg. 198.

on the southeastern coast of the Baltic Sea, and Germans emigrated there.[298] These immigrants soon started calling themselves *Preußen*—the German form of Brusi or English for Prussians.

The Turkic Tribes of Medieval Eastern Europe: The Pechenegs and the Cumans

There were two main Turkic empires that rose during the medieval period: the Pechenegs and the Cumans.[299] The Pechenegs were only a temporary arrival to Eastern Europe. They came from the Eurasian Steppe in the late 800s, fully intent on continuing their way of life. They terrorized the great states of the medieval period, such as the Byzantine Empire, Kievan Rus, and Bulgaria.

While the Pechenegs made enemies of most of the large empires of Eastern Europe, they fought lengthy wars against the Rus. In 972, the Pechenegs murdered the prince of Rus, Sviatoslav I. The khan of the Pechenegs made an example of the prince by cutting his head off and using his skull as a cup. Over the centuries, the Rus and the Pechenegs continued to fight, but the Rus never forgot this insult.

Kievan Rus grew in power and influence throughout the 11th century, and it was finally able to defeat the Pechenegs in battle. However, the strengthening of Kievan Rus was not the reason for the downfall of the Pechenegs. While engrossed in war, an outside power moving west, another Turkic tribe named the Cumans, ousted the Pechenegs from their territory on the steppe.

The Cumans, who were from the Eurasian Steppe themselves, were actually a collection of tribes that decided that there was strength in numbers.[300] They assimilated many of the Pechenegs

---

[298] Ibid., pg. 198-199.

[299] Ibid., pg.155.

[300] Ibid., pg.155-156.

into their confederation. The ones who didn't join the Cumans wandered, relocating to Bulgaria and Hungary—two empires that were their former targets. The Pechenegs assimilated into the Hungarian and Bulgarian populations, ending their two-century reign.

The Cumans managed to achieve more power than the Pechenegs ever did. They lorded over an empire from today's border between Romania and Bulgaria, across the Eurasian Steppe, past the Black and Caspian Seas, and into Kazakhstan. Just like the Pechenegs, the Cumans were raiders. They picked up where the Pechenegs left off, pillaging Byzantine, Rus, and Romania. Cuman raids took place as far west as Hungary.

Interestingly enough, the Cumans understood diplomacy and strategic alliances.[301] The nobility showcased their power and diplomatic standing by intermarrying with the Bulgarian, Rus, and Hungarian royal families. After two centuries as a dynamic power player in Eastern Europe, the Cuman Empire fell, but for what reason is anyone's guess. Over time, the Cumans migrated to the neighboring territories. The Hungarians and Bulgarians offered them protection and hired the Cumans for military service. Over hundreds of years, the Cumans naturally assimilated into Hungarian and Bulgarian culture.

The Lithuanians

In northern Eastern Europe, the Lithuanians began to organize into their own state at the end of the 12th century. This date is significant. The Lithuanians lived along the Baltic Sea as Orthodox Slavic tribes that were surrounded by enemies.[302] They were sandwiched between Kievan Rus, Poland, and German Crusader states. Around the 11th century, the Lithuanian tribes consolidated

---

[301] Ibid., pg.156.

[302] Ibid., pg.156; Liulevicius, "Clashing Golden Ages, 1389-1772." Lecture 3. *The Great Courses: A History of Eastern Europe*, 2015.

into a fighting force strong enough to protect their lands from invasion on all sides.

A century later, Lithuania had formed into a proper state. Defending its borders from the Rus and the German crusaders makes up most of its early history. Beginning in the 1230s, Lithuania started to become one of the dominant states of Europe with the help of its ruler, Mindaugas.[303] He led the Lithuanians against the Livonian Brotherhood in the Battle of Saule in 1236. This was the battle that destroyed the "Brothers of the Sword," forcing them to assimilate into the Teutonic Knights.[304] Mindaugas also successfully commanded raids against the Rus, taking some of their lands in the process.

[303] Jankowski, *Eastern Europe!*, 2015, pg.156, 200-201.

[304] Ibid., pg.156.

Chapter 5 – Enter the Mongols: The Invasion of the Mongol Horde to the Fall of Constantinople (1242–1453)

The 13th century was relatively peaceful and prosperous for Eastern Europe.[305] There were several independent states, and the region's trade routes moved people and goods. Eastern Europe was ascending but not for long.

The Mongols were coming.[306]

Bringing destruction and warfare to Eastern Europe's borders, the Mongols retreated across the Eurasian Steppe before they could completely crush the region. After the Mongols left, the states of Eastern Europe set about fixing their territories. Some states found that their fortunes would rise in the early modern

---

[305] Jankowski, *Eastern Europe!*, 2015, pg.93.

[306] Liulevicius, "Formative Migrations: Mongols to Germans." Lecture 2. *The Great Courses: A History of Eastern Europe*, 2015.

period, while others could not recover from the Mongol onslaught.[307]

The Forgotten Magyars

In 1236, a Dominican priest from Hungary, under orders from King Béla IV himself, arrived on the Volga River.[308] There, in the river valley, he found the Magyar descendants of the survivors from the defeat in Augsburg in 955. The priest returned to Hungary, informing his king what he discovered. Béla IV sent his representative back to the Volga River with an invitation for the last of the Magyars to relocate to Hungary.

On his way back to the Volga River Basin, the priest discovered that the Magyar tribes had been destroyed. The few survivors he encountered begged him to go back to Hungary and prepare for an attack.[309] A vicious horde from the east, the Mongols, also known as the Tartars, was on its way. The Mongols were quickly moving west, destroying every city in their path. The Dominican priest rushed back to Hungary, telling his king of their impending doom.

The Mongols

By 1237, the Mongols had been on the move for nearly twenty years. The Mongols were a collection of tribes who lived on the far east of the steppe in modern-day Mongolia. Genghis Khan, the mighty warrior king who brought the tribes together, formed an elite nomadic fighting force that would devastate everything in its path.

---

[307] Liulevicius, "Clashing Golden Ages, 1389-1772." Lecture 3. *The Great Courses: A History of Eastern Europe*, 2015.

[308] Jankowski, *Eastern Europe!*, 2015, pg.157.

[309] Jankowski, *Eastern Europe!*, 2015, pg.157; Liulevicius, "Formative Migrations: Mongols to Germans." Lecture 2. *The Great Courses: A History of Eastern Europe*, 2015.

The Mongols set out to conquer the known world, and they did. Until it started to splinter apart in the late 14th century, the Mongol Empire was the largest in the world up to that time.[310] With his hordes of warriors on horseback, Genghis expanded the Mongol Empire east and west, conquering China and western Asia before he reached Europe. In 1219, he completed his quest in the East, bringing China under Mongol control.[311] Genghis Khan moved west into Central Asia; from there, the Mongols made their way into Eastern Europe.

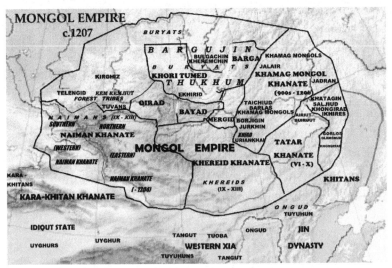

The Mongol Empire in 1207. (Credit: Khiruge, 2014)

After reaching the Black Sea, Genghis Khan sent an army north. The Mongols laid waste to the Caucasus before defeating a joint force of Cumans and Rus in 1223 at the Battle of the Kalka River. Whole states were destroyed, and the region was a wasteland.

The Mongols did not capitalize on their victory at the Kalka River. Instead, they returned to Asia, but they wouldn't be gone for long. The Mongols returned in 1229 under a new ruler: Ögedei

[310] Jankowski, *Eastern Europe!*, 2015, pg.171-173; Liulevicius, "Formative Migrations: Mongols to Germans." Lecture 2. *The Great Courses: A History of Eastern Europe*, 2015.

[311] Jankowski, *Eastern Europe!*, 2015, pg.157.

Khan.[312] He picked up where his predecessor left off. He wanted to conquer Europe all the way to the "Great Sea" (the Atlantic Ocean).

Along the Great Northern European Plain, the Mongols found the perfect space to stage its invasion of Eastern Europe.[313] The plain had ample grasses and vegetation to sustain their horses, which was the key to their power and expansion.

Over the next several years, the Mongols invaded Eurasia to the east into Asia and to the west into Eastern Europe. The Mongol forces that moved west, the Golden Horde, reached the Volga River in 1237, destroying what was left of the Magyars. The Cumans encountered the Mongols again in 1238; the Mongols pushed west, forcing the Cumans to seek sanctuary in Hungary.[314]

The Mongols continued to move west, reaching Eastern Europe. By that time, the Eastern Europeans knew the Mongols were coming. They reached Kievan Rus first, terrorizing the inhabitants and taking prisoners of war as slaves. It was there, in December 1240, that the Mongols sent King Béla IV a warning: surrender to the Mongols, or see his lands destroyed.

The Hungarian king refused the offer and prepared for the Mongol onslaught. In 1241, furious from the resistance they faced in Eastern Europe, the Mongols stormed into Eastern Europe on two fronts. One army headed toward Poland and the other toward Hungary.

---

[312] Jankowski, *Eastern Europe!*, 2015, pg.157; Liulevicius, "Formative Migrations: Mongols to Germans." Lecture 2. *The Great Courses: A History of Eastern Europe*, 2015.

[313] Liulevicius, "Formative Migrations: Mongols to Germans." Lecture 2. *The Great Courses: A History of Eastern Europe*, 2015.

[314] Jankowski, *Eastern Europe!*, 2015, pg.158-159; Liulevicius, "Formative Migrations: Mongols to Germans." Lecture 2. *The Great Courses: A History of Eastern Europe*, 2015.

Poland was still decentralized; it was a collection of smaller principalities with no cohesive leader. Without the ability to draw up a large enough army to fight the Mongols, Polish cities fell quickly. The Mongols crushed all of Poland, except for one area: Silesia in southwestern Poland. Silesia was ruled by a prince named Henryk II Pobożny, who had powerful allies. Henryk's brother-in-law was the king of Bohemia, and he sent a whole army to protect Henryk's lands. Silesia housed a hodgepodge of different forces, which were all intent on pushing back the Mongols. There were mercenaries who worked for coin and French, German, and Polish knights who fought for the glory of God. Ironically enough, European knights were often more in conflict with each other than anyone else. They called a temporary peace to join together and fight the Mongol invasion. Unfortunately for them, it would be unsuccessful.

The Mongols arrived at Silesia in April 1241. They knew how much support Henryk had inside the city of Legnica, so the Mongols tricked Henryk into thinking they were abandoning the attack. When Henryk and his forces emerged from the city, the Mongols ambushed them, which ended in a quick, crushing defeat for Henryk. The collection of armies at Legnica was the last resistance that the Mongols faced in Poland. [315] To celebrate, they decapitated Prince Henryk and stuck his head on a pike.

The Mongol forces were so vast and numerous that they could attack multiple places at the same time. While one army was crushing Prince Henryk in Silesia in southwestern Poland, another force destroyed the Hungarian forces in the northeast. At the Battle of Mohi, King Béla IV was defeated, as his ragtag collection of soldiers was not strong enough to challenge the Golden Horde. Political instability plagued Hungary before the Mongols arrived, and it interfered with Béla's ability to coordinate a successful defense.

---

[315] Legnica is also known by its German name, Liegnitz.

After it was clear that the Mongols were winning, King Béla and what was left of his army fled the battlefield. Instead of laying waste to the area, the Mongols chased the Hungarians, murdering anyone they found. Béla would remain on the run for more than a year, effectively leaving Hungary with no official government.

The Mongols swept through the Hungarian countryside, destroying land and murdering Hungarian citizens. The Mongol invasion of Hungary killed about half of its population and destroyed about 75 percent of the country. Béla returned from exile a year later, determined to rebuild his ravaged country.

Once they laid waste to Hungary, the Mongols trudged through Bulgaria and Serbia, reaching the Adriatic coast. The army that defeated Prince Henryk in Silesia had since left the area, marching through Bohemia to meet the rest of the Golden Horde in Hungary.

The Mongols were very near to conquering Eastern Europe. Nearly every campaign had resulted in absolute victory, and the Mongols swept through the region, destroying everything they could find. In March 1242, the Mongols abruptly ended their invasion.[316] They turned around and went back home, traveling east along the Great Northern Plain—the path they had used in their attempt to conquer Europe. Three months before, in December 1241, Ögedei Khan had died. Members of the upper class, the warriors who were leading the armies, all had to return home to elect the new khan.

The rest of Europe was saved from the menace of the Mongols. Although the Mongols retreated, they maintained their control over the Russian lands that they conquered before their movement into Eastern Europe. They would control modern-day Russian territory for two more centuries. This divided Russia from the rest

---

[316] Jankowski, *Eastern Europe!*, 2015, pg.159-160; Liulevicius, "Formative Migrations: Mongols to Germans." Lecture 2. *The Great Courses: A History of Eastern Europe*, 2015.

of Western and Eastern Europe, which meant that it would not experience the Renaissance or the Reformation.

Vejas Gabriel Liulevicius, a leading professor in Eastern European history, asks the most important question:

> "What if the Mongols had not turned back? Their khan had given them orders to drive all the way to the Atlantic. A shattered Europe would mean no Renaissance, no global voyagers of exploration, no Enlightenment, no scientific revolution— none of the bases of modernity so familiar to us today."[317]

Eastern Europe after the Golden Horde

After the Mongol invasions, Eastern European states started to rebuild.[318] Over the next five centuries, Eastern Europe would see the rise and decline of powerful states. These states would create their own spheres of influence over their neighbors, and they would form closer relationships with rising Western European countries. However, the Ottoman Empire would close in on the Balkans, effectively cutting it off from the rest of Eastern Europe.

Bulgaria, the Rise of Serbia, and the Battle of Kosovo

Even though the Mongols had moved out, they held their Russian lands, planning strategic raids across the border into Eastern Europe.[319] After about half a century of harassment, the Bulgarians joined forces with the Polish to force the Mongols away

[317] Liulevicius, "Formative Migrations: Mongols to Germans." Lecture 2. *The Great Courses: A History of Eastern Europe*, 2015.

[318] Jankowski, *Eastern Europe!*, 2015, pg.169, 217.

[319] Ibid., pg.174.

from their borders. While the strategy worked, another neighbor, Serbia, was growing.

For hundreds of years, Serbian influence had been limited by its more powerful neighbors. By the late 13th century, a series of powerful kings brought Serbia into the limelight. Prince Stefan Dušan came to power in 1331, extending Serbian territory into modern-day Greece, Albania, and Bulgaria. Dušan improved infrastructure with new churches and schools, bringing Serbia to the height of its power in the medieval period.

Dušan's real desire lay with the Byzantines. He wanted to conquer what was left of the failing empire and rule it as a Serbian vassal state. Although he had targeted their lands, Dušan made peace with the Bulgarians and used the alliance to attack the Byzantines. As Serbia stripped the Byzantines of their influence, Dušan made power moves that showcased his growing influence. He matched the Serbian Orthodox Church with the Eastern Orthodox Church in Constantinople, granting himself the title of "Tsar of the Serbs and the Greeks" in 1345. Threatened by Serbia's encroachment on their territory, the Byzantines imported Ottoman troops to defend their lands in 1354.[320] Stefan Dušan died the following year without having attained his goal of taking Constantinople.

The Ottomans stayed in the Balkans, taking the opportunity to conquer their own lands in Eastern Europe. After taking control of the Balkans, the Ottomans began a decades-long struggle for Bulgaria. They took city by city, and Bulgaria finally fell to the Ottomans in 1396. The Ottoman Empire would rule Bulgaria as a vassal state for the next five hundred years.

None of Stefan Dušan's successors could match his charismatic rise to power. Several weak kings ruled Serbia for the next fifty years, and the Serbian Empire slowly fell apart. One Serbian principality, Duklja, which had since renamed itself Zeta, declared

---

[320] Ibid., pg.174-177, 185.

independence from Serbia in 1360. Zeta grew, conquering parts of Albania and Kosovo. By the end of the century, it changed its name again; today, it is known by its Italian moniker, Montenegro.

Of course, the Ottomans were there to pick up the pieces as the Serbian Empire disintegrated. Throughout the 14th and 15th centuries, the Ottomans still threatened Zeta and the rest of Serbia. Zeta feared for its safety and joined Venice—the nearby Italian city-state powerhouse that was vital in trade—to push the Ottomans back in 1421. This didn't work; by the end of the century, Serbia had conquered Zeta.

The Ottomans had nothing but trouble with Montenegro. The local population constantly rebelled against their authority. The area was jagged, with lots of mountains, slopes, and hills. The Ottomans couldn't move in and occupy Montenegro easily. They decided it wasn't worth the hassle. Even though Montenegro had to pay tribute to the Ottomans, they were very rarely occupied by the Turks.

The royal family still feared the Ottomans, so they escaped into exile, and the archbishop took control of the state. Montenegro became a religious state, with the archbishop as the supreme ruler. For three hundred years, Montenegro was never free of Ottoman influence, but it was given relative autonomy compared to other Ottoman lands in Eastern Europe.

In June 1389, the Ottoman Empire delivered the decisive blow to the Serbian Empire in the Battle of Kosovo.[321] The events at Kosovo didn't seem like they would result in an Ottoman victory, as the Serbs nearly annihilated the Ottoman forces on the battlefield. The Ottomans brought in their reserve units, an advantage the Serbs didn't have. Both sides lost their heads of state in the battle; Prince Lazar of Serbia died in battle, while Sultan

---

[321] Jankowski, *Eastern Europe!*, 2015, pg.174-177; Liulevicius, "Clashing Golden Ages, 1389-1772." Lecture 3. *The Great Courses: A History of Eastern Europe*, 2015.

Murad I was murdered in retribution for the massive loss of life and freedom at the Battle of Kosovo.

Adam Stefanović, Battle of Kosovo, 1870. (Public Domain)

The Ottomans occupied parts of Serbia until the 1450s, and they finally took the rest of the empire by the end of the decade. For the next five centuries, Serbia was the center of a tug-of-war battle between the larger powers of Eastern Europe.

The Kingdom of Bosnia

Bosnia, which was originally the Roman province of Dalmatia, emerged as its own independent state in 1180 after hundreds of years of changing hands.[322] At one time or another, Bosnia was controlled by the Germanic tribes, the Byzantines, Croatians, Serbians, and Hungarians.

The events of the 13th century kept Bosnia independent. Its neighbor, Hungary, was anxious to get its hands on Bosnia again, but the Mongol invasions and other repeated incursions distracted the Hungarians from any territorial claims. Over the next century,

[322] John R. Lampe. "Bosnia and Herzegovina." *Encyclopedia Britannica.* https://www.britannica.com/place/Bosnia-and-Herzegovina; Jankowski, *Eastern Europe!,* 2015, pg.178.

three major powers in the region—the Byzantines, the Serbians, and the Hungarians—all wanted control over Bosnia.

Since Bosnia remained independent for centuries, it grew into one of the strongest states in the 14th-century Balkans.[323] Under the rule of the Kotromanić dynasty, Bosnia stretched down the east coast of the Adriatic Sea. It was around this time that Bosnia acquired Herzegovina. The rulers of Bosnia supported the local mining industry, making its precious metals a highly desirable commodity in Eastern Europe.

In 1377, Bosnia became the Kingdom of Bosnia. After King Tvrtko died in 1391, Bosnia's power started to slip. It could not hold off an Ottoman invasion in 1463, and Bosnia became an Ottoman territory by 1482.

Croatia and Dubrovnik

Beginning in the 11th century, the Kingdom of Croatia slowly disintegrated. By the 14th century, Croatia had become a Hungarian satellite state. As Croatia fell apart, it became a collection of small principalities. One of them, Dubrovnik, became a powerful regional territory in its own right.

The Byzantines took control of the strategically placed port city. In 1205, Venice took possession of Dubrovnik. Venice, a powerhouse Italian city-state that cornered Mediterranean trade, used Dubrovnik as a stopping point along its trade routes. It became one of the most frequented ports of the 14th century, which was both a good and a bad thing. It was partially responsible for the spread of the Black Plague in the middle of the 14th century. In 1358, Hungary conquered Dubrovnik, and Venice watched as the city it helped create started benefiting its rivals.

---

[323] Jankowski, *Eastern Europe!*, 2015, pg.178-79.

A photograph of Dubrovnik's old port, which is now a World Heritage Site. (Credit: Greenweasel)

One hundred years later, the Ottomans conquered Dubrovnik.[324] Much like the Hungarians, the Ottomans took a hands-off policy to their control over the port city, although the Turks did extend their protection to Dubrovnik. They guarded the port and its ships, and Dubrovnik could now trade goods from the East from trade routes controlled by the Ottomans.

Dubrovnik was infamous throughout the medieval period for its high-quality maritime technology. European nations that wanted to have the best ships and crew went to Dubrovnik first. For example, the Spanish used Dubrovnik's resources when beginning their explorations in the New World. That means that some of the first Europeans in the New World were Eastern Europeans.

In the 17th century, as more European nations devoted more resources to overseas trade, they found new, better routes to the Americas and Asia. Dubrovnik was no longer on the main trade routes, so it started to lose importance. By the 19th century,

---

[324] Ibid., pg.181.

Dubrovnik started to change hands again. First, Napoleon Bonaparte conquered the city-state in 1808. Seven years later, the Congress of Vienna granted Dubrovnik to Austria. Croatia wouldn't possess the city again until after the First World War.

Albania

For such a small country with less than desirable terrain, Albania sure caused a lot of problems. Albania lies in a strategic spot north of Greece where the Adriatic Sea and the Ionian Sea meet. Most of the major powers of the ancient period and the medieval period had their eyes on Albania, from the Greeks, Romans, and Byzantines to the Serbs, Turks, and Germans.

Albania was originally part of the Byzantine Empire.[325] In the 11th century, Albania's neighbor Serbia started challenging the Byzantines for possession of it. Soon, both powers had to contend with the French, who crossed the southern edge of the Adriatic, hoping to add Albania to its holdings in southern Italy.

In 1204, the capital of the Byzantine Empire, Constantinople, was overthrown by a group of French and Venetian knights who founded the Latin Empire.[326] Latin forces quickly moved into southern Eastern Europe, but the new empire was not strong enough to stand a serious challenge. Byzantine Prince Michael Komnenos joined forces with the Albanians to fight the Latin occupation. They were successful, and the Latins moved out.

After the Latins left, Albanians knew a period of relative peace. Until the 1270s, none of their neighbors encroached on their territory. In 1272, the French came back, and this time, they were successful. They captured a number of cities on the coast, uniting them all to form the Kingdom of Albania under French rule.

---

[325] Ibid., pg.182.

[326] Ibid., pg.183.

The French held onto its Albanian territory for about fifty years until the rise of the powerful Stefan Dušan in Serbia. By 1336, Dušan had defeated the French, annexing Albania for himself. Albania remained in Serbian hands for nineteen years. When Dušan died, the Kingdom of Serbia crumbled. There was constant fighting, especially between the elites in Serbia and Albania. Locals escaped the violence but not for long— the Ottomans were on their way. In 1385, the Ottoman Empire conquered Albania, making it part of their holdings in the Balkans.

Just as in every other Ottoman territory, the Albanians were forced to follow the Ottomans' *devşirme* system, where Christian families had to send their sons to the Ottomans as tribute.[327] These sons were trained to serve the state. If they were talented at reading and writing, they were trained for government positions. If the boys were athletic, they were given military training. These Christian servants to the Ottoman state were called Janissaries.

Janissaries had the best military training available at the time. They were feared throughout Europe, and their ferocity on the battlefield was unmatched. Despite their low rank in Ottoman society, some Janissaries could rise in the ranks and achieve powerful positions.

In 1443, one of these Janissaries, known as Skanderbeg, challenged his Ottoman masters and led a massive rebellion in Albania.[328] The Ottomans left, and Albania was independent once again. Skanderbeg defied Ottoman rule for the rest of his life. When Skanderbeg died twenty-five years later in 1468, the Ottomans saw their chance to regain Albania. They finally did so in 1478.

---

[327] Jankowski, *Eastern Europe!*, 2015, pg.187; Liulevicius, "Clashing Golden Ages, 1389-1772." Lecture 3. *The Great Courses: A History of Eastern Europe*, 2015.

[328] Jankowski, *Eastern Europe!*, 2015, pg.183; Liulevicius, "Clashing Golden Ages, 1389-1772." Lecture 3. *The Great Courses: A History of Eastern Europe*, 2015.

The Byzantines, the Ottomans, and the Fall of Constantinople

Gone were the days when the Byzantine Empire was the true successor of Rome. The Latin Empire had fallen, and the rightful emperor sat on the throne once again. As skilled a leader as Michael VIII Palaeologus was, even he could not save the Byzantines. Less than a century after the fall of the Latins, the Byzantine Empire was in serious jeopardy.[329] The emperor made a fatal misstep when he tried to defend his lands with Ottoman soldiers. His allies turned on him, taking the Balkans and making inroads to Eastern Europe. The Ottomans who were now invading Eastern Europe would soon spell disaster for the Byzantine Empire.

A map showing the battles between the Seljuk Turks and the Byzantine Empire in the late 11th century. (Public Domain)

The Ottoman Empire was founded in the 10th century when the warlord Seljuk started conquering lands, forming an empire that stretched from the Middle East to China.[330] In 1071, the Seljuks had encroached on Byzantine lands, defeating the empire's forces at Manzikert. The Turks also occupied Anatolia, located in modern-day Turkey. They were focused on settlement, so the

---

[329] Jankowski, *Eastern Europe!*, 2015, pg.185.

[330] Ibid., pg.186.

Seljuks imported many Turkish tribes from the Eurasian Steppe to Anatolia. These settlers would overrun the Seljuks, forming their own empire.

When the Seljuk Turks were losing power in the last years of the 13th century, a military leader named Osman founded his own state, which would become the Ottoman Empire. The first Ottoman sultans encroached on Byzantine lands, growing their territories from a small principality to a substantial empire.

The Ottoman lands grew more and more extensive each year. By the 1350s, the Ottomans took advantage of their invitation to the Balkans and started conquering the area. Over the next one hundred years, the Ottomans made more inroads into Europe. Despite a temporary setback with the rise and fall of Tamerlane, who defeated the Ottomans at the Battle of Ankara in 1402, they consistently won battle after battle, taking land after land.[331] In 1453, they set their sights on Constantinople.[332]

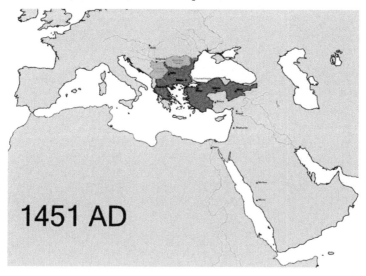

A map of the holdings of the Ottoman Empire two years before the fall of Constantinople. (Credit: Chamboz, 2016)

[331] Ibid., pg.186-187.

[332] Liulevicius, "Formative Migrations: Mongols to Germans." Lecture 2. *The Great Courses: A History of Eastern Europe*, 2015.

While the Ottomans had been glorious in their imperialist ambitions, the Byzantine Empire had not.[333] They lost a significant amount of their territory; all that was left was the city of Constantinople. In 1453, Sultan Mehmed II, also known as Mehmed the Conqueror, stormed the walls of Constantinople, which had stood (and kept invaders out) for centuries. Mehmed had gathered the best scientists, technicians, and military strategists in the world. He had ten times the number of soldiers, as well as something that had rarely been seen before in Europe: cannons. The walls of Constantinople crumbled under the siege, and eighty thousand Ottoman soldiers stormed the city. The last Byzantine emperor, Constantine XI, was killed in battle, ending the one-thousand-year reign of the Eastern Roman Empire. The Ottomans would hold Constantinople, which they renamed Istanbul, for the next five hundred years until the fall of the Ottoman Empire after World War I.[334]

---

[333] Jankowski, *Eastern Europe!*, 2015, pg.185.

[334] Liulevicius, "Formative Migrations: Mongols to Germans." Lecture 2. *The Great Courses: A History of Eastern Europe*, 2015; Liulevicius, "Clashing Golden Ages, 1389-1772." Lecture 3. *The Great Courses: A History of Eastern Europe*, 2015.

Fausto Zonaro, Sultan Mehmed II Entering Constantinople.
(Public Domain)

Chapter 6 – Eastern Europe Meets Early Modern Europe: The 15th and 16th Centuries in Eastern Europe

The fall of Constantinople is not the end of the Ottomans' story.[335] While it is known as their most famous effort, they were expansionists at heart. From Constantinople, the Ottomans pushed west, reaching Eastern Europe. This would have long-standing consequences for Hungary and Bohemia. Another power was on the rise, and they challenged the Ottoman advance and dominated Eastern Europe for the next two centuries. This power was the Habsburgs.[336]

---

[335] Jankowski, *Eastern Europe!*, 2015, pg.186.

[336] Ibid., pg. 195.

The Hungarians: The Last Stop for the Ottomans

After the Mongols left their destruction of Hungary behind, the country had more than its fair share of rebuilding to do.[337] The chaos of picking up the pieces of a broken country, in turn, broke the Árpád dynasty, which died out at the dawn of the 14th century. Instead of tempting more civil war, Hungary asked the French Anjou dynasty to take the throne. The eighty-year period of French rule did much to help Hungary recover. Using sophisticated state-building methods, the French built Hungarian relationships with their neighbors. By the end of the 14th century, Hungary was strong enough to resist Ottoman intervention.

After Anjou rule, Hungary was ruled by another foreign king: Sigismund from the Luxembourg royal family. His reign was most remembered not for his successes but his failures, like the 1396 defeat at the Battle of Nicopolis. Hungary continued its pattern of foreign rule, choosing a Polish king, Władysław III, in 1437. He also failed to push back the Ottomans, although he organized a crusade to return the Balkans to Eastern Europe.[338] In November 1444, Władysław died on the battlefield in the Battle of Varna, which was one of the last battles of the Crusades. His general, John Hunyadi (also written as János Hunyadi), returned to Hungary and ruled over the country as a governor.

In 1456, under John Hunyadi, the Hungarians stopped the Ottomans at Belgrade.[339] This would be the first but not the last time that the Hungarians would stop Ottoman plans for domination of Eastern Europe. Not only would Hungary successfully defend its lands, but it would also grow under John Hunyadi's son, King Matthias Corvinus (r. 1458–1490).

---

[337] Ibid., pg. 192.

[338] Ibid., pg. 193.

[339] Ibid., pg.186-187, 193-194.

A 15ᵗʰ-century image of Matthias Corvinus. (Public Domain)

Matthias Corvinus was responsible for the cultural growth of Hungary, building libraries full of Renaissance texts and bringing in the shining stars of the architectural world to beautify the country. Matthias Corvinus conquered new lands, making Hungary larger and more powerful than it had ever been. Most importantly, he kept the country safe from the Ottomans.

A map showing the territories Matthias Corvinus added to Hungary during his reign. (Credit: Viztarp, 2010)

After Matthias Corvinus died, Hungary went into decline. It had its share of domestic unrest, and the Ottomans would take advantage of that. In 1526, the Ottomans laid a decisive blow to the Hungarian forces at the Battle of Mohács. There was nothing stopping the Ottomans from moving into Europe.

The Ottomans reached as far inland as Austria. Using the Danube River, the Ottomans arrived in Vienna in 1529. The plague stopped any designs the Ottomans had on the city, though. As it was, the Ottoman Empire stretched well into Eastern Europe. The 16th century saw the area from the Balkans to European (western) Russia under Ottoman dominion.

Surprisingly, despite the constant warfare, Christians and Jews thrived under Ottoman rule.[340] Uninterested in conversion, the Ottomans labeled them *dhimmi*, a special group of the population that was under Ottoman protection in exchange for tax payments called jizya. *Dhimmi* included Christians and Jews, who both found safe havens in Ottoman lands as they escaped violence and persecution in their homes in Europe. Jews formed the merchant class of most Ottoman cities, finding more economic opportunities than they could in Christian Europe.

In the Balkans, this tax was paid in the form of both money and Christian children. Christians had to send their sons to the Ottoman Empire, where they were taught military strategy and defense and became valued members of the Janissaries. Although this may sound harsh, very few Balkan Christians converted to Islam to avoid the tax.

Religious Warfare in Bohemia: The Hussite Wars

When King Louis II of Hungary (r. 1490-1516) died in the Battle of Mohács, he also left the throne of Bohemia empty.[341] The power of Hungary would soon shatter into a fractured territory, and Bohemia would emerge from religious warfare to foreign rule.

Luckily, Bohemia didn't have much recovering to do after the Mongol invasions.[342] However, the country would soon be split apart by religious warfare. Since the 10th century, Bohemia had been a Christian nation closely allied with the Holy Roman Empire. The most famous of the medieval kings, Ottokar II of Bohemia (r. 1253-1278), was a "conversion by conquest" king. He conquered Silesia and eastern Austria, hoping the growth of his

---

[340] Liulevicius, "Clashing Golden Ages, 1389-1772." Lecture 3. *The Great Courses: A History of Eastern Europe*, 2015.

[341] Ibid., pg. 194-195.

[342] Ibid., pg. 196.

Christian lands would help him become Holy Roman emperor. In 1273, Ottokar lost his bid for that title to Rudolf of Habsburg. For five years, Ottokar stewed in his defeat and prepared for battle. In 1278, he met Rudolf at the Battle on the Marchfeld in the modern-day Czech Republic. Unfortunately, Rudolf had the better army, and he slew the Bohemian forces; Ottokar lay among the dead on the battlefield. In the aftermath of the battle, Rudolf took Austria from the Bohemian landholdings. Austria would famously remain in Habsburg hands until the end of World War I.

A king of Bohemia would eventually become the Holy Roman emperor but not until almost a century later.[343] Přemyslid rule died out in Bohemia in 1310, and the throne passed to a member of the royal family in Luxembourg. What is special about this dynasty is that it would achieve Ottokar's goals.

In 1346, Prince Charles of Luxembourg was crowned king of Bohemia after his father died in battle. Born and raised in Prague, he spent his reign beautifying the city. In 1355, he was the first king of Bohemia to become the Holy Roman emperor. Crowned Charles IV, he remained loyal to Prague, ruling the Holy Roman Empire from there.[344] That means that the center of Christian Europe lay just at the western boundary of Eastern Europe, not in Rome.

Soon, Bohemia would become the center of religious turmoil that would escalate into warfare. At the turn of the century, a religious reformer named Jan Hus started spreading ideas about the corruption of the Catholic Church. Spearheading the ideas of John Wycliffe from England, Hus stirred up resentment toward the church in Bohemia, which led to unrest.

---

[343] Ibid., pg. 197.

[344] Jankowski, *Eastern Europe!*, 2015, pg. 197-198; Liulevicius, "Clashing Golden Ages, 1389-1772." Lecture 3. *The Great Courses: A History of Eastern Europe*, 2015.

Hus found allies in the royal family of Bohemia, but they were also anxious to end the burgeoning tensions in the country.[345] At the end of 1414, King Wenceslaus IV (r. 1378–1419) and his brother Sigismund (who was the king of Hungary) promised Hus he would be safe if he addressed the Council of Constance in southern Germany. King Sigismund himself presided over the council. When Hus arrived, he was arrested. Hus was burned alive for heresy in 1415. How much Wenceslaus IV and Sigismund protested is up for debate.

Johann Hus auf dem Konstanzer Konzil ("Jan Hus at the Council of Constance"). Karl Friedrich Lessing, 1842. (Public Domain)

The execution of Jan Hus could not silence his followers.[346] The Hussites were incensed by the betrayal of their leader and attacked city officials, throwing them out of windows. Hus had not chosen someone to continue his movement after his death, so factions of

[345] Jankowski, *Eastern Europe!*, 2015, pg. 198; "Wenceslas, king of Bohemia and Germany." *Encyclopedia Britannica.* https://www.britannica.com/biography/Wenceslas

[346] "Czechoslovak History: The Hussite Wars." *Encyclopedia Britannica.* https://www.britannica.com/topic/Czechoslovak-history/The-Hussite-wars; Liulevicius, "Clashing Golden Ages, 1389-1772." Lecture 3. *The Great Courses: A History of Eastern Europe*, 2015; "Wenceslas, king of Bohemia and Germany." *Encyclopedia Britannica.*

Hussites spread throughout Bohemia, ranging from moderate to radical. These factions still had to contend with fervent Catholics who still lived in the country.

An image from a 15th-century manuscript, the Jena Codex, showing the burning of Jan Hus. (Public Domain)

Decades of struggle and tensions took a toll on the king of Bohemia. When King Wenceslaus IV died in 1419, the Hussites lost their king and a powerful ally. Although he was married twice, he never had any children. Sigismund was Wenceslaus's heir, and the throne of Bohemia automatically passed to him. Due to his role in Hus's assassination, the Hussites rejected Sigismund's ascension to the Bohemian throne. Fed up with the turmoil that divided the country, Sigismund launched several crusades against them over the next fifteen years. The Hussites, as divided as they were, recognized their common enemy, and they fought together to drive the Catholic forces back.

Another image from the Jena Codex showing a battle from the Hussite Wars. (Public Domain)

In 1434, the Catholic forces finally defeated the Hussites.[347] They were down, but they were not out. Hussite support remained so strong in Bohemia that it would eventually become a state-protected religion. In the 15th century, about one hundred years before the Protestant Reformation, Bohemia became the first country in Europe where Protestantism was practiced.

The Restructuring of Bohemia and Hungary

The Ottomans understood the importance of controlling Hungary. It was centrally located within Eastern Europe; if they could control Hungary, the Ottomans would have a stable footing in Europe.[348] However, the circumstances surrounding the outcome of Mohács made this impossible.

The Habsburgs didn't want the Ottomans to come too far east, so they snatched up the crown of Bohemia, which also extended their power. The Habsburgs saw themselves as the inheritors of the Carolingians and the Franks, who were the stalwart defenders of Christendom. This would eventually destroy Bohemia's place as the first practicing Protestant country.

However, in Hungary, it wasn't as easy as snatching a crown and occupying a country. Louis II's death led to a brutal civil war.[349] As it was, Louis was the last of his line, and there were multiple rivals for the throne. Each claimant, John Zápolya and Ferdinand I, each had their own support among the Bohemian elite. Their struggles ended in a stalemate. Bohemia turned to the other great power in the region to negotiate for them: Suleiman the Magnificent, the sultan of the Ottomans and the victor of the Battle of Mohács.

---

[347] Jankowski, *Eastern Europe!*, 2015, pg. 198.

[348] Ibid., pg. 195.

[349] "Hungary: The Period of Partition." *Encyclopedia Britannica.*
https://www.britannica.com/place/Hungary/The-period-of-partition

The trouble was, Suleiman didn't want a united Hungary to challenge his power. So, he recognized both claims. After occupying the center of the country himself, Suleiman created a vassal state out of southern Hungary, effectively separating John's and Ferdinand's claims in half. Western Hungary belonged to the Habsburg dynasty, and the east was renamed Transylvania. John died in 1540, passing his claim to his newborn son. This allowed the sultan to turn Transylvania into a vassal state of the Ottomans, and it was ruled by the Hungarian nobility.

The Romanian States under Ottoman Control

Despite the Ottoman threat to their security, the first Romanian states (Wallachia, Transylvania, and Moldavia) were the products of making the best out of a bad situation.[350] Cooperating with powers like the Ottomans and the Hungarians, they were able to enjoy some freedom in ruling themselves.

Desperate to avoid another Mongol invasion, Hungary and its neighbor Poland drove the Mongols out of Eastern Europe. To keep the Mongols away, Hungary bargained with the Vlachs, creating the states of Wallachia and Moldavia. They were the first line of defense against another Mongol invasion, allowing the Hungarians and the Poles to organize their defenses.

While this was a good plan, the people of Wallachia and Moldavia didn't see it that way. By the mid-14th century, they resisted Hungarian domination and created their own independent states.[351] Independence came at a cost, though, as they had to deal with the Ottomans alone. After a brief alliance with the Hungarians to resist the Ottomans at the Battle of Nicopolis in 1396, Wallachia

---

[350] Jankowski, *Eastern Europe!*, 2015, pg.187.

[351] Ibid., pg. 187-188.

succumbed to the Ottoman hold on the area, paying tribute to keep the Ottomans out of their lands.[352]

Throughout the rest of the 14th century, Moldavia avoided Ottoman domination because it was farther inland than Wallachia. However, as the Ottomans spread west from the Black Sea and dominated Wallachia, the Moldavians were in trouble. Instead of succumbing to the Ottomans, Moldavia sought protection from Poland.[353]

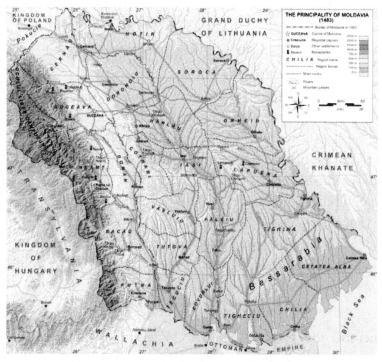

A map of Moldavia in 1483. (Credit: Spiridon Manoliu, 2009)

In Moldavia, Stephen III (r. 1457–1504) would become legendary for his resistance to the Hungarians and Ottomans. The Ottomans tightened their grip on the Balkans, but Stephen stopped both the Ottomans and the Hungarians from invading his lands. Fourteen years into his embattled rule, he formed an alliance with

---

[352] Ibid., pg. 188-189.

[353] Ibid., pg. 190.

a weakening Wallachia. His efforts fell short, and another invasion from the Ottomans, which lasted from 1484 to 1486, made Stephen realize that help wasn't coming. The other nations of Christian Europe, as much as they supported the Crusades, were surprisingly quiet when the Ottomans were encroaching on Christian nations in Eastern Europe. After years of struggle, Stephen finally gave in, negotiating a tribute to the Ottomans to end the hostilities. Wallachia and Moldavia would soon find themselves under direct Ottoman control. After the Ottoman victory at the Battle of Mohács and with their hold on the area nearly secure, Ottoman soldiers permanently occupied the territories.

It was in this period that the three Romanian states would unite under one rule, even though it only lasted a few years.[354] At the close of the 16th century, the Ottomans placed Michael the Brave on the throne of Wallachia. It was a mistake because Michael had his own plans. Instead of playing the puppet to the Ottomans, he brought both Transylvania and Moldavia under his rule. It was the first time Romania would be united. Unfortunately, Michael was murdered in 1601, and the Ottomans quickly moved in and reclaimed their hold on the territory.

The Introduction of Prussia

Remember the Teutonic Knights? When we saw them in the last chapter, they were founding Crusader states along the Polish-Lithuanian-Kaliningrad border.[355] The German Crusader states made it easier for the Teutonic Knights to defend the Polish border, and they dominated the southern Baltic. These states formed the beginnings of the new states of Prussia.

---

[354] Ibid., pg. 190-191.

[355] Ibid., pg. 198-199.

However, these Teutonic Knights were anything but holy. They may have started out that way, but they soon became obsessed with secular power. The knights conquered cities, building up their own control over the Baltic through military invasions and occupations. They soon became *persona non grata* in Eastern Europe and the target of a wide-reaching alliance.

Poland grew alarmed at the rate that the Teutonic Knights acquired territory.[356] It had already lost its northern borders to the knights, and it feared losing more. The apprehension among the northern Eastern European states made allies out of traditional enemies, as they were all united in a common cause.

The three major powers in the Baltic region—Poland, Lithuania, and the Novgorod Republic (a former state of Kievan Rus located in modern-day western Russia that had carved out its own autonomy against the Mongol Horde)—united against the Teutonic Knights. That wasn't the only problem the knights had; they were also starting to irritate their own people. The Teutonic Knights heavily taxed the German workers, craftsmen, and merchants who settled their lands, and they eventually rebelled against the knights.

---

[356] Ibid., pg. 199-200.

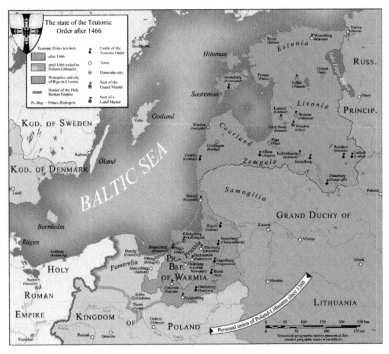

*A late 15th-century map of the territories held by the Teutonic Order.
(Credit: S. Bollman, 2010)*

This early period in Prussian history laid the groundwork for what was to come. The Prussia of later centuries would use both military force and commercial endeavors to spread its influence throughout Europe. Memories of the Teutonic Knights would reverberate through the centuries, inspiring a cult of personality and warrior mentality of later Prussian monarchs. The rise of the Hanseatic League would produce a new type of foreign policy, one focused on a global economy.[357]

The Hanseatic League

The Baltic Sea was a highly concentrated area of trade, one that drew people to the region. Goods from all over Eurasia made their way to the Baltic after traveling along the Silk Road and other trade highways.

---

[357] Ibid., pg. 203.

Most of the Germans who moved to live in the Crusader states were merchants. The sheer amount of them meant that the Teutonic Knights could tax them enough to raise money for their wars. However, it ruined the merchants' ability to make a living.

A map showing the territories of Northern Europe that were part of the Hanseatic League in 1400. (Credit: Droysen/Andrée, 1886)

The Hanseatic League, founded in 1267, was an organization of trade cities that stretched from England to Eastern Europe. It included all the major trade areas that could be reached by land and sea. The Hanseatic League effectively acted as its own state. It had an organized military designed to defend merchant ships against pirate attacks, as well as enforced agreed-upon terms with other league cities. Traders associated with the league enjoyed several benefits, such as protection in other countries and no restrictions or taxes on their products.

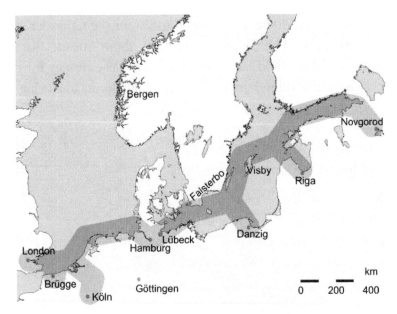

The trading routes used by the Hanseatic League. (Credit: Flo Beck, 2006)

Almost two hundred cities belonged to the Hanseatic League when it was at its most powerful in the 1300s. During the medieval period, many states were not strong enough to offer the type of protection that the league provided. For this reason, it lasted until the 1660s.[358] By this time, countries were stronger and able to control their own trade. Although it didn't last, the Hanseatic League was instrumental in protecting the burgeoning Baltic trade. It would flourish under the league's direction.

Russian Beginnings: Novgorod and Muscovy

Kievan Rus was a shell of what it once was.[359] The former Viking states that had united into a force that dominated Eastern Europe at the height of the Middle Ages was now a wasteland. The Mongol invasion had ripped through Rus, decimating everything in their

---

[358] Ibid., pg. 204.

[359] Ibid., pg. 208.

path. The survivors then had to suffer the indignity of Mongol occupation.[360] The Rus states were forced to submit and offer yearly tributes as vassal states. The Mongols cemented the fall of Kievan Rus, which was already in decline.[361]

The Novgorod Republic

To the north, the Novgorod Republic escaped the Mongol Horde.[362] The city-state paid off their attackers if they would leave them in peace, which became a repeating theme throughout Eastern Europe. The Mongols got what they wanted: wealth, riches, and submission to their authority.

Since it escaped the Golden Horde unscathed, Novgorod could focus on building itself up. It had been on the rise since the 12th century, flourishing from its important trade relationships. Located to the east of the Gulf of Finland, which is a smaller body of water connected to the eastern Baltic Sea, it benefited from its prime location in the Baltic trade. Although Kievan Rus had severely declined by the time the Mongols showed up, the cities that escaped the Mongols' wrath were able to prosper.

Using its wealth from trade, Novgorod invested in itself, building up its defenses and training its military. In the 1240s, it had pushed back invasions from both the Swedes and the Teutonic Knights. Thanks to the victories by Prince Alexander Nevsky, Novgorod was in the perfect position to expand. It was already a metropolis in Eastern Europe, with trade being the key to its success. Of course, the people of Novgorod would want to defend it. Traders from all over Eurasia did business there. It gained even more power and influence thanks to its membership in the Hanseatic League. With its success on the battlefield and its riches from trade, Novgorod spread out, conquering lands in every direction. Over the years,

---

[360] Liulevicius, "Clashing Golden Ages, 1389-1772." Lecture 3. *The Great Courses: A History of Eastern Europe*, 2015.

[361] Jankowski, *Eastern Europe!*, 2015, pg. 210.

[362] Ibid., pg. 208.

Mongol power faded. They went from keeping their lands on a tight leash to barely exerting any control at all. As Lithuania started spreading to the east, conquering the western border of the Rus lands, the Mongols pulled back. They rebuilt their center of power southeast of Novgorod in a smaller settlement: Moscow.

Muscovy Russia under the Rurik Princes

As Mongol power fell in the region, their control was relegated to a series of successor states that tried to keep their dominance. Rus city-states also became major powers.[363] Moscow was only one of many city-states that exerted its influence in former Rus lands. Established on the Volga River in the 12th century, Moscow thrived as a trading center.[364] Soon, it became the dominant Rus city-state in the region. The Mongols showed a preference for Moscow, allowing the city's officials to collect their tributes.[365]

Ivan III and the "Gathering of the Russias"

The Rurik dynasty princes would come to power in Moscow in the early 15th century, and they would define modern Russia.[366] Just like Novgorod, Moscow used its wealth to build its defenses and expand its dominions.[367] The second Rurik prince, Ivan III, took on the Golden Horde and won in 1480.[368]

[363] "Russia." *Encyclopedia Britannica.* https://www.britannica.com/place/Russia

[364] Jankowski, *Eastern Europe!*, 2015, pg. 208.

[365] Jankowski, *Eastern Europe!*, 2015, pg. 208; Liulevicius, "Clashing Golden Ages, 1389-1772." Lecture 3. *The Great Courses: A History of Eastern Europe*, 2015.

[366] "Russia." *Encyclopedia Britannica.*

[367] Jankowski, *Eastern Europe!*, 2015, pg. 208.

[368] Jankowski, *Eastern Europe!*, 2015, pg. 208; Liulevicius, "Clashing Golden Ages, 1389-1772." Lecture 3. *The Great Courses: A History of Eastern Europe*, 2015.

A photograph taken of Ivan III featured on the "Millennium of Russia" monument, located in Veliky Novgorod, Russia. (Credit: Дар Ветер, 2010)

Ivan III was the strong leader that the fledgling Rus states needed. His wife was a Byzantine princess, and he longed to replicate the power of Constantinople in his domain. He spread out the Rurik landholdings, and he built the city of Moscow to be the most beautiful and modern city in the region.

Under Ivan's leadership, Moscow developed into the state of Muscovy. Muscovy and the Novgorod Republic became rivals, and their enmity ended in a showdown in the late 15th century. Muscovy was victorious, establishing its place as a force to be reckoned with in Eastern Europe. By the end of the 1470s, Moscow had defeated its two most intimidating foes: Novgorod and the Mongols. Ivan's "Gathering of the Russias" initiative pulled the rest of the Rus territories under his rule. While this may have given Ivan III his nickname of "The Father of Russia," his grandson is the more well-known of the Rurik princes. His grandson was none other than Ivan IV, better known as Ivan the Terrible.

The Terrifying Reign of Ivan IV

Ivan IV continued his grandfather's work in consolidating the Russian state.[369] Through warfare and terror, he created a centralized state that would become a major force in Europe. The territories gained by both Ivan III and Ivan IV set the course for the formation of the Russian Empire at the beginning of the 18th century.

Despite his success in expanding and centralizing the state, Ivan the Terrible had a series of hits and misses on the battlefield. He fought several conflicts during his lifetime, destroying the Russian landscape and taxing Russian resources.[370] His wars with Poland and Sweden were failures, but he had more success with subduing the successor Mongol states east of Muscovy.

---

[369] "Ivan the Terrible." *Encyclopedia Britannica.*
https://www.britannica.com/biography/Ivan-the-Terrible

[370] Jankowski, *Eastern Europe!*, 2015, pg. 208; "Ivan the Terrible." *Encyclopedia Britannica.*

Ivan IV "the Terrible." Viktor Vasnetsov, 1897. (Public Domain)

Between 1547 and 1550, Ivan attacked the Kazan Khanate, located along the Volga River, twice. Russian forces were pushed back on both campaigns. Finally, in 1552, the city of Kazan fell to Ivan's army after a lengthy siege. Four years later, Ivan secured control over the Volga River by conquering the Astrakhan Khanate, located at the mouth of the river. With these successes came more territory to incorporate into his realm. Ivan's control over the Volga also meant that he secured a viable trading route to the Caspian Sea.

The Livonian War

With control over trade to the east, Ivan looked west for more trading opportunities in the Baltic. He attacked the state of Livonia, located on the eastern coast of the Baltic Sea. Situated in modern-day Estonia and Latvia, Livonia was occupied by the German crusaders, the Livonian Brotherhood.

The last time we saw the Livonian Brotherhood, they had suffered a humiliating defeat at the Battle of Saule in 1236.[371] When they joined the Teutonic Knights, they changed their name to the Livonian Order. The Teutonic Order allowed the Livonians to operate independently, so the Livonian Order established a state as their base of operations: the Confederation of Livonia. It would be the last of the German Crusader states, and it was centered in present-day Estonia and Latvia.

Now that the Livonian Order had gotten their bearings, they went back to doing what they did best: terrorize pagans into submission and conversion. They were especially active in the Northern Crusades that targeted the Baltic, Finnic, and Slavic states.

The Confederation of Livonia wasn't just a religious center; it also had ties to the secular world. The German merchants who lived in the Livonian state hated war and violence; they just wanted to trade in peace. They used the Hanseatic League to ensure that the Livonian Order's crusading didn't affect their ability to do business.

And the Livonian Order listened. They established government structures designed to mediate between the Livonians and the people. This method, unlike the Teutonic method of riding roughshod over their people, actually worked. The Livonian Order and the German merchants lived in relative peace until the mid-16th century, when Ivan the Terrible set his sights on their territory.

---

[371] Jankowski, *Eastern Europe!*, 2015, pg. 202.

The Livonian War (1558–1583) was a fifteen-year conflict that the newly united Russia didn't need.[372] Although Ivan did eliminate the Livonian Order for good, that was his only real success. Things became complicated when Poland and Lithuania finally merged into one state in 1569, which we will learn about soon. Lithuania and Livonia were allies, as were Poland and Sweden. Everyone jumped into the fray, which resulted in disaster for Russia.

With their allies in tow, the Tatars of Crimea, another one of the Mongol successor states, stormed into Muscovy. From their base in the peninsula between the Black Sea and the Sea of Azov (which is now part of the modern-day borders of Ukraine), the Tatars attacked Astrakhan on the Volga, pushing further into Ivan's domain. When they reached Moscow in 1571, Ivan's beleaguered army retreated into the city. The Tatars ravaged the city, setting the city ablaze. The Fire of Moscow destroyed the city and the population. While there isn't any clear number on how many died in the attack, it is most likely that tens of thousands died in the chaos.

---

[372] Jankowski, *Eastern Europe!*, 2015, pg. 208-209; Liulevicius, "Clashing Golden Ages, 1389-1772." Lecture 3. *The Great Courses: A History of Eastern Europe*, 2015; "Ivan the Terrible." *Encyclopedia Britannica*.

The divisions of Livonia, 1600. On the map, Poland-Lithuania is marked in rose pink, the vassals of Poland-Lithuania are in magenta, the Kingdom of Sweden is in lavender, Denmark-Norway is in burnt orange, and Russia is in green. (Credit: Halibutt, 2011)

The trouble for Ivan didn't stop there. Poland attacked the Russians on their own turf while the Swedes moved in and occupied Livonia. Exhausted from years of warfare, Ivan threw his hands in the air. The Livonian War ended in 1583 with a peace treaty of humiliating terms for Russia. Ivan had to give up all of his gains made during the war. As for Livonia itself, the remnants of the state were split between Sweden and the Polish-Lithuanian Commonwealth.[373] After years of struggle, Russia was left with nothing; Ivan's attempts to reach the Baltic to capitalize on its trade had failed[374]Russian forces eventually mustered an offensive and drove the Tatars out a year later, but the damage was done.[375]

[373] Jankowski, *Eastern Europe!*, 2015, pg. 202.

[374] Jankowski, *Eastern Europe!*, 2015, pg. 208; Liulevicius, "Clashing Golden Ages, 1389-1772." Lecture 3. *The Great Courses: A History of Eastern Europe*, 2015.

[375] Jankowski, *Eastern Europe!*, 2015, pg. 209-210.

The Oprichnina

Ivan IV was a mentally unstable child-king who secured absolute power through terror and violence, and he earned his heinous nickname through his oppressive Oprichnina policy.[376] He held a horrible grudge against the nobles who fought for power during his regency. When Ivan came of age, the regent council of elites didn't want to release their hold on power. Although he was the tsar—the first Russian ruler to hold that title—Ivan was limited in what he could do.

In 1564, Ivan negotiated with the council, agreeing to grant them the power they wanted if there was a section of the country where he could rule unopposed. The nobles balked at first, but they eventually agreed.

Ivan confiscated the best lands for himself, and he ruled them with absolute power. These lands were called the Oprichnina. He established a secret police force, the Oprichnik, that ran roughshod over the lands, tormenting and assassinating who Ivan saw as an enemy. His attacks could have been defensive or not; it didn't matter. He called for someone's assassination if he thought they were talking about him, if he thought they betrayed him, or if he was in a bad mood and needed cheering up.

Ivan the Terrible used the Oprichnik to target the landowners who had been so restrictive during his regency. He used this method of rulership to eliminate his enemies or anyone he perceived as an enemy. The 1571 invasion of the Crimean Tatars into Moscow, which destroyed the city, was the turning point for Ivan's rule. Although Russian forces eventually mustered an offensive and drove the Tatars out a year later, the damage was done.[377] After nearly ten years of violence, Ivan was forced to banish his Oprichnina policy. However, it mattered little. With a

---

[376] Jankowski, *Eastern Europe!*, 2015, pg. 208-209; "Ivan the Terrible." *Encyclopedia Britannica.*

[377] Jankowski, *Eastern Europe!*, 2015, pg. 209-210.

destroyed state and a decimated population, Ivan could exact absolute power over all of Russia.

Ivan's reign of terror undoubtedly stunted Russia's growth, and it wouldn't become a major political player until the early 17th century. Ivan's disastrous reign was followed by another regency for his heirs. Known as the "Time of Troubles," regent Boris Godunov usurped power, making himself Tsar of all the Russia. From the years 1598 to 1613, Russia was engulfed in a civil war that only ended with the ascension of the most recognizable dynasty in Russian history: the Romanovs.

The Kievan Rus states at their decline in the 13th century. (Credit: SeikoEn, 2010)

Creating the Polish-Lithuanian Commonwealth

Two powers in Europe emerged after the evacuation of the Golden Horde: Poland and Lithuania. Throughout the medieval period, the neighbors expanded their territories. By the end of the 16th century, they would be a united country.[378]

Poland: A Christian Nation

In the last chapter, we saw Mieszko I turn Poland into a Christian nation.[379] Polish rulers spent nearly two centuries expanding the kingdom's territory, only for Boleslaw III's heirs to rip it apart. For over one hundred years, Boleslaw III's sons and their successors claimed their own lands and fought with each other for more territory, turning Poland into a warring collection of small states.

Until the 14th century, Poland was made up of regional territories ruled by the elite. There was no center of power in Poland for almost two centuries. The elites liked the power they wielded over their individual territories, and although members of the Piast family attempted to reclaim the monarchy, the nobles pushed back time and time again. They didn't want another king telling them what to do!

In the middle of Poland's civil war, the Mongols ripped through Poland, destroying its cities and infrastructure. The Mongols left behind a wasteland that the rulers of Poland were ill-prepared to fix.

In 1304, Poland would finally become a united country again, thanks to the campaigns of Ladislaus the Short (also known as Władysław I Łokietek). Ladislaus was a member of the Piast dynasty, and he was one of many that tried to return Poland to

---

[378] Ibid., pg. 204-208.

[379] Ibid., pg. 150-152, 204.

Piast rule. He fought off several invasions from Bohemia, Brandenburg, and the Teutonic Knights. Ladislaus lost a significant amount of border territories, but he was successful in reuniting the country under one rule. His final step in bringing the country back together was appealing to the pope to recognize Poland as a united Christian nation; the pope granted the request in 1320.

Ladislaus's son, Casimir III, succeeded his father as the king of Poland in 1333. He was a reformer, and he restored Poland's infrastructure and reorganized the legal system. One significant improvement that Casimir made was the granting of more rights to Jews who sought refuge in Poland.

Casimir III died without an heir in 1370, and the Polish crown passed to the Capetian House of Anjou. Their rule would soon meet a difficult obstacle. In 1382, the reigning Anjou king died, leaving behind only one heir: his twelve-year-old daughter, Jadwiga (also known as Hedwig in Hungary).

As a reigning monarch, Jadwiga was one of the most eligible women in Eastern Europe. Her marriage could change the fate of nations. Soon after taking the throne, she received a very unexpected marriage proposal.[380]

[380] Jankowski, *Eastern Europe!*, 2015, pg. 204-205; Liulevicius, "Clashing Golden Ages, 1389-1772." Lecture 3. *The Great Courses: A History of Eastern Europe*, 2015.

This map shows how Lithuania expanded from the 13ᵗʰ to 15ᵗʰ centuries. It was once the largest territory in Europe. (Credit: M.K., 2006)

Lithuania: A Growing Pagan Power

In the 13ᵗʰ century, Lithuania had grown to dominate Eastern Europe, thanks to the efforts of its king, Mindaugas. After defeating the Livonian Brotherhood in 1236, Mindaugas set his sights on creating his own empire.[381]

He acquired neighboring lands through alliances and conquests, shoring up Lithuanian power. The Livonian Brotherhood, now merged with the Teutonic Knights and known as the Livonian

---

[381] Jankowski, *Eastern Europe!*, 2015, pg. 200-201.

Order, was still a significant threat from the west, so the Lithuanian king did an about-face.[382] In the 1250s, he converted to Christianity.

Now that Lithuania was a Christian nation, the Livonian Order no longer encroached on Mindaugas's territory. The king turned east, pushing the Mongols back across the Baltic Sea. He even took some of their Russian territories in the process.

After Mindaugas died in 1263, Lithuanian rulers rejected Christianity. Since they returned to paganism, they lost their titles as kings of a Christian nation. During the reign of Gediminas (r. 1316–1341), Lithuania expanded into the largest territory in Europe. He conquered the lands to the south, reaching the Black Sea. He also absorbed the western lands of former Kievan Rus.

Gediminas did something unique among rulers that would have long-term effects on Eastern Europe today. He now had a large population of Slavs living in his dominions, and they spoke a language called Ruthenian. Instead of forcing them to assimilate, Gediminas gave them important political and civil rights. Among the freedoms the Slavs enjoyed was that they could retain their language and culture. Gediminas went a step further, adopting Ruthenian as Lithuania's state language. This Slavic population would eventually become two distinct cultures of their own. The Slavs living in areas closer to Moscow, in lands that were still under Mongol occupation, would become Russians. To the west, the Slavs living in Lithuanian lands would develop into the people of Ukraine and Belarus.

After Gediminas died in 1341, his son Algirdas continued his expansionist policies, but their neighbors were growing too. Lithuania soon faced the increasing influence of the Teutonic Knights, as well as Poland and Muscovy Russia. When Jogaila ascended the throne in 1377, Lithuania was strong, but it had enemies on all sides.

---

[382] Jankowski, *Eastern Europe!*, 2015, pg. 200-201; "Mindaugas." *Encyclopedia Britannica.* https://www.britannica.com/biography/Mindaugas

Poland-Lithuania: A Marriage of Monarchs and Territories

In 1384, Jogaila approached his neighbor, Poland, with a marriage proposal.[383] He wished to marry Jadwiga of Poland—the first female monarch of the country. He was the twenty-six-year-old grand duke of Lithuania. Jadwiga was only about eleven years old, but she was hardly the passive party. She may have just arrived in the country she was meant to rule, but she was crowned "Rex"—a title reserved for kings.

Such marriages were commonplace in the medieval period. What was so shocking about this union was that Jadwiga was a Christian while her proposed husband was a pagan. The marriage proposal was simple. After Jogaila and Jadwiga married, he would be crowned king of Poland, and they would rule together. In exchange, Jogaila would Christianize Lithuania.[384] Both countries would form a union, but each would retain its own identity and culture.

The marriage proposal was accepted, and the union between Poland and Lithuania was finalized with the Union of Krewo in 1385. After his conversion, Jogaila took the name King Władysław II Jagiełło of Poland. He also remained Lithuania's ruler, retaining the title of grand duke. Although the Union of Krewo formalized the alliance between Poland and Lithuania, they were both still distinct states with their own rulers; sometimes, as was the case with Jogaila, the same monarch would rule both states.[385] Together, the two countries would have the power to resist their enemies and retain and even extend their borders. The marriage between Jogaila and Jadwiga founded the Jagiellonian dynasty, a line of

---

[383] Jankowski, *Eastern Europe!*, 2015, pg. 204-205; Liulevicius, "Clashing Golden Ages, 1389-1772." Lecture 3. *The Great Courses: A History of Eastern Europe*, 2015

[384] Jenkins, *Short History of Europe*, 2019, pg. 102.

[385] "Jagiellon dynasty." *Encyclopedia Britannica*.
https://www.britannica.com/topic/Jagiellon-dynasty

kings and queens that would rule as the dukes of Lithuania and the kings of Poland, as well as the monarchs of Hungary and Bohemia.[386]

The most significant benefit of Poland-Lithuania was that both countries could now defend their lands against the Teutonic Order. Although Poland-Lithuania was technically a Christian nation and had been since the marriage of Władysław II Jagiełło and Queen Jadwiga, the Teutonic Order was still interested in expanding its territory.[387] The knights took advantage of a family rivalry between Jogaila and his cousin Vytautas to threaten the borders of Poland-Lithuania.[388] Ruling two countries took its toll on Jogaila, and he appointed his cousin as his regent in Lithuania. Despite the tensions between the cousins, they took their rulership seriously, and they put aside their squabbles for the good of the union.[389]

Tensions continued to brew between Poland-Lithuania and the Teutonic Order for the next ten years, culminating in the Battle of Grunwald in 1410.[390] It was a devastating loss for the knights. In just six hours, the Polish-Lithuanian forces decimated the Teutonic Order's high command, leaving the order essentially headless.

The Teutonic Order was down, but it wasn't out. The Teutonic Knights were not as powerful as they had been, though, and they would never expand into Eastern Europe again. However, they could still muster an offense. They antagonized Poland-Lithuania

[386] Liulevicius, "Clashing Golden Ages, 1389-1772." Lecture 3. *The Great Courses: A History of Eastern Europe,* 2015; Jankowski, *Eastern Europe!,* 2015, pg. 207; "Jagiellon dynasty." *Encyclopedia Britannica.*

[387] Mark Cartwright. "Teutonic Knight." *World History Encyclopedia.*

[388] Jankowski, *Eastern Europe!,* 2015, pg. 205-206.

[389] Liulevicius, "Clashing Golden Ages, 1389-1772." Lecture 3. *The Great Courses: A History of Eastern Europe,* 2015.

[390] Jankowski, *Eastern Europe!,* 2015, pg. 206; Liulevicius, "Clashing Golden Ages, 1389-1772." Lecture 3. *The Great Courses: A History of Eastern Europe,* 2015; Jenkins, *Short History of Europe,* 2019, pg. 102.

for years, taxing the residents of the lands to raise money for defenses. In 1440, the Prussian merchants tried to protect themselves against the knights' brutal taxation laws, forming their own union called the *Preußischer Bund* (also known as the Prussian Confederation). By 1454, the merchants had had enough of the heavy-handed Teutonic Knights and rebelled against them.

That same year, the Thirteen Years' War (1454–1466) began. When the Prussian Confederation rebelled against the Teutonic Order, they asked Poland-Lithuania's king, Casimir IV Jagiellon (r. 1447–1492 as king of Poland; r. 1440-1492 as grand duke of Lithuania), if he would rule them. The king accepted, and Poland-Lithuania and the Teutonic Knights went to war.

The war concluded in 1466, resulting in Prussia being split into two territories. Western Prussia (known as "Royal Prussia") was under Casimir's control, while the Teutonic Order remained overlords of Eastern Prussia ("Ducal Prussia"). Although the knights still had control over Ducal Prussia, they were a vassal to Poland.

Hostilities continued between Poland-Lithuania and the Teutonic Order for nearly six decades until they went to war again in 1520. This time, the Polish-Teutonic War was a much shorter affair, lasting until 1521. By the end of it, the Teutonic Order disintegrated, losing its lands in Ducal Prussia to Poland. Prussia was now completely under Poland-Lithuania's control, and it would remain so until 1657.

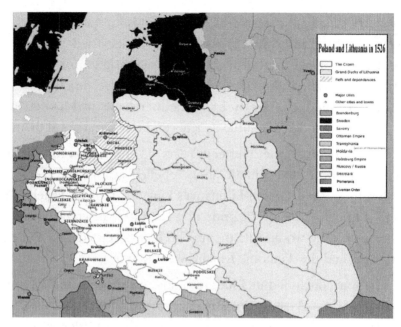

A map of Poland-Lithuania in 1526. The lands of Poland are in beige, and the land of Lithuania is in bright yellow. The vassal states are in yellow and brown lines. (Credit: Halibutt, 2009)

Although the union between Poland and Lithuania could be considered a successful one, Lithuania was always worried it would lose part of its identity to Poland.[391] Throughout the years of the union, Lithuania protested any attempt by Poland to overwhelm its government structure and culture. Even though Lithuania was triple the size of Poland, the connection forced out many Lithuanian customs.

These points of contention made themselves known early. During Władysław II Jagiełło's reign, his cousin, Vytautas, convinced Władysław to grant Lithuania more rights than it had under the original union treaty. Yet, the Jagiellonian dynasty reigned over both countries for almost two hundred years. It was inevitable that the countries would merge and share political, economic, and social characteristics.

[391] Jankowski, *Eastern Europe!*, 2015, pg. 207; Liulevicius, "Clashing Golden Ages, 1389-1772." Lecture 3. *The Great Courses: A History of Eastern Europe,* 2015.

The matrimonial merger had proved to be a fruitful one, at least by political standards. Poland-Lithuania's power grew, and its coffers filled up with wealth from trade with other European nations. The last king of the Jagiellonian dynasty, Sigismund II, knew that he would die without a successor, so he took steps to protect Poland and Lithuania.[392]

In 1569, despite heavy protests from Lithuania, he signed the Union of Lublin. The document officially joined Poland and Lithuania as the same country; it was known as the Polish-Lithuanian Commonwealth. Although Sigismund II was the first ruler of the commonwealth, he wouldn't be for long. He died without heirs in 1572, and the Jagiellonian dynasty died with him. However, his preemptive plan to officially unite Poland and Lithuania had its benefits. The two countries of the commonwealth wielded much more power together than they ever had before. The Polish-Lithuanian Commonwealth became a major political player until the mid-17th century.

---

[392] Jankowski, *Eastern Europe!*, 2015, pg. 208; "Jagiellon dynasty." *Encyclopedia Britannica*; "Sigismund II Augustus." *Encyclopedia Britannica*. https://www.britannica.com/biography/Sigismund-II-Augustus

Chapter 7 – The Turning Point: The 17th and 18th Centuries in Eastern Europe

By the year 1600, the territories of Eastern Europe had recovered from the Mongol invasions, with some turning into major regional powers.[393] At this time, there were four major political players in the region: the Habsburg dynasty, the Ottoman Empire, Sweden, and the Polish-Lithuanian Commonwealth.

These powers would decline during this period. However, Russia was on its way to becoming a major world power. Meanwhile, the Ottomans continued stomping over Eastern Europe, attempting to continue their glory from the fall of Constantinople. It was only a matter of time before they, too, would enter their own decline.

We'll start our story with the Thirty Years' War, a territorial conflict that became a continental war, with Eastern Europe caught in the crossfire.[394]

---

[393] Jankowski, *Eastern Europe!*, 2015, pg. 217.

[394] Ibid., pg. 219.

The Thirty Years' War

The Thirty Years' War (1618–1648) was a 17th-century war that pitted Catholics against Protestants in a bid to see what religion would reign supreme in Europe. Since the 15th century, Protestantism had been spreading in Eastern Europe, beginning with Jan Hus and his efforts in Bohemia.[395]

This war is one of the longest conflicts in history, and it had several theaters and offshoots.[396] The conflict actually started because of a dispute between Catholic and Protestant factions in Bohemia in the present-day Czech Republic.[397] It ended with powers all across Europe joining in on the fight, bringing religious warfare to a new level.

The Bohemian Revolt

Although they lost the Hussite Wars, the Hussites won a major victory in 1437. It remained so popular that the Bohemian government granted it legal protection as a state religion. Bohemia would become the first Protestant state in Europe, so it's fitting that the Thirty Years' War started there.

In 1526, the Habsburgs became the kings of Bohemia after the Battle of Mohács.[398] After less than one hundred years of Habsburg rule, the Bohemian elite refused to acknowledge Holy Roman Emperor Ferdinand II when he ascended the throne.[399] Instead,

---

[395] Ibid., pg. 198.

[396] Jankowski, *Eastern Europe!*, 2015, pg. 219; "Thirty Years' War." *HISTORY.* Published November 9, 2009. Last Updated August 21, 2018. https://www.history.com/topics/reformation/thirty-years-war

[397] Jankowski, *Eastern Europe!*, 2015, pg. 218-219; Jenkins, *Short History of Europe*, 2019, pg. 133-134.

[398] Jankowski, *Eastern Europe!*, 2015, pg. 217; Liulevicius, "Clashing Golden Ages, 1389-1772." Lecture 3. *The Great Courses: A History of Eastern Europe*, 2015.

[399] Jenkins, *Short History of Europe*, 2019, pg. 133.

they chose someone else: Frederick V of the Palatinate.[400] Their choice makes sense; Ferdinand was a devout Catholic, while Frederick was a Protestant.

Ferdinand dispatched representatives to pressure the Bohemians into submission. When Ferdinand's men reported to Prague Castle, the emperor's threats and strong-arming didn't work.[401] The Bohemian elites threw the representatives out of a window! Luckily for the emissaries, they survived; a pile of horse waste broke their fall.

In 1618, the noblemen of Bohemia threw Holy Roman Emperor Ferdinand II's envoys out of a window at Prague Castle. This event, commemorated in this 17th-century woodcut, is known as the 1618 Defenestration of Prague. (Public Domain)

---

[400] Ibid., pg. 134.

[401] Jankowski, *Eastern Europe!*, 2015, pg. 218-219; Liulevicius, "Clashing Golden Ages, 1389-1772." Lecture 3. *The Great Courses: A History of Eastern Europe*, 2015.

Even though the representatives didn't die, Ferdinand was furious at the disrespect. He invaded Bohemia in 1618, beginning the first phase of the Thirty Years' War.[402] The Bohemians gave Ferdinand's forces a tough fight for two years. In 1620, at the Battle of White Mountain, the Protestants were defeated.

Ferdinand didn't take this humiliation lightly, and the elites of Bohemia paid for it dearly. His revenge was punitive and bloody; Ferdinand stripped the elites of their lands and titles, which were then given to Habsburg supporters. In a final twist of vengeance, he ordered twenty-seven nobles to be marched out to the city square, where they were murdered. Ferdinand quickly subdued the rest of the territory. It would be a vassal to the Habsburgs until the dismantling of their empire in 1918.

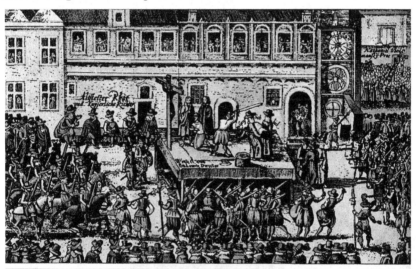

This image depicts the execution of twenty-seven Bohemian nobles at Holy Roman Emperor Ferdinand II's order. (Public Domain)

[402] Jenkins, *Short History of Europe*, 2019, pg. 134.

The Struggle for Transylvania

The Ottoman Empire took control of Transylvania after its victory at the Battle of Mohács.[403] While the Ottomans were in charge, the Hungarians were given relative freedom in their own affairs.[404] The Hungarian elite was in charge of the government in the Ottoman vassal territory, which was governed by the Báthory family.

The Báthorys

Stephen Báthory ruled Transylvania, along with his other territories, including the Polish-Lithuanian Commonwealth, from 1571 to 1586, making him one of the most powerful men in 16th-century Eastern Europe. During this time, Transylvania expanded its borders into Slovakia and Ukraine. But Stephen's name has a negative connotation thanks to his niece, Elizabeth Báthory.

A portrait of Stephen Báthory. Attributed to Jost Amman, 1585. (Public Domain)

---

[403] Jankowski, *Eastern Europe!*, 2015, pg.187, 194.

[404] Ibid., pg. 221-222.

Elizabeth married Count Ferenc II Nádasdy, a soldier for Royal Hungary, which was then controlled by Habsburgs. They lived in Csejte, Royal Hungary (present-day Čachtice, Slovakia), but he was away fighting the Ottomans for most of their marriage. In 1604, Count Nádasdy died on the battlefield.

After receiving news of her husband's death, Elizabeth reportedly started luring Slovak girls to her castle fortress, where she tortured and killed them. Elizabeth allegedly murdered hundreds of girls before the Habsburgs had her arrested. She holed up for the rest of her life in her castle, where she died in 1614.[405]

A copy of a 1585 portrait of Elizabeth Bathory when she was about twenty-five years old. (Public Domain)

[405] Jankowski, *Eastern Europe!*, 2015, pg. 221-222; Rachel L. Bledsaw, "No Blood in the Water: The Legal and Gender Conspiracies Against Countess Elizabeth Bathory in Historical Context" (2014). *Theses and Dissertations.* 135, pg. 1-2.

Elizabeth Báthory is perhaps one of the most controversial women in history. While she is infamously known as the "Blood Countess" and has a reputation for bathing in the blood of her victims, there is no factual evidence to back this up. The first mention of her draining the blood of her victims doesn't appear in the historical record until 1760, nearly a century and a half after she died.[406]

A Territory in Transition: Wallachian, Habsburg, and Hungarian Rule in Transylvania

The first years of the 17th century brought a turbulent rule to Transylvania. In 1599, the prince of Wallachia invaded Transylvania and took control for a time. His reign would only last two years. In 1601, the Habsburgs stepped in and assassinated him. The Habsburgs used the opportunity to run roughshod over Transylvania. Pogroms took place all over the region, and the Habsburgs eliminated anyone who was not Catholic or didn't support them.

The Habsburgs enacted three years of terror in Transylvania. In 1604, the Hungarians—under Stephen Bocskay—defeated the Habsburg forces. The region went back to Ottoman control, returning some peace and stability, as well as autonomy, to Transylvania. However, the region was on a path to losing that independence.

---

[406] Bledsaw, "No Blood in the Water," 2014, pg. 5.

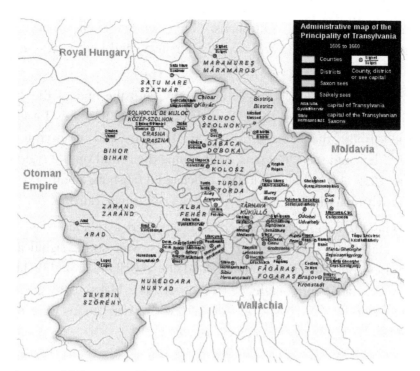

A map of 17th-century Transylvania, from 1606 to 1660. (Credit: Andrei nacu, 2008)

In 1613, the Ottomans placed Gabriel Bethlen on the throne. When the Thirty Years' War broke out five years later, he campaigned against the Habsburgs. He won several victories, but he didn't defeat them. However, the Hungarian elite was a fickle bunch, and they didn't support Bethlen's campaigns; they would only openly back him if he won against the Habsburg forces. Even though he had the support of the Ottoman Empire, Bethlen's forces were an unorganized bunch. He never could secure a definitive victory. In 1626, the Habsburgs obtained peace with Bethlen, and he retired.

When Bethlen died in 1629, he was succeeded by the Rákóczi family. They mostly abstained from the rest of the Thirty Years' War, preferring to secure their control over Transylvania. Several years after the war ended, the Rákóczis got ambitious; in 1657, they joined Sweden in an invasion of the Polish-Lithuanian Commonwealth. The Hungarians suffered a humiliating defeat, which incensed the Ottomans. They ended their policy of autonomy, secured control over the territory, and kept a close eye on the Rákóczis.

Transylvania slowly lost its autonomy, and the end of the 17th century brought the decisive blow. In the War of the Holy League (1683-1699), the Habsburgs invaded Hungary and Transylvania. They defeated the Ottomans, establishing their hold on the region. The 1699 Treaty of Karlowitz officiated Habsburg control over Transylvania, pushing the Ottomans out of Eastern Europe.

The Protestant elite resisted and launched a rebellion against the Habsburg rule in 1703. The nobles won some significant victories, but the Habsburgs crushed the rebellion in 1711. The days of relative independence were over. The Habsburgs enacted direct rule over Transylvania—something the Hungarians were not used to.

The Decline of the Polish-Lithuanian Commonwealth:

In the 17th century, the Polish-Lithuanian Commonwealth dominated Eastern European affairs.[407] However, during this period, it would enter a phase of decline that would preempt its downfall. It was a time of foreign kings and warfare that would permanently weaken the state.

---

[407] Jankowski, *Eastern Europe!*, 2015, pg. 230-234.

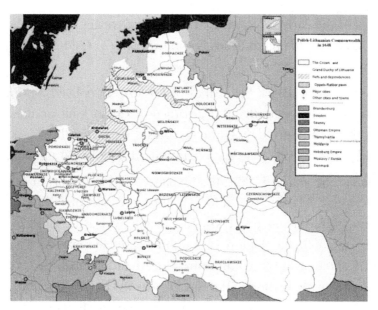

The borders of the Polish-Lithuanian Commonwealth in 1648, the year that the Khmelnytsky Uprising began. (Credit: Mathiasrex/Halibutt, 2009)

The beginning of the end came with the Khmelnytsky Uprising of 1648-1657. When King Sigismund II died in 1572, it brought the Polish-Lithuanian Commonwealth into a period of foreign rule. The Polish nobility asked Sigismund II's brother-in-law, Stephen Báthory (r. 1576-1586), to take the reins; as a result, Báthory became the ruler of the commonwealth. He was the king of Poland and the grand duke of Lithuania, in addition to being the prince of Transylvania.[408] That's a lot of titles!

Stephen Báthory ruled the three territories efficiently for the next ten years until he died in 1586. The nobles sought out another foreign king from the House of Vasa, the royal family of Sweden. While the Vasa dynasty introduced a new line of kings that would rule for almost one hundred years, it was quite possibly the worst thing that could have happened to the commonwealth. Under Vasa rule, the commonwealth was pulled into wars between Sweden and

[408] Jankowski, *Eastern Europe!*, 2015, pg. 230-234; "Stephen Báthory." Encyclopedia Britannica. https://www.britannica.com/biography/Stephen-Bathory

Russia in the early 17th century. However, a greater threat lay to the east that would break the commonwealth's hold on Eastern Europe.

North of the Black Sea, tribes of Eastern Slavs lived a nomadic life on the steppe under the jurisdiction of no king or master.[409] Occupying modern-day Ukraine, these warriors, the Cossacks, would become both an asset and a bother for Poland-Lithuania.

Since the early 1300s, the expanse of land that makes up modern-day Ukraine was under Lithuanian control.[410] The Grand Duchy of Lithuania put Ukraine on a long leash, letting it rule itself. In 1569, the Union of Lublin passed control of Ukraine from Lithuania to the commonwealth, which changed the policies in dealing with Ukraine. Instead of leaving the lands alone, the commonwealth occupied them. To encourage settlement, the state granted the nobility tracts of land in Ukraine. The nobles used these new estates to subdue the local population, forcing them into labor and converting them to Christianity.

Despite the new expansionist policy, the commonwealth still kept a light hold on Ukraine. It was the perfect spot for those who existed on the fringes of society who felt threatened by the status quo. Local Ukrainians developed their own communities and welcomed all nationalities and ethnic groups.

These new settlements protected their way of life through military training and preparedness. They learned how to raid cities, fight on horseback, and use weapons. Settlements planned their own defenses and kept a regular supply of weapons, food, and supplies in order to withstand attacks. These new warriors on horseback were called Cossacks, and they were a formidable enemy to the nations that surrounded them. They also made great allies, and they hired themselves out to anyone who could pay.

---

[409] Liulevicius, "Clashing Golden Ages, 1389-1772." Lecture 3. *The Great Courses: A History of Eastern Europe*, 2015.

[410] Jankowski, *Eastern Europe!*, 2015, pg. 237-238.

The kings of the Polish-Lithuanian Commonwealth hired the Cossacks as auxiliaries in times of war.[411] However, they often found themselves on the wrong side of the Cossacks. The commonwealth was too persistent in trying to get the Cossacks to accept Christianity and abandon their nomadic lifestyle. The commonwealth should have known not to go after the people they relied on for their defenses.

The Cossacks turned on their former employers, using the traits the Polish-Lithuanian Commonwealth valued against them. In 1648, communications between the rulers of the commonwealth and the Cossacks soured, and the Cossack chief, Bogdan Khmelnytsky, declared war on the Polish-Lithuanian Commonwealth. The nomads rode in from the east from a wide expanse of land the commonwealth called the "Wild Fields." They had the organization and discipline of a well-trained army.

After winning several victories against the Polish-Lithuanian Commonwealth, Bogdan Khmelnytsky made a triumphant march into Kiev (Kyiv). Entrance of Bohdan Khmelnytsky to Kyiv, Mykola Ivasyuk. (Credit: Palukopa, 2009)

---

[411] Jankowski, *Eastern Europe!*, 2015, pg. 233, 237-238; Liulevicius, "Clashing Golden Ages, 1389-1772." Lecture 3. *The Great Courses: A History of Eastern Europe*, 2015; "Ukraine: The Cossacks." Encyclopedia Britannica. https://www.britannica.com/place/Ukraine/The-Cossacks

At first, Khmelnytsky's rebellion was successful, but it quickly fizzled out. A year into the conflict, the Cossacks pushed the Polish-Lithuanian forces out of Ukraine. This new freedom would only last for two years. The commonwealth army came back and crushed the Cossacks.

The Cossacks refused to suffer the indignity of foreign rule by the country that defeated them, and they continued to resist for the next three years. The Cossacks approached Russia in 1654, signing an alliance that would have long-term ramifications. To this day, there is debate on the exact nature of the agreement between the Cossacks and the Russians. While the Russians claim that Ukraine passed its sovereignty to the Russian crown, the Ukrainians maintain that they signed the alliance with the agreement that Ukraine would remain autonomous.

The commonwealth was furious, and it soon went to war with Russia. The war between Russia and the Polish-Lithuanian Commonwealth lasted for one year, with no clear victor. In 1655, Sweden invaded the commonwealth over a separate issue—a succession dispute. Russia and the Polish-Lithuanian Commonwealth signed a peace treaty, ending their conflict and turning their attention to Sweden.

The Cossacks couldn't do anything about Russia's about-face because a period of civil strife damaged their leadership. Until the end of the 1660s, a series of rival commanders challenged each other for control over the Cossacks. This destroyed any campaign it could have made to secure its position.

In 1667, the Polish-Lithuanian Commonwealth and Russia officially divided Ukraine between them. The Cossacks still refused to admit defeat, and they approached the Ottomans to help attack their enemies. Hoping it would give them another route into Eastern Europe, the Ottomans agreed, reigniting the conflict in 1672. An exhausted Polish-Lithuanian Commonwealth finally made peace with the Ottomans four years later in 1676[412]

This wasn't the end of the story. With the Russians, Ukraine got more than it bargained for. With Russia's participation in the conflict, it saw an opportunity to extend its borders. Throughout the rest of the 17th century and into the 18th century, Russia spread into present-day Ukraine, taking control of most of the territory where the Cossacks lived.[413] The Russians saw the benefit of the Cossacks just as much as their lands, and the Russians incorporated the nomads into the Russian police force to serve the Russian tsar.

As for the Polish-Lithuanian Commonwealth, the state barely survived.[414] The commonwealth came out of the Cossack conflict with no money, no resources, and a fractured army. The last Vasa king, John II Casimir Vasa (r. 1648–1668), botched the war effort, abdicating in humiliation in 1668.[415] The Polish nobles had enough of foreign rule and chose to elect their next monarch from their own ranks.[416] In 1674, the nobles elected one of its most well-known members, John III Sobieski, to the throne.[417] He was exactly what the commonwealth needed. John had proven himself on the battlefield during the Cossack conflict, and his reign was a

---

[412] Jankowski, Eastern Europe!, 2015, pg. 233, 237-238; Liulevicius, "Clashing Golden Ages, 1389-1772." Lecture 3. The Great Courses: A History of Eastern Europe, 2015; "Ukraine: The Cossacks." Encyclopedia Britannica. https://www.britannica.com/place/Ukraine/The-Cossacks; Alex Gendler. "A Day in the Life of a Cossack Soldier." TED-Ed. August 2019.

[413] Jankowski, Eastern Europe!, 2015, pg. 238, 241; Liulevicius, "Clashing Golden Ages, 1389-1772." Lecture 3. The Great Courses: A History of Eastern Europe, 2015.

[414] Jankowski, Eastern Europe!, 2015, pg. 233.

[415] "John II Casimir Vasa." Encyclopedia Britannica. https://www.britannica.com/biography/John-II-Casimir-Vasa

[416] Jankowski, Eastern Europe!, 2015, pg. 233.

[417] Jankowski, Eastern Europe!, 2015, pg. 233; "John III Sobieski." Encyclopedia Britannica.

temporary reprieve from the constant wars it had been pulled into for most of the 17th century.

The commonwealth regained some of its glory and reputation under John's leadership. He would play a crucial role in ending Ottoman supremacy in Eastern Europe. Until his death in 1696, the Polish-Lithuanian Commonwealth enjoyed its last years as one of Eastern Europe's dynamic powers.

The Ottomans, the Battle of Vienna, and the Great Turkish War

This period would mark the beginning of the end for the Ottoman Empire. It would lose Montenegro, deal with chaos in its territories in both Wallachia and Moldavia, and lose the decisive Battle of Vienna.[418] By the end of the 17th century, Ottoman supremacy in Eastern Europe was threatened.

The Ottomans in the Romanian Lands

After the debacle of Michael the Brave, in which the ruler of Wallachia brought both Transylvania and Moldavia under his control, the Ottomans knew they had to take a more hands-on approach in the Romanian lands. Although Michael the Brave would unite Romania, it wouldn't remain so for long.

The Ottomans quickly moved in after Michael's assassination, taking advantage of the resulting power vacuum. While the Ottomans retained their hold on Moldavia and Wallachia, they did allow them some opportunities for self-rule. However, when the Ottomans found out that the Moldavian and Wallachian princes supported a 1711 Russian invasion of their lands, the Turks quickly changed their tune.

---

[418] Jankowski, *Eastern Europe!*, 2015, pg. 190-191, 223-224, 241-244.

The Moldavian prince escaped into exile rather than face the Ottomans' wrath. The Wallachian prince was not so lucky; the Ottomans sentenced him to death. With the thrones of Moldavia and Wallachia empty, the Ottomans installed their own line of puppet rulers, the Phanariots.[419]

A portrait of a 19ʰ-century Greek Phanariot family. Theodoros Vryzakis, 19ʰ century. (Public Domain)

The Phanariots were Greek merchants from Constantinople who only cared about trade. Most importantly, they didn't play politics, which is what the Ottomans needed in their Romanian lands. The Phanariots would rule Moldavia and Wallachia until 1821, encouraging trade relationships between Eastern Europe and the Ottoman Empire.

Ottoman Failures in Eastern Europe: The Loss of Montenegro and the European Challenge

Like other Ottoman territories in Eastern Europe, Montenegro enjoyed the Ottoman methods of indirect control.[420] The former Serbian territory of Zeta had been independent since the 14ᵗʰ

[419] Jankowski, *Eastern Europe!*, 2015, pg. 223-224; "Phanariote." *Encyclopedia Britannica.* https://www.britannica.com/topic/Phanariote

[420] Jankowski, *Eastern Europe!*, 2015, pg. 177, 225.

century; since then, it had turned into a religious state ruled by archbishops. By the 18ᵗʰ century, Montenegro was still under the control of its archbishops.

That doesn't mean the Ottomans didn't try to reassert their authority. By the early 18ᵗʰ century, the Ottomans took the Montenegrin capital of Cetinje three separate times: twice in the 17ᵗʰ century (in 1623 and 1687) and once in the 18ᵗʰ century (in 1712). Each time, the Ottomans failed to secure any more of the territory than the city borders.

The 18ᵗʰ century also brought a change in fortune for Montenegro. The Montenegrins constantly resisted Ottoman rule, but their independence movement really took off after they allied with Russia.[421] The Russians provided soldiers, weapons, and money to support Montenegrin independence from Ottoman rule, which the Ottomans would finally recognize in 1799. Independence was relatively easy to achieve since the archbishop kings had lost their power over Montenegro throughout the 18ᵗʰ century. The territory descended into civil war, with the tribal families all competing for control of the territory.

The Battle of Vienna (1683)

This change of fortune was devastating for the Ottomans. For hundreds of years, the Ottoman Janissaries terrified the powers of Europe.[422] These elite armed forces were trained in the top military technology and strategy available, outperforming any European army on the battlefield. However, in the 17ᵗʰ century, that started to change.[423]

[421] Jankowski, *Eastern Europe!*, 2015, pg. 177, 225; "History of Montenegro." *Encyclopedia Britannica.* https://www.britannica.com/place/Montenegro/History

[422] Jankowski, *Eastern Europe!*, 2015, pg.187; Liulevicius, "Clashing Golden Ages, 1389-1772." Lecture 3. *The Great Courses: A History of Eastern Europe*, 2015; "Janissary." *Encyclopedia Britannica.* https://www.britannica.com/topic/Janissary

[423] Jankowski, *Eastern Europe!*, 2015, pg. 241.

A drawing of a mid-17th-century Ottoman Janissary. (Public Domain)

European countries (both in Eastern and Western Europe) were starting to modernize, building their own efficient armies. While Europe was moving forward, the Ottomans remained stagnant.[424] Soon, the powers of Europe were worthy competitors. The Ottomans started losing battles, and their military supremacy was threatened by Christian nations.

---

[424] Ibid., pg. 241-242.

This was something that Merzifonlu Kara Mustafa Paşa could not tolerate.[425] The grand vizier to Sultan Mehmed IV (r. 1648–1687), Kara Mustafa Paşa, wanted to demonstrate Ottoman supremacy in Eastern Europe. The only way he felt he could do that was by finally taking the city of Vienna. Of course, the sultan was not on board with this plan. Mehmed was a bumbling, ineffectual ruler, more interested in life's pleasures than actually ruling an empire. Under the influence of ambitious advisors, the sultan was powerless to stop Kara Mustafa Paşa's plan to siege the city. In 1683, the Ottomans attacked Vienna again, trying to recreate a victorious version of their 1529 attempt.[426]

In the 17th century, Vienna was the center of Austria and the base of operations for the Habsburgs; it had been the capital of Habsburg power since the 15th century.[427] An Ottoman attack so far inland set the other Christian nations of Eastern Europe on alert. Putting aside their own rivalries, they united against their common enemy.

Luckily, the Habsburgs had powerful friends. One of them was King John III Sobieski of the Polish-Lithuanian Commonwealth.[428] Although John was a king, he was a warrior through and through. Interestingly enough, he wasn't enthusiastic about a Habsburg alliance.[429] During his reign, John originally sought peace with the Ottomans, but their continued attacks on Christian nations changed his mind. In April 1683, he signed a peace accord with the Habsburgs. John and Holy Roman Emperor Leopold I

---

[425] Jankowski, *Eastern Europe!*, 2015, pg. 242-243; "Mehmed IV." *Encyclopedia Britannica.* https://www.britannica.com/biography/Mehmed-IV

[426] Jankowski, *Eastern Europe!*, 2015, pg. 242-243; Liulevicius, "Clashing Golden Ages, 1389-1772." Lecture 3. *The Great Courses: A History of Eastern Europe*, 2015.

[427] Jankowski, *Eastern Europe!*, 2015, pg. 255; Liulevicius, "Clashing Golden Ages, 1389-1772." Lecture 3. *The Great Courses: A History of Eastern Europe*, 2015.

[428] Jankowski, *Eastern Europe!*, 2015, pg. 233.

[429] "John III Sobieski." *Encyclopedia Britannica.*

(himself a Habsburg) agreed to defend each other from any attack. It wouldn't take long for the Ottomans to come knocking.

In 1683, the Ottoman army reached the city of Vienna, completely surrounding the city. Frans Geffels, The Relief of Vienna, ca. 1683–1694. (Public Domain)

In July 1683, the Ottomans and their 150,000 soldiers arrived at the gates of Vienna.[430] Holy Roman Emperor Leopold I left the city as soon as he heard the Ottomans were coming. When John III Sobieski and his allies arrived in September, the Ottomans had already started digging under the walls of Vienna, bringing them closer to success than they had been before. John led the offensive himself, commanding an army of Polish and German forces. [431] With joint forces of the Holy Roman Empire and the Polish-

---

[430] Jankowski, *Eastern Europe!*, 2015, pg. 242-243; Jenkins, *Short History of Europe*, 2019, pg. 145; "Siege of Vienna, 1683." *Encyclopedia Britannica.* https://www.britannica.com/event/Siege-of-Vienna-1683

[431] Liulevicius, "Clashing Golden Ages, 1389-1772." Lecture 3. *The Great Courses: A History of Eastern Europe*, 2015; "Siege of Vienna, 1683." *Encyclopedia Britannica;* "John III Sobieski." *Encyclopedia Britannica.*

Lithuanian Commonwealth that were eighty thousand strong, John broke the Ottoman siege at the ensuing Battle of Vienna.[432]

John III Sobieski at the Battle of Vienna. Jerzy Siemiginowski-Eleuter, 1686. (Public Domain)

The Ottomans were so surprised (and terrified) that they fled the city. Grand Vizier Kara Mustafa Paşa famously ordered such a quick retreat that he left all of his personal belongings behind. With an expert cavalry contingent, Sobieski and his army pushed

---

[432] Jankowski, Eastern Europe!, 2015, pg. 233, 242-243; Jenkins, *Short History of Europe*, 2019, pg. 145; "Siege of Vienna, 1683." *Encyclopedia Britannica*; "John III Sobieski." *Encyclopedia Britannica*.

the Ottomans out of Austria.[433] They would never travel so far west again.

The Fate of Nations: The Ottoman Empire, the Polish-Lithuanian Commonwealth, and the Habsburgs after the Battle of Vienna

The Battle of Vienna had different effects on the Ottoman Empire, the Polish-Lithuanian Commonwealth, and the Habsburgs. While the Ottomans and the Poles foundered, the Habsburgs entered the 18th century as one of the dominant landholders in Europe.

The Ottomans were absolutely the loser of this conflict. Not only did their assault on Vienna fail, but the failed campaign cost the Ottomans their reputation.[434] They were no longer the feared army on the battlefield; John III Sobieski's leadership proved that European armies could decisively win battles against the terrifying Ottoman forces.

Both Kara Mustafa Paşa and Mehmed IV would suffer personally. For his failure to take the city, Mehmed IV had Kara Mustafa Paşa executed in December 1683.[435] Mehmed's downfall wasn't far behind. After the Christian nations of Europe declared war on the Ottoman Empire, Mehmed IV lost his crown in 1687.[436]

---

[433] Liulevicius, "Clashing Golden Ages, 1389-1772." Lecture 3. *The Great Courses: A History of Eastern Europe*, 2015; "John III Sobieski." *Encyclopedia Britannica*.

[434] Jankowski, *Eastern Europe!*, 2015, pg. 242-243.

[435] Ibid., pg. 243-244.

[436] "Mehmed IV." *Encyclopedia Britannica*.

Defeating the Ottomans was the moment of which Christian kings had been dreaming[437] The foiled siege of Vienna and subsequent Ottoman failures on the battlefield inspired revitalized notions of a truly Christian Europe without Ottoman interference[438] The Christian nations of Eastern Europe—the Polish-Lithuanian Commonwealth, Austria, and Russia—united as the Holy League, and it had one goal in mind: drive the Ottomans out of Eastern Europe for good.[439]

For the rest of the 17th century, the Great Turkish War (1684–1699) pitted the Holy League against the Ottoman Empire.[440] Unfortunately, it would destroy what was left of the Polish-

---

[437] Jankowski, *Eastern Europe!*, 2015, pg. 242-243.

[438] Ibid., pg. 233, 242-243.

[439] "Treaty of Carlowitz." *Encyclopedia Britannica.* https://www.britannica.com/event/Treaty-of-Carlowitz

[440] Jankowski, *Eastern Europe!*, 2015, pg. 242-243; "Treaty of Carlowitz." *Encyclopedia Britannica.*

Lithuanian Commonwealth[441] The war was largely a failure for King John III Sobieski—a disappointment considering his early military successes against the Ottomans[442] He launched several unsuccessful campaigns into Ottoman-held Moldavia (1684-1691), failing to liberate the territory. The Polish-Lithuanian Commonwealth was completely stripped of its resources, but 't still got involved in another conflict. As a Russian ally, the commonwealth was pulled into the Great Northern War (1700-1721) between Russia and Sweden, which would cement Russian supremacy over the Baltic Sea region[443]

After decades of warfare, the commonwealth was a fractured state that was barely hanging on[444] Its alliance with Russia quickly became one-sided, with Russia treating the commonwealth like one of its territories. It wasn't strong enough to repel Russian influence, so it had to accept its new reality[445] Russian interference would characterize the last century of the Polish-Lithuanian Commonwealth, which would lead to its downfall completely by the end of the 18th century[446]

If there was a "winner" of the Great Turkish War, it was the Habsburgs. As the Ottomans tried to piece together their hold over their lands, the Holy League challenged the Ottoman presence in Eastern Europe[447] After fifteen years of fighting, the Holy League won the war when Habsburg forces defeated the Ottomans at the

---

[441] Jankowski, *Eastern Europe!*, 2015, pg. 233.

[442] "John III Sobieski." *Encyclopedia Britannica.*

[443] Jankowski, *Eastern Europe!*, 2015, pg. 234-235.

[444] Ibid., pg. 235.

[445] "Poland: Augustus II." *Encyclopedia Britannica.*
https://www.britannica.com/place/Poland/Augustus-II

[446] Jankowski, *Eastern Europe!*, 2015, pg. 235-236; Liulevicius, "The Great Crime of Empires: Poland Divided." Lecture 4. *The Great Courses: A History of Eastern Europe,* 2015.

[447] Liulevicius, "Clashing Golden Ages, 1389-1772." Lecture 3. *The Great Courses: A History of Eastern Europe,* 2015.

Battle of Zenta in modern-day Serbia[448] On the battlefield, the Ottoman charge descended into chaos. As the army realized they were losing, the Janissaries assassinated their commander. Ottoman Sultan Mustafa II knew his chances of winning the war were over, and he agreed to surrender[449]

The Habsburgs didn't forget the assault on their home in Vienna[450] They proposed humiliating terms; in the Treaty of Karlowitz (1699), the sultan made many concessions, losing more territory than the Ottomans had in centuries. The Ottomans gave up their lands in Transylvania and Hungary.[451] They also lost control of Serbia, but this would only be temporary.

Of course, the Austrians benefited the most from the Ottoman surrender. They received Hungary and Transylvania, bringing the Habsburgs to the forefront of European politics. Perhaps the most significant effect of the Great Turkish War was that the Holy League managed to push the Ottomans behind the Danube River, ending Ottoman dominance in Eastern Europe. They would enter the 18th century on a sour note, as their defeat against the Holy League began its decline[452]

While the 18th century was the beginning of the end for the Ottomans, it cemented the rise of Habsburg power. This was the culmination of a slow process over hundreds of years[453] Even though the family could boast a Holy Roman emperor (the first of many)— Rudolf Habsburg became Holy Roman Emperor Rudolf I in 1278—the family wouldn't achieve supremacy in Europe for

[448] "Battle of Zenta." *Encyclopedia Britannica.* https://www.britannica.com/event/Battle-of-Zenta

[449] "Treaty of Carlowitz." *Encyclopedia Britannica.*

[450] Liulevicius, "Clashing Golden Ages, 1389-1772." Lecture 3. *The Great Courses: A History of Eastern Europe,* 2015.

[451] Jankowski, *Eastern Europe!,* 2015, pg. 242-243; Liulevicius, "Clashing Golden Ages, 1389-1772." Lecture 3. *The Great Courses: A History of Eastern Europe,* 2015.

[452] Jankowski, *Eastern Europe!,* 2015, pg. 243-244.

[453] Ibid., pg. 251.

another four hundred years. In that time, the Habsburgs built an impressive empire by marrying their children into wealthy noble and royal families and accumulating crucial lands through victories on the battlefield[454]

By the 16th century, the Habsburgs had so much land in their possession that they had to split it up[455] Holy Roman Emperor Charles V (r. 1519–1556) commanded the lands of the Holy Roman Empire in addition to lands in modern-day Hungary, Bohemia, Austria, Spain, Italy, the Netherlands, Luxembourg, and France. When Charles stepped down, he divided the Habsburg lands into two distinct powers. He left Bohemia, Austria, Hungary, and the Holy Roman Empire to his brother, Ferdinand I, and the rest of his lands to his son, Philip II. These two empires became known as the Spanish Habsburgs and the Austrian Habsburgs. For our purposes, we will only be looking at the Austrian Habsburgs and their role in Eastern European history.

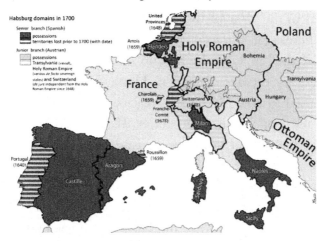

A map showing the Habsburg lands in the year 1700. The lands of the Austrian line are in yellow, and the lands of the Spanish line are in red. (Credit: Katepanomegas/Alphathon, 2013)

---

[454] Jankowski, *Eastern Europe!*, 2015, pg. 253; Jenkins, *Short History of Europe*, 2019, pg. 112.

[455] Jankowski, *Eastern Europe!*, 2015, pg. 253-254; Jenkins, *Short History of Europe*, 2019, pg. 126.

Beginning in the 17th century, Austria grew in power and influence, making the Habsburgs a family to watch[456] The Spanish Habsburg dynasty died out in 1700, which increased Austrian Habsburg power over Europe. This coincided with the Austrian victory as part of the Holy League in the Great Turkish War. The Habsburgs seemed unstoppable.

Using their far-flung lands, the Habsburgs encouraged German settlement throughout their empire. In 1740, when the most memorable Habsburg queen, Empress Maria Theresa, ascended to the throne, the Habsburg holdings included Austria, Bohemia, Croatia, Hungary, and Transylvania, and other smaller territories.[457] During Maria Theresa's reign, the Germans spread out among the Habsburg lands. Germans arrived in Transylvania and the Banat (the corner of modern-day Hungary, Romania, and Serbia), Croatia, and Bukovina (the border of Ukraine and Romania).

However, this was also the same year that all of Europe became embroiled in the War of the Austrian Succession—a conflict with Maria Theresa at the center.[458] When Holy Roman Emperor Charles VI died in 1740, he had no direct male heirs, leaving his empire to his capable daughter, Maria Theresa. When Maria Theresa tried to take her father's place as queen of the Habsburg Empire, the opportunistic Frederick II of Prussia attempted to knock down Austrian influence in Europe by challenging Maria Theresa's inheritance. He invaded Silesia, one of the Habsburgs' most valuable territories. It set off a chain of events in which both Austria's and Prussia's allies joined the war. The conflict, which had major theaters in Europe and North America, ended in 1748;

[456] Jankowski, *Eastern Europe!*, 2015, pg. 255-256.

[457] Liulevicius, "Clashing Golden Ages, 1389-1772." Lecture 3. *The Great Courses: A History of Eastern Europe*, 2015.

[458] Jankowski, *Eastern Europe!*, 2015, pg. 255-256; Jenkins, *Short History of Europe*, 2019, pg. 158-160; "War of the Austrian Succession." *Encyclopedia Britannica*. https://www.britannica.com/event/War-of-the-Austrian-Succession

although Frederick kept Silesia, Maria Theresa inherited the bulk of her father's estate.

The Rise of Prussia

The War of the Austrian Succession had one long-lasting effect: it made Prussia an influential world power. Prussia came out of the former German Crusader states, which had been controlled by the Teutonic Knights and the Livonian Order. However, over several centuries, the German Crusaders lost their influence.[459] Since the mid-15th century, Prussia had been a vassal state of the Polish-Lithuanian Commonwealth, a move orchestrated by merchants of Prussian lands to challenge the rule of the Teutonic Knights.[460]

The Hohenzollerns

By the beginning of the 17th century, a new royal dynasty had come to power in Prussia: the Hohenzollerns.[461] The family achieved their position the way most heads of state did during this period: through marriage.[462] In 1594, the elector of Brandenburg, one of the states of the Holy Roman Empire, married the daughter of the duke of Royal Prussia, Anna Marie of Brunswick-Lüneburg. (As a side note, electors were a part of the electoral college that elected the Holy Roman emperor.) Anna's father died in 1618, making her husband both the elector of Brandenburg and the duke of Prussia.

Thanks to this auspicious marriage, the Hohenzollerns would rule Prussia and Brandenburg together until 1918.[463] While the family still carries royal titles to this day, they are largely nominal

---

[459] Liulevicius, "Clashing Golden Ages, 1389-1772." Lecture 3. *The Great Courses: A History of Eastern Europe*, 2015.

[460] Jankowski, *Eastern Europe!*, 2015, pg. 206; Liulevicius, "Clashing Golden Ages, 1389-1772." Lecture 3. *The Great Courses: A History of Eastern Europe*, 2015.

[461] Jenkins, *Short History of Europe*, 2019, pg. 137; "Prussia." *Encyclopedia Britannica.* https://www.britannica.com/place/Prussia

[462] Jankowski, *Eastern Europe!*, 2015, pg. 256-257.

[463] Jankowski, *Eastern Europe!*, 2015, pg. 256-257; "Prussia." *Encyclopedia Britannica.*

without any political power.[464] However, in the 17th century, these Prussian princes became very powerful. They used the Khmelnytsky Uprising of 1648-1657 to campaign for self-rule. In exchange for military support, the Polish-Lithuanian Commonwealth agreed to grant Prussia its independence in 1657.[465]

As much as the Prussians fought against their former Crusader overlords, the Prussians inherited the Crusader spirit. While other kings built up their military for defensive purposes, the military was a crucial part of the Prussian state. Prussian kings spent four-fifths of their budget on training soldiers, acquiring weapons, and studying military strategy. The idea of service to the state prevailed throughout Prussian society.

Frederick the Great

Perhaps the most famous Hohenzollern is Frederick II (r. 1740-1786), also known as Frederick the Great[466] He was the king of Prussia that we mentioned in the previous section, the one that was all too eager to snatch Silesia from Empress Maria Theresa. Thanks to his father, Frederick William I, Frederick II took command over one of the best-trained armies in Europe.

---

[464] "Prussia.eu - The Official Site of the House of Hohenzollern."
https://www.preussen.de/en/

[465] Jankowski, *Eastern Europe!*, 2015, pg. 232-233; Liulevicius, "Clashing Golden Ages, 1389-1772." Lecture 3. *The Great Courses: A History of Eastern Europe*, 2015.

[466] Jankowski, *Eastern Europe!*, 2015, pg. 257; "Prussia." *Encyclopedia Britannica*.

Adolph von Menzel, Frederick the Great Playing the Flute at Sanssouci, ca. 1850. Not only was Frederick the Great one of the best military minds of his age, but he was also devoted to arts, music, and education. In this painting, he is playing the flute for an audience at his palace, Sanssouci.

Under his leadership, Prussia grew larger and more powerful, commanding the battlefield in the War of the Austrian Succession. Unfortunately, they didn't have the same luck during the Seven Years' War (1756-1763). Prussia became a dominant European power by the end of the 18th century with the Partition of Poland. The pieces of Poland that Prussia gained united all the Prussian lands together, making them a regional power on the southeastern edge of the Baltic Sea.

Russia Builds an Empire

At the beginning of the 17th century, Russia was barely a blip on the radar of Eastern Europe.[467] It couldn't compete with powerhouses like the Ottoman Empire or the Polish-Lithuanian Commonwealth. After the reign of Ivan the Terrible, Russia was weakened by civil strife. Things got worse in 1591 when Ivan's

---

[467] Jankowski, *Eastern Europe!*, 2015, pg. 244.

youngest son, Dmitri Ivanovich—the next heir to the throne after his brother—died; he was presumably murdered (or disposed of) by the regent Boris Godunov, clearing the way for Boris to claim the throne.[468] The other European powers could smell blood in the water, and they put forward their own "Dmitris" as challengers to the throne. This phase of the "False Dmitris" would result in both the Polish-Lithuanian Commonwealth and Sweden invading Russia to place their candidates on the throne.

In 1591, the political instability in Russia got worse after the death (most likely murder) of Ivan the Terrible's heir, Tsarevich Dmitry. Death of Tsarevich Dmitry, ca. 1890. (Public Domain)

[468] Jankowski, *Eastern Europe!*, 2015, pg. 246; "Dmitry Ivanovich." *Encyclopedia Britannica.* https://www.britannica.com/biography/Dmitry-Ivanovich

In 1610, forces from the Polish-Lithuanian Commonwealth occupied Moscow, where they would remain for two years. The Russian nobility, led by Mikhail Romanov, would force them out in 1612. Mikhail would become the next tsar of Russia the following year, founding the Romanov dynasty that would reign for the next three hundred years. The first Romanovs were relatively weak rulers who tried to rebuild a country that was in shambles.

It was during this period that Russia would unlock the potential of Siberia.[469] Beginning with Ivan the Terrible, Russian tsars would support expeditions to claim that untamed land. For hundreds of years, the Russians moved deeper and deeper into Siberia. This had two benefits. First, it expanded Russian landholdings exponentially. Second, it had military value, providing land for retreating armies to fall back and further drawing the enemy into inhospitable conditions.

Peter the Great

Under Peter the Great (r. 1682–1725), Russia would make up for its years of stagnation.[470] He was the first monarch to modernize Russia. Peter the Great improved Russia's military standing by hiring Western professionals to build the country's first navy, bring in new technology, and train soldiers in the latest military strategies.[471] The new Russian army was now so well-trained that when Sweden tried to invade Russia in 1708, the Russian forces under Peter the Great successfully pushed them back. His success in the Great Northern War made Russia a major player on the world stage.[472] Peter had succeeded where Ivan the Terrible had not; he made inroads in the Baltic, claiming lands that lie in

---

[469] Jankowski, *Eastern Europe!*, 2015, pg. 247-248.

[470] Jankowski, *Eastern Europe!*, 2015, pg. 247-248; Jenkins, *Short History of Europe*, 2019, pg. 159-160; Liulevicius, "Clashing Golden Ages, 1389-1772." Lecture 3. *The Great Courses: A History of Eastern Europe*, 2015.

[471] Jenkins, *Short History of Europe*, 2019, pg. 156.

[472] "Second Northern War." *Encyclopedia Britannica*. https://www.britannica.com/event/Second-Northern-War

modern-day Latvia and Estonia.[473] In 1721, Peter proclaimed his expanded territories to be the "Russian Empire."

One of the best-known images of Peter the Great is attributed to Jean-Marc Nattier; it was completed in the early 18ʰ century. (Public Domain)

Success on the battlefield wasn't enough. Russia needed to give the appearance of a modernized state, and it couldn't do that when it was still rooted in traditional practices.[474] He introduced Western

[473] Liulevicius, "Clashing Golden Ages, 1389-1772." Lecture 3. *The Great Courses: A History of Eastern Europe*, 2015

[474] Jankowski, *Eastern Europe!*, 2015, pg. 247-248; Jenkins, *Short History of Europe*, 2019, pg. 155-156.

culture to Russian society, enforcing it in his new capital of St. Petersburg.

Between 1703 and 1712, architects and professionals from Russia and abroad labored on Peter's new city. The tsar conscripted peasant labor to do the heavy lifting, proclaiming his namesake city the capital of Russia, which it would remain until 1918.

The Five Empresses

After Peter the Great died in 1725, Russia saw a new phase of rulership under the empresses.[475] From 1725 to 1796, five women ruled Russia with varying degrees of success. Peter's widow Catherine I (r. 1725–1727) would reign for two years before her death in 1727.[476] She was unanimously put forward by several prominent court officials and high-ranking members of the army. Not bad for a former peasant!

The second wife of Peter the Great became the first of five women who would rule Russia after his death in 1725. She ruled as Catherine I. Jean-Marc Nattier, Portrait of Catherine I of Russia, 1717. (Public Domain)

---

[475] Jankowski, *Eastern Europe!*, 2015, pg. 249.

[476] Jankowski, *Eastern Europe!*, 2015, pg. 249; "Catherine I." *Encyclopedia Britannica.* https://www.britannica.com/biography/Catherine-I

Before she died, Catherine made her husband's grandson (through his daughter born to his first wife) her heir, who ruled as Peter II (r. 1727-1730). Peter also had a short reign, and he was succeeded by Peter the Great's niece, Anna Ivanovna (r. 1730-1740).[477] When the Supreme Privy Council offered her the throne, they made her sign off on their control over the government, effectively making her a figurehead. Anna soon learned that she had support for her rule among the army and the landowners. She destroyed the contract and overthrew the council, establishing herself as an absolute monarch.

Anna was not as well-liked as her later successors would be. She didn't have much talent for ruling and used her German advisors to rule the country. Russia fought two major conflicts during her reign, the War of the Polish Succession (1733-1735) and the Russo-Turkish War (1736-1739). Both wars were successful for Russia. The War of the Polish Succession put a Russian-supported monarch on the thrones of the commonwealth, giving Russia massive influence there. The Russo-Turkish War gave Russia some territory but not access to the water trade routes it wanted. Anna further alienated the population by her lavish spending at court, which she funded through taxing the peasantry.

In 1740, Anna Ivanovna named Ivan VI (r. 1740-1741), the infant son of her niece, Anna Leopoldovna, as her heir. Ivan became emperor as a baby, with a named regent.[478] However, Anna Leopoldovna overthrew her son's regent and became the power behind the throne herself. She would never reign as empress, though.

Peter the Great had another daughter through his marriage with Catherine I: Elizabeth. Elizabeth became a powerful woman at court, and she formed an opposition to Anna Leopoldovna's

[477] Jankowski, *Eastern Europe!*, 2015, pg. 249; "Anna, empress of Russia," *Encyclopedia Britannica*. https://www.britannica.com/biography/Anna-empress-of-Russia

[478] "Elizabeth, empress of Russia." *Encyclopedia Britannica*. https://www.britannica.com/biography/Elizabeth-empress-of-Russia

regency. Elizabeth especially took issue with Anna's reliance on German advisors. In 1741, Elizabeth (r. 1741–1762) orchestrated a coup. After she arrested Anna Leopoldovna, Ivan VI, and their court, she had herself proclaimed the new empress.

Unfortunately, Elizabeth wasn't the ideal empress either. Like her niece, she preferred to leave the ruling in the hands of her council. She put the time she wasn't ruling to good use by funding Russian art and architecture and supporting a return to her father's policies. Elizabeth reigned longer than any of her empress predecessors; she presided over a twenty-one-year reign, during which Russia became a major force in European politics.

After Elizabeth was another formidable empress, who is slightly better known: Catherine the Great.[479] Elizabeth's heir was her nephew Peter, who was crowned Peter III in 1762. He wouldn't sit on the throne for long. Peter's wife, Catherine, led a coup against him six months after he took the throne. With the support of the military, she had Peter arrested and forced him to abdicate. She was proclaimed the next empress, Catherine II (r. 1762–1796). To avoid any challenge to her claim, Peter was arrested and quietly disposed of in the Russian countryside. According to some sources, she ordered his death herself.

[479] Jankowski, Eastern Europe!, 2015, pg. 249-250; Jenkins, *Short History of Europe*, 2019, pg. 163; "Catherine the Great." *Encyclopedia Britannica*. https://www.britannica.com/biography/Catherine-the-Great

One of the most famous Russian monarchs is Catherine the Great, the last of the five empresses. She greatly expanded Russia's territory during her reign, and she was a patron for artists and Enlightenment thinkers. Aleksey Antropov, Portrait of Catherine II of Russia, ca. late 18ᵗʰ century. (Public Domain)

Catherine the Great ruled over Russia for thirty-four years, during Russia's greatest period of growth. Through war and conquest, she added hundreds of thousands of miles of territory to the Russian Empire, snatching land from the Ottoman Empire and the Polish-Lithuanian Commonwealth. Catherine was undoubtedly committed to public works projects. She invested a significant amount of the treasury into building new cities and improving the infrastructure of old ones. Considering herself the true heir to Peter the Great, Catherine the Great reformed the Russian military, updating it with the best technology and retraining it with the best strategists.

At this time, Russia was experiencing a cultural flowering; it was successful on the battlefield, and the royal court was a beacon for intellectuals of the Enlightenment. However, the end of Catherine's reign cast a dark shadow. The French Revolution struck fear into the hearts of monarchs across Europe, and Catherine was no different. She was terrified of losing her crown and her head, especially considering she was not a native (Catherine was German-born) of a land where the people had perfected the art of the peasant uprising. Before she could ascertain whether her throne was in jeopardy, Catherine died in 1796. She passed the crown to her son, Paul, thus ending the decades-long period of women rulers.

Chapter 8 – The Partition of Poland and the Long 19th Century (1772–1914)

The period between 1800 and 1914 is often called the "Long 19th Century" for a good reason.[480] It was a turbulent time, with all sorts of changes and shakeups that would lead Europe into its bloodiest conflict yet.

We'll begin this chapter on the Long 19th Century a little earlier with the destruction of the Polish-Lithuanian Commonwealth. The Partition of Poland set the tone for the changes and powerplays that would happen throughout the rest of the 19th century.

---

[480] Jankowski, *Eastern Europe!*, 2015, pg. 265-266.

The End of the Polish-Lithuanian Commonwealth

Throughout the 17th and 18th centuries, the Polish-Lithuanian Commonwealth always seemed like they were at war with someone.[481] Persistent warfare with Eastern Europe's most powerful states, such as the Ottomans, the Swedes, and the Russians, had depleted the commonwealth's resources. By the early 18th century, the people and the state were exhausted. Between 1708 and 1712, a plague hit Poland during the Great Northern War, killing 25 percent of the inhabitants.[482]

The Beginning of the End

Poland-Lithuania had one enemy that resided inside the state that helped lead to its downfall: the meddlesome nobility. Members of the elite held so much power that they controlled the government. At a moment's notice, a monarch could lose their favor. The nobles would then reach out to other heads of state, inviting them to come and rule in the current king's place as long as they favored the elite in their policies. The chance to rule another country and gain more territory was too good of an opportunity to pass up for many.

The nobility held so much power in the Polish-Lithuanian Commonwealth that they could stop proceedings on debates and polices in Parliament simply by stating their objection.[483] This

---

[481] Jankowski, *Eastern Europe!*, 2015, pg. 235-236; Liulevicius, "The Great Crime of Empires: Poland Divided." Lecture 4. *The Great Courses: A History of Eastern Europe*, 2015.

[482] Liulevicius, "The Great Crime of Empires: Poland Divided." Lecture 4. *The Great Courses: A History of Eastern Europe*, 2015; Isis Davis-Marks." Construction in Poland Reveals Graves of 18th-Century Plague Victims." *Smithsonian Magazine.* Published August 25, 2021. https://www.smithsonianmag.com/smart-news/workers-unearth-remains-18th-century-grave-plague-victims-180978510/

[483] Liulevicius, "The Great Crime of Empires: Poland Divided." Lecture 4. *The Great Courses: A History of Eastern Europe*, 2015.

tradition, the *liberum veto*, greatly affected the commonwealth's ability to become a more egalitarian society. It also left the commonwealth's governing body open to external control. Foreign powers started bribing the nobility into passing legislation that was favorable to them and protesting the legislation that wasn't.[484] The Russians, the Prussians, and the Austrians all had members of the Polish elite in their pockets.

At the end of the 1700s, the Polish-Lithuanian Commonwealth was ripe for the picking by its foreign enemies. The commonwealth was dismantled in three stages between 1772 and 1795, and the Partition of Poland was a dark end to a once illustrious empire.

The Partition of Poland

In the late 18th century, Russia held the most influence in the Polish-Lithuanian Commonwealth. The Russians held both the nobles and the king in their power, and they could manipulate the government to set favorable conditions for themselves. Catherine the Great of Russia (r. 1762-1796) placed one of her favorites, Stanislaw August Poniatowski, on the throne in 1764.[485] By making him king, she guaranteed that she would inevitably have control over the territory.

Yet, Prussia and Austria still had their own hands to play. Frederick the Great of Prussia (r. 1740-1786) and Empress Maria Theresa of Austria (r. 1740-1780) had their own designs on Poland as well. As the 1760s rambled on, some members of the Polish nobility grew fearful of the foreign powers. The seeds of rebellion were starting to grow.

---

[484] Liulevicius, "The Great Crime of Empires: Poland Divided." Lecture 4. *The Great Courses: A History of Eastern Europe*, 2015; Jankowski, *Eastern Europe!*, 2015, pg. 234-235.

[485] Liulevicius, "The Great Crime of Empires: Poland Divided." Lecture 4. *The Great Courses: A History of Eastern Europe*, 2015; Jenkins, *Short History of Europe*, 2019, pg.175.

Meanwhile, Catherine the Great's puppet, Poniatowski, was actually doing his job as king—and doing it well. He initiated several reforms to modernize the country, which alarmed Catherine, Frederick, and Maria Theresa. The key to their power was destroyed if there were any major political changes.[486] They needed to be able to keep the Polish nobility at their beck and call.[487]

Members of the Polish elite united against Russia, Prussia, and Austria, forming the Bar Confederation in 1768. It went to war with the foreign powers, protesting their control over the commonwealth's government. Despite winning several victories on the battlefield, the nobles didn't stand a chance against the powerful armies of Russia, Prussia, and Austria.

In 1772, using the War of the Bar Confederation to their advantage, Russia, Austria, and Prussia invaded the Polish-Lithuanian Commonwealth.[488] The three powers slowly chipped away at the commonwealth, taking the most desirable lands for themselves.

---

[486] Jankowski, *Eastern Europe!*, 2015, pg. 235.

[487] Liulevicius, "The Great Crime of Empires: Poland Divided." Lecture 4. *The Great Courses: A History of Eastern Europe*, 2015.

[488] Liulevicius, "The Great Crime of Empires: Poland Divided." Lecture 4. *The Great Courses: A History of Eastern Europe*, 2015; Jankowski, *Eastern Europe!*, 2015, pg. 235; Jenkins, *Short History of Europe*, 2019, pg.175.

A 1773 allegorical image of Catherine the Great, Joseph II of Austria (Maria Theresa's son and heir), and Frederick of Prussia (left to right, respectively) fighting over lands of the commonwealth. (Public Domain)

About 30 percent of the commonwealth woke up to new masters. Austria occupied the south, adding to lands it already held. Prussia had been a collection of broken-up territories along the Baltic Sea until the First Partition of Poland. Now, they took the lands that separated their own, spreading east and occupying the coast. Finally, Russia extended its borders west, taking sections of Lithuania located in modern-day Belarus and Ukraine.

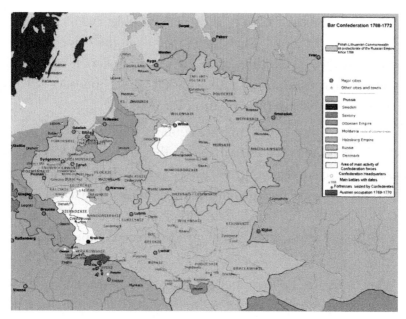

A map of the Polish-Lithuanian Commonwealth during the War of the Bar Confederation, 1768-1772. (Credit: Maciej Szczepańczyk, 2007)

Heads of state across Europe screamed in protest; if Russia, Austria, and Prussia could invade the commonwealth, then no one's lands were safe. Catherine, Frederick, and Maria Theresa had a big problem on their hands; their invasion looked like a land grab (which it undoubtedly was). However, appearances were all that mattered. The heads of state demanded that the Polish pass legislation that allowed them to take the lands.

In 1773, the nobles reported to a meeting of Parliament; it was just a formality, as most of the nobles had capitulated, agreeing to approve the bill that authorized the invasion.[489] There was only one who protested. A member of the Polish elite, Tadeusz Rejtan, refused to go along with the plan. He collapsed on the floor, standing in front of the door and ripping his shirt open in protest of the act. The performance didn't work, and Parliament still passed the legislation.

---

[489] Liulevicius, "The Great Crime of Empires: Poland Divided." Lecture 4. *The Great Courses: A History of Eastern Europe*, 2015.

Tadeusz Rejtan wasn't the only noble who protested Parliament's decision. Many members of the elite left the commonwealth, preferring exile to living under foreign rule. Tadeusz Kosciuszko, for instance, left with hundreds of his countrymen to fight in the American Revolution.

The elite who stayed in the country tried to fix a broken commonwealth. By changing the state, they may have been able to make it strong enough again to resist foreign rule. The progressive elite passed several reforms, including drafting a new constitution. Just like before, this worried the other powers. To enforce their rule, Russia, Austria, and Prussia invaded the commonwealth again in 1792.

This time, the Polish rebelled against the invasion. Under the leadership of Tadeusz Kosciuszko, who had returned from the newly formed United States, the rebellious factions were united.[490] The rebellions were concentrated in the capitals of both Poland and Lithuania, which were Warsaw and Vilnius, respectively.

[490] Jankowski, *Eastern Europe!*, 2015, pg. 235; Liulevicius, "The Great Crime of Empires: Poland Divided." Lecture 4. *The Great Courses: A History of Eastern Europe*, 2015.

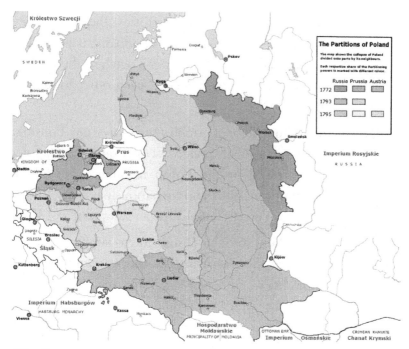

The Partition of Poland. This map shows how much territory Russia, Austria, and Prussia acquired during the Three Partitions of Poland, which took place between 1772 and 1795. (Credit: Halibutt, 2005)

Kosciuszko attracted more allies among the population by promising serfs their freedom. The Jews, who had found sanctuary in Poland for hundreds of years, were quick to defend their adopted homeland; in Warsaw, the Jewish population formed their own armed contingent. By 1794, the rebellion was over.[491] The Polish lost their high command when Kosciuszko was captured in battle. The Russian army invaded Warsaw, massacring the population in retaliation for the rebellion.

The following year, the empires defeated the rest of the opposition. They moved in, dividing up the rest of the lands. Dismantling the Polish-Lithuanian Commonwealth was the worst thing Russia, Prussia, and Austria could have done. No matter how

---

[491] Liulevicius, "The Great Crime of Empires: Poland Divided." Lecture 4. *The Great Courses: A History of Eastern Europe*, 2015; Jankowski, *Eastern Europe!*, 2015, pg. 235-236.

direct their rule was over their new territories, they could never control their new subjects. The Poles and Lithuanians were always rebelling and conspiring against their rule. Together, the countries had taken the territory; now, they needed each other to keep the peace.

Although they didn't have a country anymore, the Polish still played a vital role in global politics. For example, Napoleon Bonaparte was impressed by the Polish regiments. He adopted them as auxiliary troops in 1797, and he famously brought 100,000 Polish soldiers with him on his failed Russian campaign in 1812.

In 1802, he sent them to Saint-Domingue to suppress the slave revolt, but they joined the slaves in fighting for their freedom—a cause the Polish knew intimately.[492] Two years later, Saint-Domingue defeated the last of the French forces and declared its independence from France. The Poles who survived yellow fever and the war stayed behind, making their new home in Haiti. In the Haitian massacre of 1804, when the new leader of Haiti, Jean-Jacques Dessalines, purged the island of the remaining whites as punishment for centuries of abuse to African slaves, he guaranteed the Polish legions his protection. They were the only whites he didn't have murdered, and he granted them citizenship rights as Haitians.

Back in Europe, the Polish still reeled from the loss of their homeland.[493] The Congress of Vienna—the peacekeeping meeting between the powers of Europe in the aftermath of Napoleon's reign—gave European countries back what Napoleon had taken. It was conspicuously silent on reforming the Polish-Lithuanian Commonwealth.

---

[492] Dubois, Laurent. *Haiti: The Aftershocks of History*. New York: Metropolitan Books, 2012, pg. 41.

[493] Liulevicius, "The Great Crime of Empires: Poland Divided." Lecture 4. *The Great Courses: A History of Eastern Europe*, 2015.

The Polish never gave up, and they continued to rebel. They wanted their freedom, but more importantly, they wanted their home back. Polish intellectuals wrote and created art that celebrated their past. The Lithuanians went even further back, wishing they had never even met the Poles. The Jews of the former commonwealth had an even worse time. The Russians passed discriminatory laws that restricted their movements. Anti-Semitism was in full swing, and the Jews resented their intolerant new overlords. This was not the sanctuary they had found when they arrived in Poland after leaving persecution in Western Europe.

"The Long 19th Century"

The Long 19th Century begins with Europe dealing with the aftereffects of Napoleon.[494] His campaigns permanently altered the face of Europe. He didn't just take territory; he tried to change the way society worked. While this may have terrified the crowned monarchs of Europe, it inspired the seed of revolution in the minds of the public.

After Napoleon's fall from grace in 1814, the European powers didn't want to go back to decades of war and instability.[495] So, they worked together to make sure it didn't happen again. Representatives from Austria, Russia, and Prussia joined delegates from Great Britain and France at a series of meetings in Vienna. Led by the Austrian foreign minister, Klemens von Metternich, the Congress of Vienna reorganized power in Europe. They believed that by making sure all of the countries had the same amount of power, they would keep the peace and prevent war from breaking out again.

The nations of Europe had an opportunity at the Congress of Vienna to institute wide-sweeping reforms that would have benefited all of society.[496] The problem was, they didn't even

---

[494] Jankowski, *Eastern Europe!*, 2015, pg. 265-266.

[495] Jankowski, *Eastern Europe!*, 2015, pg. 268.

[496] Ibid., pg. 268-269.

investigate why the people were so dissatisfied with their lives. Instead of considering the population, they worried about themselves and their own influence. The result would be a new phase of revolution.

The first phase of the 19th century was filled with ups and downs, from orchestrating peace to the outbreaks of revolution. This period of revolution would greatly impact European countries and how they related to each other. According to Tomek Jankowski, after the Revolutions of 1848, "European governments were as much focused on whether their own peoples would rise up against them as what other countries did."[497]

In Eastern Europe, the four main powers were still in control: the Ottoman Empire, Prussia, Austria, and Russia. The first stirrings of revolution would begin in the Balkans. Their desire for self-rule led to activist groups, some with violent methods.[498] The revolutionary movements in the Balkans would inspire the rest of Eastern Europe, as they started to agitate for freedom too.

The Great Powers redrew the map of Europe, 1815. (Credit: Alexander Altenhof, 2016)

[497] Ibid., pg. 265-266.

[498] Ibid., pg. 268-269.

Nationalism

A major component of independence movements is nationalism. According to Professor Vejas Liulevicius, that is when "...an 'imagined community' of language, ancestry, history, and customs unites a people."[499] The 19th century brought changes in the way people related to their state. The elite believed they were the ones who could change things and that no one else mattered. Influenced by the ideas of liberty and fraternity from the American and French Revolutions, the people clamored for recognition, claiming their participation and voice were just as important as anyone else's.[500]

Nationalism developed across Europe in three ways; these methods are found throughout all independence movements, and they speak to the power of how others recall the past. Nationalism starts with activism. Artists, scholars, and public figures refer to the past, examining the connections between people. These connections are the product of a common experience, language, and/or ethnicity. Works of literature, new and old, were written and published in local, vernacular languages, engaging the masses and inspiring national pride. Activists then use this ideology and bring it into the real world, convincing others that they are stronger together than apart.[501] When this happens, there is a challenge to the existing order, as activists show their supporters the alternative to the way things are. This challenge can turn violent, though.

Nationalism was on the rise throughout Eastern Europe, where there was no political support for it. In many places, ideas of self-

---

[499] Liulevicius, "The Origins of Nationalism, 1815-1863." Lecture 5. *The Great Courses: A History of Eastern Europe*, 2015.

[500] Jankowski, *Eastern Europe!*, 2015, pg. 268-269; Liulevicius, "The Origins of Nationalism, 1815-1863." Lecture 5. *The Great Courses: A History of Eastern Europe*, 2015.

[501] Liulevicius, "The Origins of Nationalism, 1815-1863." Lecture 5. *The Great Courses: A History of Eastern Europe*, 2015.

rule and national identity that created these imagined communities were a threat to the status quo.[502]

Nationalist movements were influenced by Romanticism, an artistic movement that made its way through Europe. Compared to the Enlightenment's focus on intellectual growth, the Romantic period emphasized the emotional reaction one has to life. With a focus on feelings instead of thoughts, Romantics pressed the importance of living authentically; there is freedom in living as you were meant to.

The Revolutions of 1848

The Revolutions of 1848, which spread from France to Eastern Europe, threatened the monarchical order. [503] The revolutions would reach Poland, Austria, and the German principalities (the remnants of the Holy Roman Empire, which was dismantled by Napoleon in 1806).

One could see why a revolution had appeal. After centuries under foreign domination, revolutionaries supported any rebellion against monarchies that weren't working in their best interests. They believed people should establish democratic governments where everyone had a say in the process.

Romantic thinkers promoted the idea of a pan-revolutionary movement. They believed that if all the people throughout Europe, no matter where they were from or where they lived, rose up together against monarchies and unfair governments, the revolutions would be more effective. However, the revolutionary groups couldn't get along well enough to form any kind of coherent global movement. For the most part, the Revolutions of 1848 didn't work. Monarchies reclaimed their power and brutally put down revolutionary activity.

---

[502] Jankowski, *Eastern Europe!*, 2015, pg. 271.

The Hungarian Revolution

While most of the 1848 rebellions were squashed before they could really get started, Hungary formed its own revolutionary government for six months. Reaching Vienna first, the revolution spread to the Hungarians. As poets and other revolutionaries mused on the events in Vienna, they suggested the same reality for Budapest. These artists recalled the days of Magyar Hungary before rule by the Ottomans and the Habsburgs.

In 1849, Hungary declared its independence from Habsburg rule. Even though the coup had been nonviolent, Polish soldiers, whose memories of their former country burned strong, came to help the Hungarians with their revolution. The new government passed a series of reforms, including voting rights for all men, the end of serfdom, and a free press.

---

[503] Liulevicius, "The Origins of Nationalism, 1815-1863." Lecture 5. *The Great Courses: A History of Eastern Europe*, 2015.; Jenkins, *Short History of Europe*, 2019, pg.210-212.

During the 1848 Revolutions, the Hungarian Revolution was a bloodless coup that wrestled power away from Habsburg rule. The Hungarians founded a democratic government, establishing their first parliament and passing laws that guaranteed suffrage and freedom of the press. This painting shows the first meeting of the Hungarian Parliament, with its officials standing on the balcony above. August von Pettenkofen, Opening Ceremony of the Hungarian Parliament in 1848. (Public Domain)

Habsburg Emperor Franz Josef (r. 1848–1916) knew he couldn't put down the revolutionary government alone. He approached the emperor of Russia, Nicholas I, for help. Nicholas I (r. 1825–1855) had just as much to lose by the success of the Hungarian revolt. Just like any monarch who ruled with absolute power, he didn't want the revolution to spread to his lands that had once been the Polish-Lithuanian Commonwealth.

Nicholas offered Franz Josef 100,000 soldiers to overthrow the revolutionary government. The joint forces of the Russian and Austrian armies met the Hungarians in battle in July 1849. The Hungarian revolutionaries lost, and they were forced to surrender.

Out of spite, they handed their weapons over to the Russian army.[504]

The next phase brought an exacting and bloody vengeance upon the Hungarians. Over the next ten years, the Austrian government sanctioned cruel repression over the Hungarian population. What was significant about this blowback is that the Habsburgs' violent reaction was unjustified for what had caused it.[505] The overthrow of the monarchy had been a bloodless event, where the revolutionaries simply snatched control of the government. The Habsburgs responded with violence. Prince Felix Schwarzenberg, who served as the Austrian minister of foreign affairs as well as the prime minister, and Baron Julius von Haynau, the field marshal of Austrian forces on the ground in Hungary, issued a widespread order to crush any opposition to Habsburg rule.[506] They started at the top, executing army generals and members of the government. To quell any rebirth of the revolution, the Austrians terrified the Hungarians into submission, ordering massacres and forced imprisonment of civilians.

The Counter-Revolution: Conservative Monarchies Rise Again

After 1848, the main monarchies of Eastern Europe had a powder keg on their hands. More often than not, "estate or class very often overlapped with ethnicity. In such a setup, social tensions or resentments could immediately take on an ethnic charge, making nationalism even more potent."[507] Each major power took a different approach to reestablishing its authority.[508]

---

[504] Miklos Molnar, *A Concise History of Hungary*, Cambridge: Cambridge University Press, 2001, pg. 199.

[505] Liulevicius, "The Origins of Nationalism, 1815-1863." Lecture 5. *The Great Courses: A History of Eastern Europe*, 2015.

[506] Molnar, *A Concise History of Hungary*, pg. 191, 194, 199.

[507] Liulevicius, "The Age of Empires, 1863-1914." Lecture 6. *The Great Courses: A History of Eastern Europe*, 2015.

[508] Jenkins, *Short History of Europe*, 2019, pg.214; Liulevicius, "The Age of Empires, 1863-1914." Lecture 6. *The Great Courses: A History of Eastern Europe*, 2015.

The common element is that they tried to make their lands ethnically homogenous; by making everyone the same, it would eliminate any sense of ethnic nationalism that was still lingering. However, this amounted to destroying cultures and identities.

Russification and Anarchy

After Russia confiscated the western lands of the Polish-Lithuanian Commonwealth, rebellions against its rule were common. Initially, Russia granted the former lands of the commonwealth a great degree of autonomy. Over several decades, the Russian tsars, Paul I, Alexander I, and Nicholas I, encroached on the commonwealth's independence. This bred resentment among the population, which was relatively left to its own devices.

Marcin Zaleski, Capture of the Arsenal, 1831. (Public Domain)

In 1830, the November Uprising began in Poland.[509] The Polish soldiers raided the military barracks for weapons and secured control of Warsaw, winning some key victories. Unfortunately, the rebels were poorly organized and did not have effective leadership. In February 1831, Tsar Nicholas I's army invaded former Poland-Lithuania, sparring with the revolutionaries until October. In

---

[509] Jankowski, *Eastern Europe!*, 2015, pg. 318; "November Insurrection." *Encyclopedia Britannica.* https://www.britannica.com/event/November-Insurrection

retaliation for their disorder, the tsar passed more repressive laws against the Poles. He sent soldiers to occupy the country and placed the former commonwealth under direct rule.

The November Uprising may have lacked confident leadership, but it spawned several national heroes whose exploits are celebrated by Poles and Lithuanians. In spring 1831, a noblewoman named Emilia Plater gathered an army of peasants armed with scythes. She led them in several campaigns, earning her the nickname the "Lithuanian Joan of Arc." Jan Rosen, Emilia Plater Conducting Polish Scythmen, ca. 19ᵗʰ century. (Public Domain)

This was not the only act of brutal repression during Nicholas's reign.[510] When his son, Tsar Alexander II, succeeded Nicholas in 1855, he was determined to reform society, but the seeds of discontent had been growing for decades. Alexander was not as despotic as his predecessors, and he eased the restrictions on non-

---

[510] Jankowski, *Eastern Europe!*, 2015, pg. 318-319; Liulevicius, "The Age of Empires, 1863-1914." Lecture 6. *The Great Courses: A History of Eastern Europe*, 2015.

Russians across his lands.[511] In turn, ideas of nationalism spread again, leading to another rebellion.

In 1863, soon after Russia had been humiliated in the Crimean War, losing to the Ottoman Empire, Great Britain, and France, the Poles rebelled again.[512] This time, the rebellion spread among students and young professionals, people who were most likely too young to remember the 1830 uprising.[513] All they knew was cruelty and repression by the Russians.

As the revolutionaries started leading demonstrations against the government, Russian official Aleksander Wielopolski instituted a draft of young men into the Russian army as a way to get rid of the revolutionaries.[514] There was a massive outcry against this conscription, and the rebels armed themselves, preparing for war with Russian forces. The rebellion quickly spread to Lithuania and made its way east into modern-day Ukraine and Belarus.

Although the revolutionaries lost several battles, they managed to stay together until the following year. Disappointed in the progress of the rebellion, many Poles left Russian-held lands. By 1864, the Russians had reclaimed their authority over Poland.

Although Alexander II had been more lenient with the Poles than his predecessors, he didn't tolerate insurrection. He executed the leaders of the resistance in August 1864, placing Poland under military occupation. Poland was divided into smaller districts so

[511] Liulevicius, "The Age of Empires, 1863-1914." Lecture 6. *The Great Courses: A History of Eastern Europe*, 2015.

[512] Liulevicius, "The Age of Empires, 1863-1914." Lecture 6. *The Great Courses: A History of Eastern Europe*, 2015.; Jankowski, *Eastern Europe!*, 2015, pg. 312, 319; Jenkins, *Short History of Europe*, 2019, pg. 216.

[513] Liulevicius, "The Age of Empires, 1863-1914." Lecture 6. *The Great Courses: A History of Eastern Europe*, 2015.; "January Insurrection." *Encyclopedia Britannica.* https://www.britannica.com/event/January-Insurrection

[514] Liulevicius, "The Age of Empires, 1863-1914." Lecture 6. *The Great Courses: A History of Eastern Europe*, 2015; "January Insurrection." *Encyclopedia Britannica;* Jankowski, *Eastern Europe!*, 2015, pg. 312-313, 319.

Russia could control them better. After the leaders of the insurrection were executed, thousands of revolutionaries and their supporters were shipped to Siberia to live in exile.

Aleksander Sochaczewski, Farewell Europe! Painting, 1894. (Public Domain)

The Russians then passed a series of reforms that attempted to make everyone the same. This process is called Russification. They forbade speaking or writing in any language that was not Russian. The population also could not celebrate or honor any ethnic background, history, or traditions that were not distinctly Russian.

Russification took place all over the empire. In Lithuania, the Russians tried to eliminate the Lithuanian language by making printing and speaking in Lithuanian illegal. Only Russian and the Cyrillic alphabet could be spoken or written. This law remained on the books for forty years before it was finally abolished in 1904. In defiance of the law, Lithuanian revolutionaries smuggled books into their territory. The Russians also passed legislation to eliminate the German language in their Baltic territories, namely in modern-day Latvia and Estonia.

Russification saw protests in Ukraine as well. Ukrainians saw themselves as different from the Russians, but Russians refused to acknowledge it. In the Austrian-held part of the territory, ethnic nationalism was allowed to spread on account of the Austrian government being less restrictive than the Russians. While the

Ukrainians wanted their own history, territory, and identity, the Russians pushed their Russification through religion. Some Christian populations still remained in Ukraine—an inheritance from the Byzantine Empire. Russia outlawed all Christian churches, making Russian Orthodoxy the only legal state religion.

In the aftermath of the Polish rebellion, those who hadn't joined the fighting but supported the revolution found refuge in politics. By slowly pushing laws through Parliament that benefited all members of society, they believed they could eventually overcome foreign rule. This took too long, though, and many Poles lost heart that anything would ever change. Some established an activist group called the National Democrats, which was a purely Polish group that supported resisting Russification.

Pan-Slavism in Austria and Russia

Pan-Slavism, which supports the belief that all Slavic peoples had a common background, grew among the South Slavs and the West Slavs.[515] Pan-Slav activists pushed rhetoric that all Slavs should work together to gain more political rights in their respective nations.

In 1848, as revolution rocked Vienna, the Slavs met in Prague to work out their plans for moving forward. They encouraged the study of Slavic history and language to honor their ethnic heritage, but they also wanted to gain equal rights under the Austrian government.

---

[515] "Pan-Slavism." *Encyclopedia Britannica*. https://www.britannica.com/event/Pan-Slavism

A drawing depicting the first Pan-Slav Congress in Prague, 1848. (Public Congress)

The Slavs of Austria turned to Russia to pressure Austria into giving them rights. Russia encouraged pan-Slavism, as it knew it couldn't succeed at becoming a dominant power in Europe without Slavic help. But while Russia supported a pan-Slavic union, the Slavic peoples would still remain under Russian domination. By accepting Russia's help, the Slavs of Eastern Europe would trade one set of overlords for another.

Pan-Slavism gradually waned throughout the rest of the 19th century. In the years before World War I, there was a resurgence among Eastern European Slavs, but there were too many different viewpoints to create a cohesive movement.[516]

Pan-Germanism, Prussia, and Austria-Hungary

When Napoleon reached the Rhine in 1805, he found hundreds of small dukedoms, principalities, and states with little in common other than the fact they spoke German.[517] For nearly a century and a half, they created their own traditions and cultures

---

[516] Jankowski, *Eastern Europe!*, 2015, pg. 299.

[517] Liulevicius, "The Age of Empires, 1863-1914." Lecture 6. *The Great Courses: A History of Eastern Europe*, 2015., Jankowski 294-296, 300.

with no thought of uniting together. The inhabitants of these states saw themselves as a product of their land; they weren't ethnically connected.

Napoleon's restructuring of these areas into larger groups changed ideas of what made a state, and the events of his domination over the area helped develop feelings of pan-Germanism. The people of the Holy Roman Empire, which Napoleon would break up the following year in 1806, now began to see themselves as Germans.[518]

Prussia and Austria received these German states as part of their restored territories from the Congress of Vienna. Prussia received more of these states, but Austria still held a significant amount of them to the south. After all, Prussia had played a major role in defeating Napoleon.[519] The Prussian army was part of the invading force that took Paris in 1814, and it defeated Napoleon at Waterloo. These victories helped Prussia grow in power and influence. It became the most powerful of the German states, while Habsburg Austria ranked a close second.[520] For this reason, the two states were at war just as much as they were at peace.

Prussia and Austria still had their eye on one more state to make their control over the region complete: Schleswig-Holstein. In two wars that lasted intermittently between 1848 and 1864, Prussia and Austria gained control over these two territories; each power took one of the duchies for themselves. Schleswig-Holstein was important because it was the boundary between the German states and Denmark.

---

[518] Jankowski, *Eastern Europe!*, 2015, pg. 294; Liulevicius, "The Age of Empires, 1863-1914." Lecture 6. *The Great Courses: A History of Eastern Europe*, 2015.; Jenkins, *Short History of Europe*, 2019, pg.220.

[519] Jankowski, *Eastern Europe!*, 2015, pg. 257.

[520] Jankowski, *Eastern Europe!*, 2015, pg. 294-295; Liulevicius, "The Age of Empires, 1863-1914." Lecture 6. *The Great Courses: A History of Eastern Europe*, 2015.

The territory of Schleswig-Holstein was the buffer state between Denmark and the German states. On this map, Schleswig is marked in light pink, and Holstein is marked in light blue. (Credit: Malte89, 2016)

Neither Prussia nor Austria could agree on what to do with Schleswig-Holstein, which ended up causing the Austro-Prussian War of 1866.[521] Austria lost against Prussia, which means it also lost its control over the German states. Prussia snatched them up, dissolving the Habsburg German Confederation (the *Deutscher Bund*), which was an association of German-speaking states.

[521] Liulevicius, "The Age of Empires, 1863-1914." Lecture 6. *The Great Courses: A History of Eastern Europe*, 2015.; Jankowski, *Eastern Europe!*, 2015, pg. 296, 304.

Prussia formed its own organization, the North German Confederation, in 1867.

After Austria lost most of its territory, it was in danger of collapsing. It struck a deal with another Habsburg territory, Hungary, granting the territory status as a full kingdom if they could form a dual monarchy. Its new name was Austria-Hungary, but both nations were still distinct entities. What they had in common was the same ruler and common goals in defense and foreign policies. Meanwhile, Prussia was stronger than ever. It became the most prominent state in the North German Confederation, and it was controlled by the "Iron Chancellor," Otto von Bismarck (in off. 1871–1890).[522]

Austria-Hungary and Prussia embraced pan-Germanism, but they had different views on how to implement it.[523] The Austrians celebrated German culture, but Prussia saw the political potential of uniting the German states. The idea of a united Germany grew in popularity, even though it would include non-Germans.

---

[522] Jenkins, *Short History of Europe*, 2019, pg.221-224.

[523] Jankowski, *Eastern Europe!*, 2015, pg. 304.

A map of the German Empire from its founding in 1871 to its dissolution in 1918. The empire stretched from the southern coast of the Baltic Sea to the North Sea coast. (Credit: kgberger, 2009)

After Prussia completed its domination over the German states, Otto von Bismarck eliminated the North German Confederation and established the German Empire in 1871.[524] This new empire was hardly homogenous. Its territories included a significant number of Poles and other ethnic minorities who didn't respond well to Germanization. Similar to Russification, this process tried to eliminate ethnic diversity and make the whole population German.[525] The German Empire only taught German language and literature, and non-German languages and traditions were banned. The empire also ordered a reordering of populations and society,

---

[524] Jankowski, *Eastern Europe!*, 2015, pg. 304; Jenkins, *Short History of Europe*, 2019, pg.227.

[525] Jankowski, *Eastern Europe!*, 2015, pg. 297.

importing Germans to settle in targeted areas and pushing the non-German minorities out.

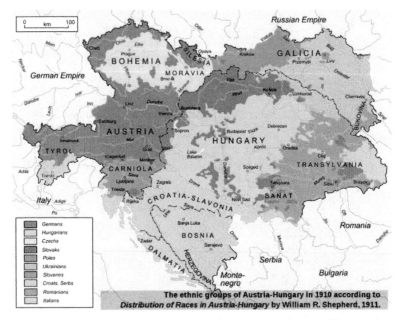

A map showing the demographics living in the Austro-Hungarian Empire. (Public Domain)

Austria-Hungary was much more ethnically diverse than the German Empire was, so they had their own unique experience with pan-Germanism. With its new dual monarchy, the country became host to Hungarians, Czechs, Poles, and Ukrainians—just to name a few. For the most part, the Hungarians were happy with their union with Austria because it gave them more power as a kingdom. However, they were not pleased by its Germanization policies because more than 50 percent of Austria-Hungary's new residents were non-Germans.

The Ottomans vs. the Balkans

These ideas of independence especially spoke to the residents of the Balkans.[526] Throughout this book, we've seen how many different ethnic groups, languages, and experiences that the people of the Balkans shared. All they wanted was freedom from the Ottomans. Even though the Turks were famously tolerant of other cultures and religions, the Balkans wanted self-determination.

The Ottomans had held the Balkans for hundreds of years. When you think about it, that's a really long time to hold a territory that is not your own. The Ottomans were horrible administrators; they were more focused on collecting lands than making sure their territories were being governed correctly.[527]

The powers of Europe started modernizing while the Ottomans lagged behind. Since other countries had better military technology and strategy, the Ottomans started losing on the battlefield. The Russians saw a great opportunity to bring more Slavic populations under their rule. Their rival in the Balkans, Austria-Hungary, didn't care about the Slavs; however, they did care about Russia growing too powerful and themselves not being powerful enough.

---

[526] Liulevicius, "The Origins of Nationalism, 1815-1863." Lecture 5. *The Great Courses: A History of Eastern Europe*, 2015.

[527] Jankowski, *Eastern Europe!*, 2015, pg. 271

In response to the Greek independence movement, the Ottomans unleashed untold atrocities on Greeks living in their empire. In Constantinople, the Ottomans executed the head of the Orthodox Church and terrorized Greek communities. Houses were burned, and people were assaulted and killed—even women and children. (Public Domain)

The Balkan independence movements started in Greece.[528] In 1821, Greece rebelled against Ottoman rule. Twelve years later, the Greeks had their independence. This kickstarted a series of tumultuous events that lasted decades.[529]

While the Greeks had won their independence, it only applied to Greeks who lived in Greece. The 60 percent of Greeks who resided in the Balkans lived outside of Greece, meaning they were still under foreign rule.

---

[528] Liulevicius, "The Origins of Nationalism, 1815-1863." Lecture 5. *The Great Courses: A History of Eastern Europe*, 2015.; Jankowski, *Eastern Europe!*, 2015, pg. 274.

[529] Liulevicius, "The Age of Empires, 1863-1914." Lecture 6. *The Great Courses: A History of Eastern Europe*, 2015., Jankowski, *Eastern Europe!*, 2015, pg. 271-276.

The Struggle for Serbia

While the Ottomans were dealing with one rebellion, they had another on their hands. Serbia initiated two periods of independence movements from 1804 to 1830.[530] It all started in the last years of the 18th century when the Ottoman Janissaries invaded Serbia. The Janissaries had once been the valued fighting force of the Ottomans, but they had descended into corruption and greed. They took control of Serbia to make their own state, but they had to deal with the local population first.

The Janissaries brutally persecuted the Serbian Christian population for decades. Tired of the abuse that basically amounted to slavery, Serbian Christians rebelled against the Ottoman Empire in 1804. The Ottomans refused to defend Christians against Muslims, no matter what the Janissaries had done. In retaliation, the Ottomans invaded and defeated the rebellion. This experience was responsible for the birth of Serbian pride and nationalism that would result in their independence.

The Serbians had a valuable ally in Russia. Djordje Petrović led a campaign that eliminated the Ottoman presence in Serbia by 1806. The Ottomans came back in 1812 to subdue the population in a punitive campaign. The Russians were no help this time; they were distracted by Napoleon's invasion, so the Serbians lost their support. The Ottomans regained control of Serbia the following year, and Djordje Petrović escaped to Austria-Hungary.

In 1814, another Serbian uprising would run through the country and successfully push the Ottomans out. The leader of this uprising was Miloš Obrenović. Petrović tried to come back and start another rebellion, but Obrenović assassinated him before he could do anything.

---

[530] Jankowski, *Eastern Europe!*, 2015, pg. 274-277.

Mór Than, The Assassination of Karadjordje, 1863. Djordje Petrović was known by the name Karadjordje. When he returned to Serbia to launch another rebellion, his rival, Miloš Obrenović, had him executed. (Public Domain)

While Obrenović commanded a substantial defense, the Russians reappeared. Having dealt with Napoleon, they strong-armed the Ottomans into backing off and giving Serbia its independence.[531] In 1830, the Ottomans finally capitulated, and they evacuated the country and allowed the Serbians to govern themselves.

The Serbians spent the next forty-five years building themselves up into a regional power.[532] Until 1875, Serbian nationalists wanted to recreate medieval Serbia, rejoining all its lands back together. Serbia would make many enemies in its goal of rebuilding the medieval Serbian empire. Other Christian nations in Europe didn't have a problem with this reordering of states, as long as the

[531] Jankowski, *Eastern Europe!*, 2015, pg. 279.

[532] Jankowski, *Eastern Europe!*, 2015, pg. 277-279.

Serbians were confiscating lands in the Ottomans' possession. The problem came when Serbia had designs on its former lands that were now part of other Christian nations.

Serbia was also occupied by internal struggles. Once the Congress of Berlin forced the Ottomans to formally recognize Serbian independence, the country descended into a decades-long rivalry between the successors of both Miloš Obrenović and Djordje Petrović.[533] In 1903, members of the Serbian Army stormed the royal residence, murdering everyone they found.

In 1903, King Alexander I of Serbia (Alexander Obrenović) and his wife, Queen Draga, were executed, along with most of their royal court. (Public Domain)

[533] Jankowski, *Eastern Europe!*, 2015, pg. 277, 280.

Among the dead were King Alexander Obrenović of Serbia, the queen, and their family members and close advisors. A new dynasty came to the Serbian throne, but the country would soon join with other Balkan states to push the Ottomans out once and for all.

The Ottoman Target

The next major challenge for the Ottomans was the Crimean War (1853–1856).[534] By the mid-19th century, religious tensions between Russia and the Ottoman Empire exploded into conflict.[535] Russia wanted a foothold in the Middle East and to its sacred sites, which were under Ottoman control. When the Ottomans refused to grant access to the Russians, Tsar Nicholas I invaded and captured Wallachia and Moldavia.[536] The Ottomans declared war, and they found allies in Britain and France. While the war was a victory for the Ottomans (and a terrible loss for the Russians), the win was barely by the skin of their teeth.

In the mid-19th century, Russia, Great Britain, and France had been wondering what to do with the foundering Ottoman Empire.[537] The fall of the empire would leave an opening to command Eastern Europe, and all three wanted a piece of the action. The British and the French worried about Russia's expansionist designs, so they preferred having the Ottoman Balkans as a buffer zone.

---

[534] Jankowski, *Eastern Europe!*, 2015, pg. 274-275; "Crimean War." *HISTORY.* Published November 9, 2009. https://www.history.com/topics/british-history/crimean-war

[535] "Crimean War." *HISTORY;* Jenkins, *Short History of Europe*, 2019, pgs.215-216.

[536] Jankowski, *Eastern Europe!*, 2015, pg. 274-275; "Crimean War." *HISTORY.*

[537] Jankowski, *Eastern Europe!*, 2015, pg. 274-275; Jenkins, *Short History of Europe*, 2019, pg.227.

The Russo-Turkish War and the Congress of Berlin

The end of the 19th century brought more war and revolutions. Restless populations in Bosnia-Herzegovina and Bulgaria rose in rebellion against the Ottoman Empire in 1875.[538] The Ottomans had had enough; they moved into Bulgaria, slaughtering the population. About twelve thousand Bulgarians died at Ottoman hands.[539]

A map showing the provinces of the Ottoman Empire, 1900. (Credit: Julieta39, 2016)

The Russians were appalled at the Ottomans' behavior in Bulgaria.[540] They formed an alliance with Bulgaria, Bosnia-Herzegovina, and Serbia, and they declared war on the Ottoman Empire. The Russo-Turkish War (1877–1878) ended with an Ottoman defeat. The Treaty of San Stefano forced the Ottomans to relinquish Bulgaria to Russia. That same year, Otto von Bismarck hosted the Congress of Berlin. This conference

[538] Jankowski, *Eastern Europe!*, 2015, pg. 274-275, 279.

[539] Jenkins, *Short History of Europe*, 2019, pg. 227.

[540] Jenkins, *Short History of Europe*, 2019, pg.227; Jankowski, *Eastern Europe!*, 2015, pg. 274-275.

attempted to settle the disputes in the Balkans.[541] Bismarck forced the Ottomans to declare Serbia, Montenegro, Wallachia, and Moldavia (the latter of the two joined together to form Romania) as independent states, while Austria-Hungary obtained Bosnia-Herzegovina.

By the 1890s, the Ottomans were hanging on by a thread, and tensions throughout Europe simmered for several years. They no longer controlled the Balkans, and their British and French allies soon joined forces with Russia to combat the growth of the German Empire's armed forces and weapons. More trouble was coming. The Ottomans would soon be pushed out of Eastern Europe completely by the Balkan Wars (1912–1913).[542]

The Balkan Wars

In 1908, the Bosnian Crisis seemed to be the fuse that would make the Balkans explode. Austria-Hungary officially annexed Bosnia-Herzegovina after controlling it for three decades.[543] This outraged Serbia because it wanted Bosnia-Herzegovina too. Serbia's reasoning for wanting this territory was both personal and political. Bosnia-Herzegovina would allow Serbia to reach the Adriatic Sea, but it couldn't do that with Austria-Hungary in control of it. As a compromise, the powers agreed to carve out another state that granted coastal access: Albania.

Russia was Serbia's ally, so it promised to come to Serbia's aid if war broke out. It also had its own designs on Bosnia-Herzegovina. Control over the territory would give expansionist Russia the foothold in Eastern Europe it desperately wanted, plus it would *really* needle their long-standing enemy in Europe, Austria-

---

[541] Jankowski, *Eastern Europe!*, 2015, pg. 275-276, 279; Jenkins, *Short History of Europe*, 2019, pg.227.

[542] "Balkan Wars." *Encyclopedia Britannica.* https://www.britannica.com/topic/Balkan-Wars

[543] Jankowski, *Eastern Europe!*, 2015, pg. 280; Jenkins, *Short History of Europe*, 2019, pg.236-237.

Hungary. As it was, all sides prepared for a conflict. To avoid war in the Balkans, the German Empire stepped in and made Russia back off.

Over the next several years, conflicts broke out across the Balkans. This stemmed from political instability in the Ottoman Empire that reverberated throughout Eastern Europe.[544] Since the 1870s, the Young Turks, members of a movement that sought to update Ottoman social and political institutions, were the real power of the Ottoman state.[545] The sultan was forced to make several compromises, including heading a constitutional monarchy (instead of an absolute monarchy) and answering to a parliament.[546] The Young Turk movement was too immovable to rule over a multi-ethnic empire.[547] They stripped Christians and other non-Muslim communities of their rights, which was a far cry from how the empire had handled things.

Revolutionary groups rose in Ottoman lands with Christian communities, including Macedonia, Bulgaria, and Serbia.[548] These organizations didn't have a common goal; each was devoted to their own nationalist movements. By 1911, however, they all realized that they could work together to completely free themselves from Ottoman hold. In 1912, with Russian backing, Bulgaria, Greece, Montenegro, and Serbia joined forces and created the Balkan League to crush Ottoman rule over Macedonia.[549] The Ottoman Empire was distracted by another war, so the Balkan League was successful in the First Balkan War (1912–1913). The members of the league managed to amass an

[544] Jankowski, *Eastern Europe!*, 2015, pg. 276.

[545] Jenkins, *Short History of Europe*, 2019, pg. 236.

[546] Jankowski, *Eastern Europe!*, 2015, pg. 276.

[547] Jankowski, *Eastern Europe!*, 2015, pg. 276; "Balkan Wars." *Encyclopedia Britannica.*

[548] Jenkins, *Short History of Europe*, 2019, pg.236; "Balkan Wars." *Encyclopedia Britannica.*

[549] Jenkins, *Short History of Europe*, 2019, pg.236-237; "Balkan Wars." *Encyclopedia Britannica.*

army of three-quarters of a million soldiers, which they used to conquer Ottoman-controlled lands in modern-day North Macedonia, Bulgaria, Greece, Turkey, and Albania. By December, the Balkan League's efforts forced the Ottoman Empire to capitulate.

As a result of the complete failure in the First Balkan War, the Young Turks led a coup and overran the Ottoman government in January 1913. They also went to war with the Balkan League again.[550] The Balkan League was successful once more, capturing more lands in Greece and Turkey.[551] The war was over by May; the resulting peace treaty divided Macedonia among the powers of the Balkan League. The Ottoman Empire was stripped of the rest of their lands in Eastern Europe except for their lands in Thrace, which was northeast of the Aegean Sea.[552]

[550] Jankowski, *Eastern Europe!*, 2015, pg. 276; "Balkan Wars." *Encyclopedia Britannica;* Jenkins, *Short History of Europe,* 2019, pg.236-237.

[551] "Balkan Wars." *Encyclopedia Britannica.*

[552] Jenkins, *Short History of Europe,* 2019, pg.236-237; "Balkan Wars." *Encyclopedia Britannica.*

This postcard from 1912 shows the alliance of the Balkan League, showing soldiers from each country—Bulgaria, Serbia, Montenegro, and Greece—holding hands in friendship. Postcards like these were used as recruitment tools during the Balkan Wars. (Public Domain)

The end of the First Balkan War in 1913 proved to the Ottomans that their days were numbered.[553] Their former colonies had succeeded in defeating them, which was a huge blow to Ottoman power in Europe. The empire itself still survived but only barely. The Young Turks established a dictatorship, which would dominate Ottoman affairs until the end of World War I. The status of the Ottoman emperor, a figure who once inspired fear into the hearts of Europeans, was now only a ceremonial role.

---

[553] Jankowski, *Eastern Europe!*, 2015, pg. 276; "Balkan Wars." *Encyclopedia Britannica.*

The Balkan League would soon fall apart. Although the Balkan League worked together to push the Ottomans out of their territory, they couldn't get along well enough to make any real progress.[554] The Balkan League squabbled over how to break up Macedonia, which brought the members of the league into a war of their own!

The Second Balkan War (1913) resulted from the Balkan League's inability to agree on how to allocate the lands won in the First Balkan War. Greece, Romania, and Serbia fought over how much of Macedonia each of them would get. In June 1913, Greece and Serbia allied against Bulgaria. The king of Bulgaria went on the offensive, attacking Greek- and Serbian-occupied Macedonia. Bulgaria was victorious in its initial battles against the Serbian forces. The Second Balkan War drew in other powers such as Romania and the fledgling Ottoman Empire. Each invaded territories and staked their own claims. Bulgaria was completely surrounded by its enemies, so it ceased hostilities, and the war ended. The members of the Balkan League came to terms in August 1913; Serbia and Greece split Macedonia among themselves, granting Bulgaria a small piece of it.

---

[554] Jenkins, *Short History of Europe*, 2019, pg.237; Jankowski, *Eastern Europe!*, 2015, pg. 276.

The lands of Thrace were the only part of Eastern Europe under Ottoman control at the end of the Balkan Wars. After the end of World War I and the fall of the Ottoman Empire, this historical region would be divided between Bulgaria, Greece, and Turkey. (Credit: Пакко, 2009)

The Balkan Wars would directly contribute to the events that sparked World War I. Serbian gains in the Balkan Wars exacerbated the tensions with Austria-Hungary (who held Bosnia-Herzegovina), which would violently escalate the following year. The powers of Europe knew a war was coming. It was just a matter of when.

Chapter 9 – Stuck Between Two World Wars (1914–1945)

Scholars study World War I and World War II probably more than any other war in history. Both wars are commonly associated with their Western Fronts, but the events on the Eastern Front were just as vital to the outcome of the war. Studies of World War I often neglect the Eastern European experience.[555] The West was filled with trenches, but the East had open areas, lengthy pastures, and mountain ranges that saw combat and movement. In this chapter, we will see World War I, the interwar years, and World War II from the Eastern European viewpoint.

The Great War That Was Never Great

The international peace that the European powers dreamed of after Napoleon's defeat in 1815 was a failed experiment.[556] While tensions in the Balkans had been simmering for years, a diplomatic

---

[555] Liulevicius, "World War I: Destruction and Rebirth." Lecture 8. *The Great Courses: A History of Eastern Europe*, 2015.

[556] Jankowski, *Eastern Europe!*, 2015, pg. 330.

visit would bring the world into war and destruction.[557] In June 1914, the archduke of Austria, Franz Ferdinand, and his wife Sophie visited Sarajevo, Bosnia. As they drove through the streets in their vehicle, someone shot them dead.[558] Just four weeks later, all of Europe would be at war with each other.

Gavrilo Princip belonged to Young Bosnia, a political group that wanted to bring the South Slavs of the Balkan states together and create a coalition of states under independent rule. Ironically, this Serbian nationalist shot the archduke on the same day—June 28th—that the Serbians were defeated in 1389 at the Battle of Kosovo. Princip was one of several men who planned to execute Franz Ferdinand that day. When Princip caught up to Franz Ferdinand's car, he pointed and shot his gun, hitting both the archduke and his wife.

---

[557] Liulevicius, "World War I: Destruction and Rebirth." Lecture 8. *The Great Courses: A History of Eastern Europe*, 2015; Jankowski, Eastern Europe!, 2015, pg. 330.

[558] Liulevicius, "World War I: Destruction and Rebirth." Lecture 8. *The Great Courses: A History of Eastern Europe*, 2015., Jankowski, *Eastern Europe!*, 2015, pg. 330-331; Jenkins, *Short History of Europe*, 2019, pgs.237-238.

Archduke Franz Ferdinand, his wife Sophie, Duchess of Hohenberg, and their children, 1910. (Public Domain)

Gavrilo Princip was caught and arrested, and he stood trial for the murders. The court ruled he was too young for execution, so he was sentenced to twenty years in prison. He started his prison sentence while the war he helped to spark broke out across Europe.

The murder of the archduke and his wife created an international incident: the July Crisis of 1914. The Great Powers of Europe were interested in preserving peace, so they pressured Austria-Hungary to find a way to deal with the assassination with as little bloodshed as possible. Austria-Hungary blamed Serbia for knowing about the assassination and hiding it. However, the government was split on how to proceed: should Austria-Hungary go to war with Serbia, or should they find a diplomatic resolution?

Serbia's ally, Russia, jumped in the fray. Tsar Alexander II of Russia had been assassinated in 1881. This was not so long before the assassination of the Austrian archduke and his wife that Russians didn't remember it. Still, Russia wanted to retain the influence it had in Eastern Europe through its relationship with Serbia. Nicholas II of Russia promised to support Serbia in the event of war.

Since Austria-Hungary was facing a war against both Russia and Serbia, it called on its ally of Germany. Germany was concerned about how powerful Russia was becoming.

France had a peace alliance with Russia, which pitted it against its other ally, Germany. The French sided with the Russians, leaving Germany open to attack on both sides. Germany spent the 19th century beefing up its defenses, so it was one of the most militarized nations in the world. It had a plan of attack for a war on both sides; it was known as the Schlieffen Plan.[559] The idea behind this German military strategy was to attack France and eliminate it first. The French military was not as strong as the Russian military, so the Germans could crush the French relatively quickly. Once France pulled out of the war, then Germany could put all of its resources into defeating Russia.

The powers of Europe couldn't avoid the inevitable anymore. Austria-Hungary declared war on Serbia on July 28th, 1914—a month to the day after the assassination of Franz Ferdinand and his wife.[560] Russia followed suit, declaring war on Austria-Hungary.

---

[559] Jankowski, *Eastern Europe!*, 2015, pg. 330-331; Jenkins, *Short History of Europe*, 2019, pg.234.

[560] Jankowski, *Eastern Europe!*, 2015, pg. 331-332; Jenkins, *Short History of Europe*, 2019, pg.238.

Germany issued its declarations of war against Russia and France, and France declared war on Germany.

The war devolved into two sides, and every Eastern European country and territory was involved in some way.[561] Russia, Serbia, and their allies joined the Allied Powers, and Germany, the Ottoman Empire, Austria-Hungary, and their allies formed the Central Powers. This conflict would change the history of warfare. World War I would be the first major conflict to use new military technology on a large scale. There were new weapons like machine guns and artillery weapons, which led to a massive loss of life on all sides.

Europe split into two sides during the Great War: the Triple Alliance and the Triple Entente. This map shows how the war stretched across all of Europe. Soon, it would be a world war. (Credit: historicair/Fluteflute/Bibi Saint-Pol, 2009)

The Schlieffen Plan would commit Great Britain to the war.[562] Although Britain had its own alliances, it was appalled at Germany's first military movements. According to the Schlieffen

---

[561] Liulevicius, "World War I: Destruction and Rebirth." Lecture 8. *The Great Courses: A History of Eastern Europe*, 2015.; Jankowski, *Eastern Europe!*, 2015, pg. 331-332.

[562] Jankowski, *Eastern Europe!*, 2015, pg. 331-332; Jenkins, *Short History of Europe*, 2019, pg. 238.

Plan, Germany would move through Belgium to get to France. Days after the first declaration of war, on August 3rd, 1914, Germany invaded Belgium, and Great Britain declared war on Germany. The nations of Europe also pulled their colonies and protectorates into the fight, making the war a truly global conflict.

Germany's Schlieffen Plan didn't work. Instead of just facing French forces, Germany faced French, British, and Belgian armies as its forces moved from Belgium into France.[563] British and French soldiers stopped the German advance at the First Battle of the Marne, after which the Western Front reached a stalemate. Each side dug in—quite literally, as they fought battles from the safety of the trenches—with neither side making much progress. This unexpected development meant that Germany didn't knock France out of the war as quickly as it had planned. This allowed Russia to make valuable gains on the Eastern Front.

Despite the setbacks on the Western Front, Germany spent the first years of the war racking up victories on the Eastern Front. By August, Germany had delivered Russia a resounding defeat in the Baltic, and it occupied Russian-held Poland, Latvia, and Lithuania.[564] The Germans intended on Germanizing the Baltic and Slavic populations of these states. In combination with the territories they already had, it would make Germany the most powerful empire in Eastern Europe.

While the Germans kept Russia in check, Russia was not by any means losing the war. In September 1914, Russia tried to invade East Prussia, but the Germans pushed them back. While Russia

---

[563] Jankowski, *Eastern Europe!*, 2015, pg. 333-334; Jenkins, *Short History of Europe*, 2019, pg. 239-240.

[564] Liulevicius, "World War I: Destruction and Rebirth." Lecture 8. *The Great Courses: A History of Eastern Europe*, 2015.

suffered many defeats by the Germans, it still chipped away at the Austro-Hungarian and Ottoman defenses.[565]

Nationalism, which stoked the fire that created the mess of the Great War (another name for World War I), actually became an enemy.[566] Many people did not identify with the borders they lived in. For example, the Poles lived in Russian, Austrian, and German lands, but they still retained their identity as Poles. Jews lived everywhere, forming communities throughout Eastern Europe. Some soldiers took their enlistment seriously, serving with honor in the army they joined. Others were torn between their loyalties to themselves and the state, and they abandoned the fight.

The war brought people on every side to the brink of madness, starvation, and death. In 1915, a coalition of forces from Bulgaria, Austria, and the German Empire defeated the Serbians.[567] They escaped through the Albanian mountains in the dead of winter. The trip over the mountains was a disaster. Many Serbs died of exposure or violence from attacks by Albanians or Austrians. When the Serbian soldiers reached the Adriatic Sea, British and French ships picked them up and brought them to Greece. After they recovered, they returned to the fighting.

Austria-Hungary almost lost the war to the Russians in the Brusilov offensive, which lasted between June and September 1916.[568] This would become the most significant Allied offensive of World War I. The Allied forces would acquire more territory than

---

[565] Jankowski, *Eastern Europe!*, 2015, pg. 334-335; "The German Spring Offensive: The Kaiser's Battle." *Sir John Monash Centre. Australian National Memorial France.* Published March 5, 2018. https://sjmc.gov.au/german-spring-offensives-kaiserschlact-kaisers-battle/

[566] Liulevicius, "World War I: Destruction and Rebirth." Lecture 8. *The Great Courses: A History of Eastern Europe*, 2015.

[567] Liulevicius, "World War I: Destruction and Rebirth." Lecture 8. *The Great Courses: A History of Eastern Europe*, 2015.; Jankowski, *Eastern Europe!*, 2015, pg. 334-335, 346.

[568] Jankowski, *Eastern Europe!*, 2015, pg. 334-335, 383; "June 4, 1916: Brusilov Offensive Begins." HISTORY. Published October 28, 2009. https://www.history.com/this-day-in-history/brusilov-offensive-begins

at any other time during the war. Russia was the star of the offensive, knocking Austria-Hungary out of the war. However, these victories were overshadowed by the coming of revolution at home.

Between the end of 1916 and the beginning of 1917, Russian success on the battlefield declined. They were running out of men and resources. By February 1917, Russia was embroiled in a revolution, which pulled it out of the war effort.[569] Without Russia to stop them, the German army occupied Eastern Europe from the Baltic Sea to Ukraine.[570] With less pressure on the Eastern Front, Germany could focus on the stagnant Western Front.

It was around this time that the United States joined the Allies.[571] This would completely change the course of the war. Since the American soldiers hadn't been at war for years, they invigorated the Allied war effort. The first American soldiers started arriving in the early months of 1917, although it took some time to get the war effort up and running.[572] The Germans believed they could win the war if they took the Western Front before the United States could send all of its troops, and they launched the Spring offensive in 1918.[573]

Germany threw almost everything it had into the offensive. They deployed thousands of soldiers, along with thousands of pieces of weapons and artillery. But even with this massive undertaking, the German army still couldn't defeat the Allies. The German Spring offensive ended in July 1918. The Allies responded with an offensive of their own, knocking Germany out

---

[569] "The German Spring Offensive: The Kaiser's Battle." *Sir John Monash Centre.*

[570] Jankowski, *Eastern Europe!*, 2015, pg. 334-335; "The German Spring Offensive: The Kaiser's Battle." *Sir John Monash Centre.*

[571] Jankowski, *Eastern Europe!*, 2015, pg. 334-335; Jenkins, *Short History of Europe,* 2019, pg.242.

[572] "The German Spring Offensive: The Kaiser's Battle." *Sir John Monash Centre.*

[573] Jankowski, *Eastern Europe!*, 2015, pg. 334-335; "The German Spring Offensive: The Kaiser's Battle." *Sir John Monash Centre.*

of the war. In November 1918, the German Kaiser abdicated.[574] On November 11th, the armistice was signed, and the war ended.

Australian soldiers guard German prisoners of war, April 1918. (Public Domain)

While World War I destroyed Eastern Europe's landscape, it also brought considerable positive changes.[575] It tore apart the four empires—the German Empire, the Ottoman Empire, the Austro-Hungarian Empire, and the Russian Empire—and made room for new states.

The Russian Revolution

By 1917, Russia was losing the war. The war front and the home front suffered from poor morale and general dissatisfaction with the state. Tsar Nicholas II (r. 1894–1917) was an ineffectual leader who suffered many losses on the war front.

---

[574] Jenkins, *Short History of Europe*, 2019, pg.243; Jankowski, *Eastern Europe!*, 2015, pg. 334-335; "The German Spring Offensive: The Kaiser's Battle." *Sir John Monash Centre.*

[575] Liulevicius, "World War I: Destruction and Rebirth." Lecture 8. *The Great Courses: A History of Eastern Europe*, 2015.

The Russian failure on the battlefield reflected at home.[576] Russian citizens had no food or supplies, and they lived in poor living conditions. The people itched for more say in their government so that they could change the realities of their daily lives for the better.

In February 1917, a series of workers strikes in Petrograd turned into a rebellion. The February Revolution involved both blue-collar and white-collar workers protesting the state of the country, the state of the government, and the state of their day-to-day lives. As the protests continued, more joined in the revolution—even the soldiers sworn to protect the royal family.

An image of protestors in the February Revolution, 1917. (Public Domain)

Tsar Nicholas II abdicated from the throne in favor of a provisional government that would rule until order could be restored.[577] The leader of this provisional government, Alexander

[576] Liulevicius, "World War I: Destruction and Rebirth." Lecture 8. *The Great Courses: A History of Eastern Europe*, 2015.; Jenkins, *Short History of Europe*, 2019, pg. 241; Jankowski, *Eastern Europe!*, 2015, pg. 383.

[577] Liulevicius, "World War I: Destruction and Rebirth." Lecture 8. *The Great Courses: A History of Eastern Europe*, 2015.; Jenkins, *Short History of Europe*, 2019, pg. 242; Jankowski, *Eastern Europe!*, 2015, pg. 383-384.

Kerensky, appeased the populace by promising a switch from a monarchy to a democracy.

In November, Vladimir Lenin and his radical socialist party, the Bolsheviks, overthrew the provisional government and gained control of Russia. They established a communist state and took steps to secure their power over the country.

First, though, Russia needed to get out of the war. After negotiating with the Central Powers, Lenin signed the Treaty of Brest-Litovsk, agreeing to terms that were unfavorable to Russia.[578] Lenin didn't care, as he wanted to leave the war behind and reform the country.

The Push for Independent States

Another result of World War I is that the conflict broke down the borders of empires. Other nationalist movements couldn't grow under oppressive foreign rule, but they could when that state was taken away.

The Polish cry for independence and their own state gained traction. Poles appealed to the Western powers to get the job done. A Polish soldier named Józef Haller united Polish soldiers on both sides of the war under his command, and he brought them to the Western Front to help the Allies.[579] This gallant effort impressed the Western powers enough to support Poland in their quest for a nation of their own, which it would achieve at the end of World War I.[580]

---

[578] Jenkins, *Short History of Europe*, 2019, pg.243; Jankowski, *Eastern Europe!*, 2015, pg. 334-335, 384-385; "The German Spring Offensive: The Kaiser's Battle." *Sir John Monash Centre;* Liulevicius, "World War I: Destruction and Rebirth." Lecture 8. *The Great Courses: A History of Eastern Europe*, 2015.

[579] Liulevicius, "World War I: Destruction and Rebirth." Lecture 8. *The Great Courses: A History of Eastern Europe*, 2015.

[580] Jankowski, *Eastern Europe!*, 2015, pg. 390-392.

Surprisingly, the new state of Czechoslovakia wasn't formed in Eastern Europe at all.[581] It was the brainchild of Tomas Masaryk, a professor in Prague. Masaryk was of both Czech and Slovak descent, and he came up with the idea of a state. He traveled to the Allied powers for their opinions and support. In Philadelphia, a meeting of Americans of Czech and Slovak descent agreed on what the new state should be. In May 1918, an American document formed the state of Czechoslovakia. After the war was over, Masaryk became its first president.

The idea of a united Czech and Slovak state came from Tomas Masaryk, who served as Czechoslovakia's first president. (Public Domain)

[581] Liulevicius, "World War I: Destruction and Rebirth." Lecture 8. *The Great Courses: A History of Eastern Europe*, 2015.

Other new states grew from the chaos of the Great War.[582] Serbians and other Slavic groups agreed on a new state in July 1917 called Yugoslavia. There was finally a united Southern Slavic country. Unfortunately, it came too late for the Serbians. They would lose about 25 percent of their population during the war.

Latvia has another interesting origin story. The Latvians were split among the Germans and the Russians, just like the state they would soon call home. The Latvians who fought in the Russian army remained loyal, but the rest pushed for independence. Since the state was founded by soldiers, it was only fitting that they were the first members of the national army.

Plenty of new ideas came forth during this period that were on opposite ends of the spectrum, such as Vladimir Lenin's communist state and US President Woodrow Wilson's position on self-rule. In Eastern Europe, Wilson's goals were hard to realize. By November 1918, the guns went quiet, and the war was over.

The Interwar Years, 1918–1939

The reality of postwar Eastern Europe was very different from Western Europe.[583] Several things were happening; after all, new states meant new conflicts. The new countries that came out of the war needed to get their bearings. Also, in this interwar period, a series of dictators would rise, including the two most familiar ones: Joseph Stalin and Adolf Hitler.

---

[582] Liulevicius, "World War I: Destruction and Rebirth." Lecture 8. *The Great Courses: A History of Eastern Europe*, 2015.; Jankowski, *Eastern Europe!*, 2015, pg. 344, 347-348, 350.

[583] Liulevicius, "From Democrats to Dictators, 1918-1939." Lecture 9. *The Great Courses: A History of Eastern Europe*, 2015.

Known as the "Big Four," the leaders of Great Britain, Italy, France, and the United States controlled the Paris Peace Conference. Pictured are British Prime Minister David Lloyd George, Italian Prime Minister Vittorio Emanuele Orlando, French Prime Minister Georges Clemenceau of France, and US President Woodrow Wilson (left to right). May 1919. (Public Domain)

The Allies met for discussions and compromises that would define post-World War I life at the Paris Peace Conference of 1919.[584] The resulting Treaty of Versailles is made up of the agreements the Great Powers made.

New Countries and Borderland Disputes

It wasn't just the victors of World War I that showed up at the Paris Peace Conference.[585] The rulers of new countries also came, wanting the West's support for their new nations.

[584] Liulevicius, "World War I: Destruction and Rebirth." Lecture 8. *The Great Courses: A History of Eastern Europe*, 2015.; Jankowski, *Eastern Europe!*, 2015, pg. 334-335; Jenkins, *Short History of Europe*, 2019, pg. 243-245.

[585] Liulevicius, "From Democrats to Dictators, 1918–1939." Lecture 9. *The Great Courses: A History of Eastern Europe*, 2015.

First, though, the restructured region of Eastern Europe had to end the warfare. Even though the war ended on November 11th, 1918, there were still two more years of skirmishes and battles in Eastern Europe. Mostly, these fights were over borderlands and who would run the governments of these new states.

The Bolsheviks Centralize Power in Soviet Russia

Although Lenin was more focused on securing his power after the Russian Revolution than paying attention to what he was signing, he approved of the Treaty of Brest-Litovsk in 1918. When the war was over and the last of the Central Powers were defeated, Lenin and the Russian government threw out the treaty.

Now that they had a hold on the country, the Soviets spread out, invading new territories and trying to reclaim old ones. The Soviet Red Army invaded Germany, hoping to take control of the country while it was in the throes of rebellion. The Red Army also moved into newer states that were just getting started. They conquered Ukraine before moving on to Hungary. Hungary went along with the Russians temporarily; a Bolshevik activist, Bela Kun, established a communist government, which would soon fall.

Lenin was pleased with the results of the army's movements, even if the power was only temporary. He wanted to throw his weight around to show that his Red Army could be the most powerful force in Eastern Europe.

Lenin and the Red Army started to get a little full of themselves. In August 1920, they invaded Poland.[586] They knew they would win. When they arrived in Warsaw, the Red Army brought a ready-made package of supporters and a new head of government.

The Soviets chose the wrong country. Poland had just gotten its state back, and the people of Warsaw were fervent nationalists. The Soviets were so convinced that the Poles would welcome

---

[586] Ibid., pg.242.

them, but they were met with soldiers. The Polish army attacked the Red Army, pushing them back.

The Russians didn't give up and moved on to other countries.[587] Both Belarus and Ukraine were fervently nationalist, but they didn't stand a chance against the Red Army. The Soviets absorbed their territories into their dominion.

There was one country in Eastern Europe that didn't want independence: Austria.[588] The former dual monarchy Austria-Hungary had been divided up at the end of the world war.[589] Hungary lost most of its territory, and it was reduced down to a third of what it once was.[590] Hungary lost Transylvania to Romania, and it didn't know how to handle its independence. It had spent so long under Ottoman rule that the Hungarians didn't want to rule themselves. They tried to join with Germany, but the Great Powers put a stop to it, refusing to allow Germany or Hungary to reach for any more power.

Poland was on the opposite end of the spectrum from Hungary. It enjoyed its new borders a little *too* much. Poland wanted a larger state, and it earned many enemies in the process. They crossed into Lithuania, Germany, and Czechoslovakia, ruining their diplomatic relationships with them for a time.[591]

---

[587] Ibid.

[588] Liulevicius, "From Democrats to Dictators, 1918-1939." Lecture 9. *The Great Courses: A History of Eastern Europe*, 2015; Jankowski, *Eastern Europe!*, 2015, pg. 345-346.

[589] Jenkins, *Short History of Europe*, 2019, pg. 244

[590] Liulevicius, "From Democrats to Dictators, 1918-1939." Lecture 9. *The Great Courses: A History of Eastern Europe*, 2015.

[591] Jenkins, *Short History of Europe*, 2019, pg.244; Jankowski, *Eastern Europe!*, 2015, pg. 390-391

Eastern Europe also came into conflict with its Western neighbors.[592] When the Great Powers were carving out the new territories, they made the new Eastern European countries protect their minority populations. The new territories resented the interference, especially when the West didn't hold itself to the same standard. Conflicts in Eastern Europe were inevitable. However, if they kept fighting like they were, they wouldn't be able to prevent another war from happening.

Resettlement and Ethnic Cleansing

In the aftermath of the Great War, another smaller conflict broke out between Greece and Turkey. This little-known conflict is significant because it uprooted minority populations to create a more homogenous state. Almost half a million Macedonian Muslims arrived in Turkey, and over one million Greek Christians went to Greece. Bulgaria also had the same arrangement with Greece, so they also uprooted and resettled groups.

It is important to note that most of the people who were brought back to their "homeland" had never seen it before. Several ethnic groups were forced to move to places they had never been to or seen before. This process was not always peaceful. Ethnic cleansing was also used by some countries to force ethnicities to leave, especially if they resisted resettlement.

Dictatorships Take Over Eastern Europe

Most countries in postwar Eastern Europe were enthusiastic about their change in status. Self-determination had been something they could only dream about, and now, it was their reality. These new countries embraced social reforms, like improvements to the education system and land ownership, as well as other changes like a representative government. These

---

[592] Liulevicius, "From Democrats to Dictators, 1918-1939." Lecture 9. *The Great Courses: A History of Eastern Europe*, 2015.

democratic states were short-lived, as these new states were prone to dictatorships.

Less than ten years after the end of World War I, Poland became one of the first dictatorships in Eastern Europe. In 1926, Marshal Józef Piłsudski took control of the country, becoming Poland's first dictator.

Dictators toppled governments in other European countries. Sometimes they took strange paths. Karlis Ulmanis was a teacher in the United States before he came to power in Latvia. The Iron Guard Movement (a military fascist movement) gained traction in Romania, ending with the prime minister's assassination. Yugoslavia became a kingdom, and the king installed autocratic rule in 1929.

Albania also became a monarchy. Ahmed Zogu was from a powerful tribe in Albania. He joined the political scene before he led a coup in 1925. Three years later, he gave himself a new name: King Zog I. He was known for his repressive regime. He found allies in the Italian fascist government. However, it turns out they weren't really friends because the Italians led a coup in 1939 and ousted King Zog from power.

One state that didn't fall into the dictator trap was Czechoslovakia. The state adopted Western ideas and supported democracy.[593] That's not to say that there wasn't internal conflict.[594] The Slovaks felt like they were second-class citizens in the new country. Other members of minority populations weren't happy either.

---

[593] Jankowski, *Eastern Europe!*, 2015, pg. 344

[594] Liulevicius, "From Democrats to Dictators, 1918–1939." Lecture 9. *The Great Courses: A History of Eastern Europe*, 2015.

Joseph Stalin

In January 1924, Vladimir Lenin died.[595] His successor, Joseph Stalin, is known for his oppressive dictatorship and his brutal policies, specifically his attack on Russian farmers and the use of labor camps, which changed the face of Russia.[596]

When Stalin ascended to power, he was trying to reform society and move away from agricultural production.[597] He saw himself as a visionary that would bring the Soviet Union (the USSR) into the 20th century.

Stalin targeted wealthy farmers called kulaks. If he suspected that the kulaks were hiding food, not producing enough, or some other perceived crime against the state, Stalin had them deported to prison camps (*gulags*) in Siberia and Kazakhstan.[598] As he was dispatching farmers, Stalin still forced others to keep up with production, insisting that they double or even triple their output. Russian farmers acted out with small feats of resistance. They harvested their food slower or hid some rations.

---

[595] Liulevicius, "From Democrats to Dictators, 1918-1939." Lecture 9. *The Great Courses: A History of Eastern Europe*, 2015.; Jenkins, *Short History of Europe*, 2019, pg.250; Jankowski, *Eastern Europe!*, 2015, pg. 386-387.

[596] Jankowski, *Eastern Europe!*, 2015, pg. 387-388.

[597] Liulevicius, "From Democrats to Dictators, 1918-1939." Lecture 9. *The Great Courses: A History of Eastern Europe*, 2015.; Jenkins, *Short History of Europe*, 2019, pg.250; Jankowski, *Eastern Europe!*, 2015, pg. 388-389.

[598] Liulevicius, "From Democrats to Dictators, 1918-1939." Lecture 9. *The Great Courses: A History of Eastern Europe*, 2015; Jankowski, *Eastern Europe!*, 2015, pg. 388-389; Jenkins, *Short History of Europe*, 2019, pg. 255-256.

Prisoners at the Intalag gulag coal mine in northwestern Russia, ca. 1955. (Credit: Europeana, 2018)

Stalin's regime is closely associated with the Terror Famine or *Holodomor.* To terrify the population, Stalin sent the army through the countryside to steal grain and other food items. Even if the farmers had already given their rations to the state, their supplies were still taken. Stalin ordered the army to close down any farms where they found hidden food or if the farmers resisted. The regime even hired people to scour the countryside to look for people who were hiding food from the state.

As a result of the Terror Famine, millions died of starvation and disease. Many resorted to cannibalism to stay alive. Unsurprisingly, the Soviets denied their role in the Terror Famine for decades. They hid what they were doing from the press, and they engaged in acts of repression and terror to keep it from getting out.

Known as the "Red Train," government officials would arrive to take all of the first harvests for the state. 1932. (Public Domain)

Joseph Stalin also adopted the Russification techniques of his ancestors. When he came to power, he promised to protect the various nationalities in Soviet lands. Honestly, he didn't think it would matter once the people were working again. They would have a common goal to work toward, and their ethnicity would be the last thing they were thinking about.

Still, he followed through. He created departments to work in ethnic groups' interests. However, as he centralized his control over the government, he eliminated the differences between the people. Stalin arrested minorities, like Poles and Germans, who he thought were working against the state. To get rid of them, he deported them to the hinterland deep inside Russian borders.

Adolf Hitler

While several conditions aligned to bring Europe into the Great War, this was not the case for World War II. Every reason for the outbreak of World War II goes back to one person: Adolf

Hitler.[599] Hitler usurped power in Germany in 1933, and he was upset at the Treaty of Versailles's punitive conditions against Germany.[600] He believed that Germany deserved to be one of the Great Powers of Europe and that the other powers didn't take Germany seriously. Hitler went against the Treaty of Versailles and built up Germany's defenses.

Another point of contention for Nazi Germany was the fate of Eastern Europe. Even though Germany lost the Great War, they technically were victorious in Eastern Europe. The Germans wanted to keep the lands they had acquired in Eastern Europe, but the postwar treaties forced Germany to release them. It even had to let go of some lands that were German before World War I even started.

Since Hitler believed that parts of Eastern Europe were German by right, he just took them.[601] His plans centered around Eastern Europe; his strategy included adding Czechoslovakia, Belarus, the Baltic region, Poland, Ukraine, and the western lands of Russia to the Third Reich.[602] Hitler's goal was to take as much land as possible for the German "master race" to live in and reproduce.[603]

---

[599] Jankowski, *Eastern Europe!*, 2015, pg. 412.

[600] Liulevicius, "Caught between Hitler and Stalin." Lecture 10. *The Great Courses: A History of Eastern Europe*, 2015; Jankowski, *Eastern Europe!*, 2015, pg. 335-336, 412; Jenkins, *Short History of Europe*, 2019, pg.245.

[601] Liulevicius, "Caught between Hitler and Stalin." Lecture 10. *The Great Courses: A History of Eastern Europe*, 2015; Liulevicius, "World War II: The Unfamiliar Eastern Front." Lecture 11. *The Great Courses: A History of Eastern Europe*, 2015; Jenkins, *Short History of Europe*, 2019, pg.253-254.

[602] Liulevicius, "Caught between Hitler and Stalin." Lecture 10. *The Great Courses: A History of Eastern Europe*, 2015; Liulevicius, "World War II: The Unfamiliar Eastern Front." Lecture 11. *The Great Courses: A History of Eastern Europe*, 2015; Jankowski, *Eastern Europe!*, 2015, pg. 412.

[603] Liulevicius, "World War II: The Unfamiliar Eastern Front." Lecture 11. *The Great Courses: A History of Eastern Europe*, 2015; Jenkins, *Short History of Europe*, 2019, pg.253-254.

The other powers of Europe thought Hitler would just go away if they gave him what he wanted.[604] This appeasement policy only went so far, though, as Hitler was not the type to go away quietly.

First, Hitler targeted Czechoslovakia.[605] The Sudetes mountain range helped defend the country against attackers, and Hitler wanted access to it. He granted citizenship to Germans living in the mountain ranges (the Sudetens), and he demanded that Czechoslovakia hand it over. Naturally, the new country refused.

On September 29th, 1938, the Munich Conference attempted to quiet the tensions brewing in Eastern Europe.[606] In attendance were representatives from England, France, Germany, and Italy. All the representatives agreed that Czechoslovakia should give the Sudetenland to Germany. Unsurprisingly, the country most affected didn't have any representatives at the meeting.

British Prime Minister Neville Chamberlain thought that capitulation would have satisfied Hitler, but he was wrong. It got so much worse.

Hitler didn't just take the Sudetenland; he took the whole country, breaking the Munich Agreement of 1938.[607] He invaded Czechoslovakia in March 1939, occupying the regions of Moravia and Bohemia. He then set about Germanizing the population. After his successful takeover of Czechoslovakia, Hitler moved on

---

[604] Liulevicius, "Caught between Hitler and Stalin." Lecture 10. *The Great Courses: A History of Eastern Europe*, 2015; Jankowski, *Eastern Europe!*, 2015, pg. 424.

[605] Jankowski, *Eastern Europe!*, 2015, pg. 412-413; Liulevicius, "Caught between Hitler and Stalin." Lecture 10. *The Great Courses: A History of Eastern Europe*, 2015; Jenkins, *Short History of Europe*, 2019, pg. 256.

[606] Jankowski, *Eastern Europe!*, 2015, pg. 413; Liulevicius, "Caught between Hitler and Stalin." Lecture 10. *The Great Courses: A History of Eastern Europe*, 2015; https://www.britannica.com/event/Munich-Agreement; Jenkins, *Short History of Europe*, 2019, pg. 256.

[607] Jankowski, *Eastern Europe!*, 2015, pg. 413; Liulevicius, "Caught between Hitler and Stalin." Lecture 10. *The Great Courses: A History of Eastern Europe*, 2015; https://www.britannica.com/event/Munich-Agreement

to taking Klaipeda, a port city in Lithuania. The Lithuanians gave Hitler what he wanted.

After seeing what Hitler was doing, the nations of Europe stopped appeasing him.[608] He soon approached Poland, eyeing their port city of Danzig.[609] Poland had powerful allies in England and France, so they told Hitler no. He didn't take it well.

1939: Hitler, Stalin, and the Nazi-Soviet Nonaggression Pact

When Adolf Hitler and Joseph Stalin signed the Nazi-Soviet Nonaggression Pact on August 23rd, 1939, all of Eastern Europe waited to see what would happen.[610] The two men were as different as could be. They tormented each other publicly, and they could never agree on anything. Yet, the pact they signed would alter the face of Eastern Europe forever.

Hitler sent his foreign minister to Moscow to represent his interests. At the Kremlin, German Foreign Minister Joachim von Ribbentrop, Soviet Foreign Minister Vyacheslav Molotov, and Joseph Stalin went over the treaty, and Stalin watched as the foreign ministers signed it. With the signing of this contract, Hitler and Stalin became totalitarianism personified. This type of government structure demands enthusiastic devotion and service to the state.

[608] Jankowski, *Eastern Europe!*, 2015, pg. 413; Liulevicius, "Caught between Hitler and Stalin." Lecture 10. *The Great Courses: A History of Eastern Europe*, 2015; https://www.britannica.com/event/Munich-Agreement; Jenkins, *Short History of Europe*, 2019, pg. 257.

[609] Liulevicius, "Caught between Hitler and Stalin." Lecture 10. *The Great Courses: A History of Eastern Europe*, 2015.

[610] Liulevicius, "Caught between Hitler and Stalin." Lecture 10. *The Great Courses: A History of Eastern Europe*, 2015; Jenkins, *Short History of Europe*, 2019, pg. 257; Jankowski, *Eastern Europe!*, 2015, pg. 381, 390, 424.

The nonaggression pact covertly stated that Hitler and Stalin laid claim to parts of Eastern Europe and that each would have their own zone of influence.[611] The men divided Poland in half, with Hitler taking the west and Stalin taking the east.[612] Stalin also claimed the Baltic states of Latvia, Estonia, and Finland, while Hitler would get Lithuania.[613]

When the treaty was made public knowledge, Hitler and Stalin weren't kidding anyone. Everyone knew that there was some secret mission behind it. They had plans for Eastern Europe. Hitler and Stalin would stick to their zones, getting rid of all the Slavs and Jews that lived there so that their own nationalities could live there.

The Nazis and the Soviets Terrorize Eastern Europe

During World War I, many German soldiers refused to admit that the war was over, and they believed Germany had won.[614] These soldiers were the *Freikorps*, who were known for their violent bloodlust. They occupied the Baltic states, but the new Baltic states of Latvia, Estonia, and Lithuania defeated the Freikorps. The soldiers retreated back to Germany, and soon enough, they would find another home for their delusions: the Nazi Party.

Since Hitler had come to power, he had progressively pushed the limit on how long his neighbors would tolerate him.[615] He targeted Eastern Europe, agreeing to split control of the region with Stalin. Hitler had engaged with Poland before he signed the

[611] Jankowski, *Eastern Europe!*, 2015, pg. 381; Liulevicius, "Caught between Hitler and Stalin." Lecture 10. *The Great Courses: A History of Eastern Europe*, 2015.

[612] Jenkins, *Short History of Europe*, 2019, pg. 257.

[613] Ibid.

[614] Liulevicius, "From Democrats to Dictators, 1918-1939." Lecture 9. *The Great Courses: A History of Eastern Europe*, 2015.

[615] Liulevicius, "From Democrats to Dictators, 1918-1939." Lecture 9. *The Great Courses: A History of Eastern Europe*, 2015.

nonaggression pact. He wanted to formalize his alliance with the Soviet Union before he made any moves that would make the Soviets back out of the agreement. The pact was signed on August 23rd, 1939. Nine days later, on September 1st, 1939, Adolf Hitler invaded Poland.[616]

Hitler picked a fight with the Polish, using a flimsy excuse to invade the country. Poland wasn't prepared for the onslaught of Nazi weapons and military discipline. England and France had had enough of Hitler's antics, so they declared war on Germany. The Polish desperately tried to defend themselves, but the Red Army showed up too.

The rest of the invasion started to look like a conqueror had arrived. Hitler ordered a slaughter to break the Polish spirit.[617] The Nazis formed execution squads, the *Einsatzgruppen*, which unleashed terror on the country. The *Einsatzgruppen* moved from town to town, executing anyone who wasn't an ethnic German. Within three months of the invasion, almost sixty thousand Poles were dead.

The Nazis split up the Polish territories, occupying half of the country. (Hitler annexed the other half.) In Nazi-occupied Poland, the soldiers deported Poles and Jews so that there would be space for imported Germans to live. Some Jews tried to escape the Nazis by fleeing to the Soviet side of the country. Because of the nonaggression pact, they were turned away or brought back into the German side of the country.

The Soviets combined their part of Poland with their holdings in modern-day Belarus and Ukraine. They firmly established their own rule, deporting anyone who could be an enemy. Anyone who

---

[616] Jankowski, *Eastern Europe!*, 2015, pg. 413; Jenkins, *Short History of Europe*, 2019, pg. 258.

[617] Liulevicius, "World War II: The Unfamiliar Eastern Front." Lecture 11. *The Great Courses: A History of Eastern Europe*, 2015; Jenkins, *Short History of Europe*, 2019, pg. 253.

whispered a word against the Soviet regime or occupation was sent to prison camps in Siberia. The Soviets quickly dispatched their Polish prisoners of war to Russia, where they were murdered.

Both Stalin and Hitler were ecstatic about the fall of Poland, and they started to reorganize Eastern Europe according to the terms of the nonaggression pact. Stalin sent Germans living in his territories back to Germany. By December 1939, Hitler and Stalin also arranged for the deportation of the Germans living in the Baltic states, which destroyed communities that were centuries old.

Meanwhile, the Soviets moved into the lands assigned to them in the nonaggression pact. They incorporated parts of Romania into their Soviet satellite states. The Soviets also invaded the Baltic states. While Stalin was there, he forced all three states to allow him to build bases for the Red Army in their territories. In exchange, he would protect them. Latvia, Lithuania, and Estonia knew that Stalin wouldn't take no for an answer.

The first resistance that Stalin and the Red Army met was in Finland. The people of Finland protested against Soviet control and occupation, and the two nations went to war. The Finns pushed the Red Army out during the Winter War, but they were not completely successful. In March 1940, Stalin accepted Finland's surrender, but he did not occupy the country.

In the Baltic states, however, Stalin executed a hostile takeover. He appointed puppet governments and banned any non-communist activity. He eliminated the high command of the armies, installing Soviets in their place. The Soviets also held rigged elections to make sure their candidates were elected to positions in the government. The people of Poland were coerced into voting; if they didn't, they were accused of being an enemy of the state. Even with rigged elections, the Soviets still lied about the results. Once Soviet agents were in charge of the government, they joined the Soviet Union.

Communist agents completely took over Baltic society. They made their own curriculum in schools, took possession of businesses, and controlled the press. The Soviets targeted anyone who didn't completely support their rule, and they deported thousands of dissidents from the Baltic states.

The Eastern Front of World War II

A little over twenty years after World War I ended, Europe was at war again. The Eastern Front in this war would look much different than the Great War. The totalitarian governments changed what war looked like. It set the stage for a gruesome war, one that destroyed the people and the landscape of Eastern Europe. Years of expansion and terror couldn't have prepared the countries of Eastern Europe for what was coming.

At War with the German Reich

In September 1939, Adolf Hitler invaded Poland, exacting a bloody, brutal occupation. [618] Two days after the invasion of Poland, Great Britain and France were at war with Germany. [619] The Nazi invasion destroyed the Polish state, but the Poles played a vital role in the war effort. [620] Polish soldiers and pilots joined the British army and participated in key victories. Polish scientists also discovered how to decipher the German Enigma—a code that was supposed to be unbreakable. They gave the code to the British, who used it to sabotage German movements.

Hitler's bid for Poland was successful, and it helped him acquire more territory. In 1940, he moved into Western Europe, conquering France, Norway, Denmark, Belgium, and the

---

[618] Liulevicius, "World War II: The Unfamiliar Eastern Front." Lecture 11. *The Great Courses: A History of Eastern Europe*, 2015; Jankowski, *Eastern Europe!*, 2015, pg. 413.

[619] Jankowski, *Eastern Europe!*, 2015, pg. 413; Jenkins, *Short History of Europe*, 2019, pg. 258.

[620] Liulevicius, "World War II: The Unfamiliar Eastern Front." Lecture 11. *The Great Courses: A History of Eastern Europe*, 2015.

Netherlands.[621] When Hitler signed the Nazi-Soviet Nonaggression Pact with Stalin, he had no plans to see it through to the end of the war. Once Hitler amassed the lands he wanted, he planned to back out of his agreement with the USSR. The alliance was a means to an end, and the pact was outliving its usefulness.

Hitler in the Balkans

As Adolf Hitler was contemplating how to publicly break ranks with Joseph Stalin, he was delayed by events in the Balkans.[622] By the end of 1940, Italy, which was a part of the Axis powers, had moved into the Balkans for their own land grab.[623] In early 1941, Yugoslavia broke its alliance with Nazi Germany.[624] The original government had capitulated to the Axis powers. Revolutionaries led a coup d'état, and the new government was opposed to joining the Axis. The Führer reacted in the typical "Hitler" way: he invaded the Balkans.[625] In April 1941, Hitler took Yugoslavia and Greece, splitting Yugoslavia among Bulgaria, Hungary, and Italy.[626]

Hitler used his successes in Eastern Europe to convince other powers to join Germany in its Axis alliance. Wanting to keep Hungary in the fold, Hitler annexed the territories of Czechoslovakia with Hungarian residents to Hungary. The regent of Hungary, Admiral Miklos Horthy, thought working with Hitler was a good idea.

---

[621] Jankowski, *Eastern Europe!*, 2015, pg. 413.

[622] Jankowski, *Eastern Europe!*, 2015, pg. 413-414.

[623] Liulevicius, "World War II: The Unfamiliar Eastern Front." Lecture 11. *The Great Courses: A History of Eastern Europe*, 2015.

[624] Jankowski, *Eastern Europe!*, 2015, pg. 413-414; "Yugoslavia." *World War II Database.* https://ww2db.com/country/Yugoslavia

[625] Jankowski, *Eastern Europe!*, 2015, pg. 413-414, 435-436; "Yugoslavia." *World War II Database.*

[626] Liulevicius, "World War II: The Unfamiliar Eastern Front." Lecture 11. *The Great Courses: A History of Eastern Europe*, 2015; Jankowski, *Eastern Europe!*, 2015, pg. 413-414; "Yugoslavia." *World War II Database.*

The German Reich at its greatest extent, 1942. The lands held and administered by Germany are labeled in blue. (Credit: Goran tek-en, 2015)

In an attempt to gain allies, Hitler forced Romania to grant northern Transylvania to Hungary. He played against the Soviets, promising Romania more land when the Soviets were defeated. After getting Romania and Hungary on his side, Hitler used his German connections to manipulate Bulgaria. Meanwhile, plans moved forward for Operation Barbarossa—the invasion of the Soviet Union.[627] Hitler built himself a command center in Poland so that he could supervise the military movements of the Eastern Front.[628]

---

[627] Jenkins, *Short History of Europe*, 2019, pg. 262.

[628] Liulevicius, "World War II: The Unfamiliar Eastern Front." Lecture 11. *The Great Courses: A History of Eastern Europe*, 2015

Soviet Successes: The Battle for Moscow and the Siege of Stalingrad

In June 1941, he was ready to invade the Soviet Union.[629] On June 22nd, 1941, German, Italian, Finnish, Hungarian, Slovakian, and Romanian troops invaded the Soviet Union. This would be the largest land invasion ever seen.

Stalin couldn't believe Hitler had broken their nonaggression pact, even though he had been warned about it beforehand. Shocked by the behavior of who they considered an ally, the Soviet forces stumbled through the first armed engagements.

The Soviet satellite states couldn't have been happier, and they welcomed the Germans when they arrived. Of course, they didn't know about the Commissar Order. On June 6th, 1941, before Hitler invaded the Soviet Union, Hitler's high command issued an order that instructed the army to kill any supporter or promoter of Bolshevism. In other words, it was a blanket order to kill any Soviet they could find.

The Soviets quickly regrouped. On September 8th, 1941, the German army sieged the city of Leningrad (modern-day St. Petersburg). However, the Germans did not find an easy success, as they sieged the city for almost three years. As the siege of Leningrad commenced, Hitler's forces also attacked Moscow and invaded Crimea. Soviet forces successfully defended Moscow from October 1941 to January 1942.

Hitler was confident despite the setbacks, but the German troops in Russia couldn't advance. They suffered through the hellish winter of 1941, for which they were unprepared. December 1941 also saw the United States enter World War II, and American troops joined Allied forces in pushing the Nazis out of Western Europe. However, Hitler was still able to advance on the

---

[629] Liulevicius, "World War II: The Unfamiliar Eastern Front." Lecture 11. *The Great Courses: A History of Eastern Europe*, 2015; Jankowski, *Eastern Europe!*, 2015, pg. 413-414; Jenkins, *Short History of Europe*, 2019, pg. 262-264.

Eastern front. In 1942, the Germans moved toward Stalingrad, traveling up the Volga River toward modern-day Volgograd.[630] The Siege of Stalingrad was also a long, drawn-out affair, becoming one of the bloodiest conflicts of the war.[631] During the eight-month-long campaign, over two million died, including 800,000 civilians from warfare and starvation.

The Red Army ended the siege of Stalingrad in February 1943, taking the fight to the Eastern Front. The Soviets captured tens of thousands of Nazi soldiers at Stalingrad, which was a huge blow to the German cause. This was the point of no return; the Nazis were losing the war. In 1943, the USSR began its western advance, encroaching on Germany. The Soviets pushed the Germans back farther west, moving the Eastern Front closer to Europe.

---

[630] Liulevicius, "World War II: The Unfamiliar Eastern Front." Lecture 11. *The Great Courses: A History of Eastern Europe*, 2015; Jankowski, *Eastern Europe!*, 2015, pg. 413-414; Jenkins, *Short History of Europe*, 2019, pg. 262-264, 265.

[631] Liulevicius, "World War II: The Unfamiliar Eastern Front." Lecture 11. *The Great Courses: A History of Eastern Europe*, 2015; Jankowski, *Eastern Europe!*, 2015, pg. 413-414; "The Siege of Leningrad." HISTORY. https://www.history.com/news/the-siege-of-leningrad

A photograph from the Battle of Stalingrad, October 1942. (Credit: photographer Bauer-Altvater, German Federal Archive)

The following year delivered two final blows to Nazi Germany. The British and American campaign at D-Day freed most of France and Belgium from Nazi control.[632] The same year, the USSR invaded Eastern Europe. The Soviets completed multiple advances to liberate Poland, Czechoslovakia, Romania, Hungary, and Bulgaria from Nazi control.

---

[632] Jankowski, *Eastern Europe!*, 2015, pg. 414; Jenkins, *Short History of Europe*, 2019, pg. 267.

The Allies invaded Nazi Germany from both sides in 1945, taking all Nazi territory except for Berlin by April. Trapped in a bunker, Hitler committed suicide before he could be taken by the enemy. Before he killed himself, he put Admiral Karl Dönitz in command. Dönitz surrendered to the Allied forces in May 1945.

The Human Cost of World War II

The Germans used the lands they invaded for their resources, importing food and supplies from them.[633] This wasn't the only way the Nazi regime would forever alter the landscape; Hitler used extermination as a war tactic, killing millions in Eastern Europe.[634] Towards the end of the war, as their enemies closed in, the Nazis got desperate, exacting cleansing campaigns across the territories they occupied.[635]

As part of Hitler's war of extermination, almost no one was safe from his wrath.[636] The Germans deported millions of Eastern Europeans as prisoners of war and slave labor. It is estimated that six million Soviets were taken as prisoners of war, and about one-half starved to death in prisoner camps. Hitler also designed the Hunger Plan to cut off supplies and starve the populations of Eastern Europe to death. The only demographic that was safe were ethnic Germans. Everyone else had to go. In the lands he had conquered, Hitler had already started the process of ethnic cleansing. The assassination of Reinhard Heydrich, one of Hitler's

---

[633] Liulevicius, "World War II: The Unfamiliar Eastern Front." Lecture 11. *The Great Courses: A History of Eastern Europe*, 2015.

[634] Liulevicius, "World War II: The Unfamiliar Eastern Front." Lecture 11. *The Great Courses: A History of Eastern Europe*, 2015; Jankowski, *Eastern Europe!*, 2015, pg. 412, 450-451.

[635] Liulevicius, "World War II: The Unfamiliar Eastern Front." Lecture 11. *The Great Courses: A History of Eastern Europe*, 2015; Jankowski, *Eastern Europe!*, 2015, pg. 413-414.

[636] Liulevicius, "World War II: The Unfamiliar Eastern Front." Lecture 11. *The Great Courses: A History of Eastern Europe*, 2015; Jankowski, *Eastern Europe!*, 2015, pg. 412.

high-ranking officers in the SS—and the man who planned the mass murders of the Holocaust—was as good a reason as any.

A photograph of a Soviet soldier wearing the Star of David. He was a Nazi prisoner of war. August 1941. (Credit: German Federal Archive)

Two Czech soldiers, Josef Gabcik and Jan Kubis, bombed Heydrich's vehicle on May 27th, 1942, mortally wounding him.[637] Two days later, Joseph Goebbels, the Minister of Propaganda, openly condemned Jews for the assassination attempt. He ordered

[637] "Reinhard Heydrich." Jewish Virtual Library.
https://www.jewishvirtuallibrary.org/reinhard-heydrich-bio

the arrest of hundreds of Jews in Berlin and threatened to execute them for any further attacks on German officials. German soldiers moved through Czech lands, executing anyone they suspected was involved with the attack. The village of Lidice, right outside of Prague, was completely annihilated. German soldiers burned the villages to the ground, murdering the men and boys. The women and children were sent to concentration camps.

Soldiers lead Polish women into the forest for execution, 1940. (Public Domain)

The Nazi campaign hit Poland the worst. Six million Polish died, including three million Jews. The Polish also built the most significant resistance. They drew on their experiences after the partition to secretly organize a resistance. By 1942, there were 300,000 supporters for the end of the Nazi occupation.

The Jewish Experience

If there was one demographic that suffered the most under the oppressive totalitarian governments, it was the Jews.[638] They had lived in relative peace in Eastern Europe for hundreds of years,

---

[638] Jankowski, *Eastern Europe!*, 2015, pg. 450-456.

and now, they were treated like they were the enemy.[639] Eastern Europe has a long history of anti-Semitism, but its most disastrous hour was the Holocaust.

The Shtetl Communities of Eastern Europe

Since the 17th century, Jews had made their home in Eastern Europe. They especially found a welcoming environment in Poland-Lithuania. The Polish-Lithuanian Commonwealth was more religiously tolerant, and it welcomed Jews who wanted to settle. Every Eastern European nation had Jewish communities, though.

The Jewish communities, from territory to territory, were incredibly rich and multifaceted, each with its own traditions. Jews organized into shtetls, which were small communities of Jewish inhabitants. About four-fifths of the Jews of Eastern Europe lived in small communities like this. Shtetls were self-sufficient, and the people made their living through handicrafts or through trade contacts. They also worked as merchants and business owners.

A painting of a Jewish wedding in a shtetl. Artist: Isaak Asknaziy, 1893.
(Public Domain)

---

[639] Liulevicius, "Jewish Life in the Shtetl." Lecture 7. *The Great Courses: A History of Eastern Europe*, 2015.

When Russia took over its part of Poland after the partition, it was supposed to protect these communities. Instead, they passed anti-Semitic laws that restricted the movements of Jewish communities. Catherine the Great's 1791 Pale of Settlement had banned Jews from moving into the interior of the Russian Empire. And that was just the beginning of multiple Russian laws that restricted Jewish life and movements. The shtetls started to suffer from these restrictions.

The Pogroms

The height of shtetl life stretched over the first half of the 19th century. They started to decline after 1840 because of Russian repression. Russian anti-Semitism reached an all-time high in the 1880s, as Jews were blamed for Alexander II's assassination. Pogroms tore across the Russian landscape, attacking Jewish communities.[640] The government didn't exactly order these pogroms, but they didn't stop them.

The pogroms continued until the 20th century. In 1903, a newspaper published a story that a Christian child had been murdered. The populace immediately blamed the Jews, and violence swept across Ottoman-held Moldova. Hundreds of Jews were assaulted, and thousands of homes and businesses were attacked. The Kishinev pogrom of 1903 ended with the attackers getting a smack on the wrist—evidence of the reality Jews faced under Russian rule. Just two years later, the Russian Revolution of 1905 also brought more pogroms across the empire.

The Holocaust

After the pogroms of the late 19th and early 20th centuries, Jews found two ways to process their realities. They spread the notion of Zionism, a movement that worked toward the Jews having their own country. Most Jews also immigrated to new places. Some went

---

[640] Jankowski, *Eastern Europe!*, 2015, pg. 314.

to Palestine as part of the Zionist movement, while others left for places like the United States, England, France, and Canada.

In January 1942, the Nazi high command met at the Wannsee Conference to plan the Final Solution, the plan to murder all of the Jews left in Europe.[641] Although there were over a thousand concentration camps, there were six main extermination camps in Eastern Europe. Two of them—Auschwitz and Majdanek—were concentration camps with gas chambers on site. The other four—Belzec, Chelmno, Sobibor, and Treblinka—were used purely for killing. The Holocaust took place in Eastern Europe, where around six million Jews were killed. While Jews made up most of the targets for extermination, the Germans also killed the Roma, enemies of the state, and the mentally and physically disabled, as well as other minority groups.

---

[641] Jankowski, *Eastern Europe!*, 2015, pg. 451-452; Liulevicius, "The Holocaust and the Nazi Racial Empire." Lecture 12. *The Great Courses: A History of Eastern Europe*, 2015; Jenkins, *Short History of Europe*, 2019, pg. 264.

An illustrated map noting the locations of the six extermination camps in Poland. (Credit: Poeticbent, 2013)

The Final Solution fed into the Nazi ideology of worshiping the Aryan race. Jews were the enemy, and a perfect world without Jews was what the Aryan race needed in order to thrive. The Germans received their first experiences in systematic murder in Germany, as doctors experimented on the physically disabled. What they learned—how to kill quickly and efficiently—would help shape the Final Solution.

The Nazis used the *Einsatzgruppen* during their campaigns to eliminate the Jewish population. In 1939, the *Einsatzgruppen* followed the German army into Poland. Poland had the largest population of Jews, so some were rounded up and deported. When they were shipped to concentration camps, Germans confiscated their money, valuables, and property. Jews were also sent to ghettos, which were cramped living spaces with poor sanitation and ventilation.

The *Einsatzgruppen* also followed the German invasion of the Soviet Union in June 1941. There, they were instructed to kill Jews or anyone they considered an enemy. Those people could be communists, Roma, or the physically or mentally disabled. The *Einsatzgruppen* was famous for hiring people from the local population to help them murder Jews.[642] They also used Soviet prisoners of war.

Hitler's allies either deported Jews themselves or had their own persecution policies. Hitler's hatred of the Jewish population made itself known in his dealings with Hungary.[643] At first, Hungary was a Nazi ally. The Hungarian government believed that Hitler's strong-arm methods could help them recover their pre-World War I territories. In September 1938, Hitler returned the part of Czechoslovakia that was formerly part of Hungary. Two years later, he granted Hungary possession of Transylvania. In March 1941, Hungary and Nazi Germany invaded Yugoslavia and divided the lands among themselves. Hungary's extended territories included a significant Jewish population; many were only ethnic Jews who had converted to Christianity, some for generations. However, it mattered little to Hitler.

The Hungarian government was like-minded with Hitler in his Jewish policies. Hungary had been passing anti-Semitic laws since the late 1930s. Jews were forced into labor and banned from public and economic life. These laws restricted the movements and

---

[642] Jankowski, *Eastern Europe!*, 2015, pg. 450-451; Liulevicius, "The Holocaust and the Nazi Racial Empire." Lecture 12. *The Great Courses: A History of Eastern Europe*, 2015.

[643] "Historical Background: The Jews of Hungary During the Holocaust." Yad Vashem: The World Holocaust Remembrance Center. https://www.yadvashem.org/articles/general/jews-of-hungary-during-the-holocaust.html

activities of Jews, but violent reprisals against Jewish communities didn't begin until the 1940s when Hungary was deep in its alliance with the Nazis. Hungarian Jews were exiled to other lands, where they were assassinated, and Hungarian soldiers slaughtered Jews as enemies to the war effort.

Hungarian Jews, who had recently arrived at Auschwitz-Birkenau, are selected for labor or extermination, May/June 1944. (Public Domain)

As the Nazis started losing the war, Hungary tried to backtrack its alliance with Hitler.[644] Through their alliance, Hungarian soldiers were among the tens of thousands of casualties during the later phase of the war. Hungary's head of state, Miklos Horthy, purposely disobeyed Hitler's orders. When Hitler pressed his ally to eliminate hundreds of thousands of Jews in Hungarian lands, Horthy refused. Hitler's army invaded Hungary in March 1944 to force Horthy to remain committed to their alliance. When he gained control of the country, Hitler replaced Horthy with someone easier to control, and he deported the Jewish population to extermination camps. About half a million of the six million Jews who died during the Holocaust were Hungarian.

---

[644] Jankowski, *Eastern Europe!*, 2015, pg. 414.

The Resistance

Populations targeted by the Germans engaged in inspiring acts of resistance, especially after Germany started losing to the Soviets.[645] Perhaps the most famous example was the Warsaw ghetto uprising of 1943. On April 19th, 1943, residents of the Jewish ghetto in Warsaw, Poland, used guerilla tactics to attack the German soldiers before hiding.[646] The Germans thought they could crush the rebellion in a matter of days. It took them over a month. The Germans tried to flush out the resistance by cutting off the utilities to the buildings. When that didn't work, they burned the ghetto down.

Many Gentiles helped Jews resist or hide from the Germans.[647] Those who did risked their lives. If the Germans found anyone hiding a Jewish family, they would kill everyone. Sometimes, the easiest thing to do was run away. Many Jews who were able fled for the woods. About twenty thousand Jews lived in communities that hid in forested areas throughout the war.

---

[645] Liulevicius, "World War II: The Unfamiliar Eastern Front." Lecture 11. *The Great Courses: A History of Eastern Europe*, 2015; Jankowski, *Eastern Europe!*, 2015, pg. 413-414, 454.

[646] "Warsaw Ghetto Uprising." HISTORY. Published November 6, 2009. https://www.history.com/topics/world-war-ii/warsaw-ghetto-uprising

[647] Liulevicius, "World War II: The Unfamiliar Eastern Front." Lecture 11. *The Great Courses: A History of Eastern Europe*, 2015; Jankowski, *Eastern Europe!*, 2015, pg. 454-455.

Chapter 10 – The Postwar Years, the Fall of Communism, and the Post-Communist World

After World War II ended in 1945, Eastern Europe surveyed the devastation, questioning where it would go from here.[648] The Allied Powers questioned how Europe would be restructured after the fall of Nazi Germany. The United States, Great Britain, and the Soviet Union came to terms with how postwar Europe would look. The map was completely reimagined, with the United States and the Soviet Union claiming their own areas of influence.

---

[648] Liulevicius, "Postwar Flight and Expulsion." Lecture 13. *The Great Courses: A History of Eastern Europe*, 2015.

Finding New Countries, Finding New Homes

The shifting borders of Eastern Europe between 1938 and 1948. This would become the Eastern Bloc. (Credit: Mosedschurte, 2021)

In November 1943, Joseph Stalin furiously fought to keep the territories he received from his alliance with Hitler. After stages of grandstanding and arguing, British Prime Minister Winston Churchill recommended redrawing the borders of Europe. In order for Russia to keep its territories, Eastern Europe needed new borders, at least in some cases, showing the delicate nature of state-building.

In February 1945, the three main Allied powers—England, the United States, and the USSR—were represented at the Yalta Conference.[649] In attendance were British Prime Minister Winston Churchill, US President Franklin D. Roosevelt, and Soviet leader Joseph Stalin. They met in Crimea to settle what the postwar world would look like.

Among the many agreements made at that conference was the division of Germany and Poland. After Germany's defeat, the country would be split into zones occupied by the US, France, the USSR, and Great Britain. However, Joseph Stalin refused to compromise on Poland. He claimed that the country had been used more than once to threaten and invade Soviet borders. Stalin didn't want to return the part of Poland he controlled, but he upheld the legality of free elections. Churchill and Roosevelt gave in, supporting a new Polish government that would be an ally to the USSR, thus creating a USSR zone of influence.

The men agreed to meet at a later date but not before Roosevelt and Churchill received Stalin's agreement to join the United Nations, an international organization geared toward maintaining international peace.

The following month, Stalin made his position on Poland crystal clear. Instead of supporting a free democratic process, he sent Soviet troops to crush any criticism of the new provisional Polish government. Two years later, the "free" elections he promised were nothing more than making postwar Poland into a Soviet client state.

---

[649] Jankowski, *Eastern Europe!*, 2015, pg. 475-476; "Yalta Conference." *HISTORY.* November 4, 2019. https://www.history.com/topics/world-war-ii/yalta-conference

In July 1945, the Potsdam Conference negotiated how to resettle certain communities.[650] Germans from all over Eastern Europe were resettled with a guarantee from the Great Powers that they would be, above all, respected. The war was over, and Stalin was in a much better position to press his claims for a Soviet sphere of influence in Eastern Europe.[651] His troops were everywhere, and they were victorious. The new US president, Harry S. Truman, was less likely to bend than Roosevelt, who had died in April 1945—only weeks after his return from the Yalta Conference.

The conference ended on a sour note. In March 1946, Winston Churchill gave his iconic speech, referring to Eastern Europe as covered with an "iron curtain." This would mark the beginning of the Cold War, a decades-long phase of tensions between the democratic United States and the communist Soviet Union.[652]

---

[650] Liulevicius, "Postwar Flight and Expulsion." Lecture 13. *The Great Courses: A History of Eastern Europe*, 2015; Jankowski, *Eastern Europe!*, 2015, pg. 476; Jenkins, *Short History of Europe*, 2019, pg. 268-270.

[651] Jenkins, *Short History of Europe*, 2019, pg. 265, 273-274; "Yalta Conference." *HISTORY*.

[652] Jenkins, *Short History of Europe*, 2019, pg. 270; "Yalta Conference." *HISTORY*.

Winston Churchill, Franklin D. Roosevelt, and Joseph Stalin at the Potsdam Conference in February 1945. (Public Domain)

Of course, the peaceful resettlement of Europe was easier in theory.[653] On the ground, wartime grievances and long-standing feuds came out. Resettling became an excuse for violence. The Polish violently drove Germans out of their new territory. Poles were terrorized out of Ukraine, Lithuania, and Belarus.

Those who were displaced were piled into refugee camps until they were told where they could go. Stalin was very spirited in his demands that his people return to their homeland. Of course, no one knew he was doing that so that he could accuse them of conspiring against the state and then have them deported or executed. Until the end of the decade, the Great Powers helped Eastern Europeans resettle their populations. Many emigrated, starting new lives.

---

[653] Liulevicius, "Postwar Flight and Expulsion." Lecture 13. *The Great Courses: A History of Eastern Europe*, 2015; Jenkins, *Short History of Europe*, 2019, pg. 270.

Some of the displaced couldn't return home. The widespread destruction of the war meant that people's homes and livelihoods were gone. The Jewish survivors of World War II often didn't have homes anymore. On top of that, anti-Semitism was still alive in Eastern Europe, and several Eastern European states persecuted Jewish communities.

The Stalinization of Eastern Europe

After winning victory after victory at the end of the war, Stalin started thinking about the future. Without Germany to compete with, he wanted to expand Soviet influence across all of Eastern Europe. As the Western nations saw Eastern Europe limp back to a sense of normalcy, they tried to intervene to help Eastern Europe recover.[654]

They were immediately met with hostility, and tensions escalated on both sides. In February 1946, Joseph Stalin made his antagonism towards the West known.[655] In a speech, he stated that he fully expected the West and the East to go to war with each other. Later that month, the American diplomat George Keenan sent Washington a private dispatch—the "Long Telegram"—advising the United States on the conditions on the ground in the Soviet Union. He suggested that the US use a containment policy to keep Soviet influence from spreading.

In 1948, US President Harry Truman signed the Truman Doctrine.[656] This legislation promised US support to European countries under communist rule or under communist pressure.

---

[654] Liulevicius, "Behind the Iron Curtain, 1945–1953." Lecture 14. *The Great Courses: A History of Eastern Europe*, 2015.

[655] Jenkins, *Short History of Europe*, 2019, pg. 274; "Winston Churchill's Iron Curtain Speech—March 5, 1946." *National World War II Museum*. March 5, 2021. https://www.nationalww2museum.org/war/articles/winston-churchills-iron-curtain-speech-march-5-1946

[656] Liulevicius, "Behind the Iron Curtain, 1945–1953." Lecture 14. *The Great Courses: A History of Eastern Europe*, 2015.

However, Joseph Stalin itched for control over the whole region of Eastern Europe, and he expanded his influence through a process called Stalinization.

The recovering nations of Eastern Europe were at the whim of international politics. No matter what promises were made, the Soviet Union openly broke with the West.[657] Now, there were two spheres of influence—known as blocs—looming over Europe. One, the Western Bloc, was controlled by Europe and the United States. The other, the Eastern Bloc, was Stalin's sphere of influence, and it was dominated by the Soviet Union. Winston Churchill's iconic 1946 speech would perfectly sum up postwar Europe; he stated that "an iron curtain has descended across the continent." It marked the beginning of the Cold War, the long phase of tensions between the democratic West and the communist Soviet Union.

At first, Stalin told everyone what they wanted to hear.[658] He agreed with the democratic process. He wanted the nations of Eastern Europe to have independence. However, the whole time, he was planning to add a collection of satellite states to the Soviet Union. Stalin itched for control over the whole region of Eastern Europe, and he established communist regimes through a process called Stalinization.[659, 660] Yet, Stalin was still Stalin, and he didn't trust any foreign communists.

[657] Jenkins, *Short History of Europe*, 2019, pg. 270, 273; "Yalta Conference." *HISTORY;* "Winston Churchill's Iron Curtain Speech—March 5, 1946." *National World War II Museum.* March 5, 2021.

[658] Liulevicius, "Behind the Iron Curtain, 1945-1953." Lecture 14. *The Great Courses: A History of Eastern Europe,* 2015; "Yalta Conference." *HISTORY.*

[659] Liulevicius, "Behind the Iron Curtain, 1945-1953." Lecture 14. *The Great Courses: A History of Eastern Europe,* 2015; Jenkins, *Short History of Europe,* 2019, pg. 273-274.

[660] Liulevicius, "World War II: The Unfamiliar Eastern Front." Lecture 11. *The Great Courses: A History of Eastern Europe,* 2015.

Stalinization happened slowly, with Stalin's agents slowly taking control of the state.[661] When Stalin sent non-Soviet communists back home, they would gain the favor of state institutions by, for instance, securing army and government positions. Once they had these in place, the communists then used them to eliminate any protest against communist regimes.

The agents would engage with the population, passing popular reforms to get their support. When they had the support of the population, the communists took control of the government. By slowly infiltrating the political scene, the Soviet Union could spread its influence in a much more sustainable way than by invading and subduing a population.

Stalin had control of most of Eastern Europe by 1948, the same year US President Harry Truman signed his Truman Doctrine, which was legislation promising American support to European countries under communist rule or pressure. The only two countries Stalin couldn't infiltrate were Finland and Austria. Three countries—Czechoslovakia, Hungary, and Poland—fell in line with the Western Bloc to establish democracy as soon as the war was over. These governments didn't last, and they soon became client states of the Soviet Union. However, all three countries would flirt with democracy throughout the Cold War.

The Stalin-Tito Split of 1948

The first direct challenge to Stalin's authority would come from Yugoslavia.[662] The leader of Yugoslavia, Josip Broz Tito, refused to cower to Stalin's demands. When Stalin tried to force Tito to fix Yugoslavia's economy to benefit the Soviet Union, Tito refused. If anyone was going to benefit from Yugoslavia's economy, it was

---

[661] Liulevicius, "Behind the Iron Curtain, 1945-1953." Lecture 14. *The Great Courses: A History of Eastern Europe*, 2015.; Jenkins, *Short History of Europe*, 2019, pg. 273-274.

[662] Liulevicius, "Behind the Iron Curtain, 1945-1953." Lecture 14. *The Great Courses: A History of Eastern Europe*, 2015.; Jenkins, *Short History of Europe*, 2019, pg. 273-274.

going to be Yugoslavia. When Stalin suggested signing an alliance with Bulgaria, Tito said no.

Stalin was so furious that he withdrew his agents from Yugoslavia. He tried to get Tito to toe the line by using other powerful communists. In retaliation, Tito had Stalin's supporters in Yugoslavia arrested. The US heard about Yugoslavia's defiance, and it sent help to Tito. He would never return to Stalin's sphere of influence.

Daily Life in Postwar Eastern Europe

Much planning and delegation had gone into restructuring Europe after World War II. But what did daily life look like for most Eastern Europeans?[663]

Twentieth-century Eastern Europe would have to constantly reevaluate itself. After the war was over, constant warfare and skirmishes over territories defined the Eastern European experience. For those who lived under the Soviet Bloc, Stalin resisted any kind of Western items or ideas. Communist rhetoric often focused on complete devotion to the state. To keep people in line, these nations had a secret police force. Communist nations ruled through fear or repression and were usually led by someone who had a cult of personality.

Nikita Khrushchev, the "De-Stalinization" of Eastern Europe, and the Hungarian Revolution of 1956

In 1953, Nikita Khrushchev would bring the Soviet Union a new type of leadership, as he broke away from Stalinization.[664] In the aftermath of Stalin's death, Khrushchev openly condemned Stalin's policies, initiating a phase of modernization throughout the

---

[663] Liulevicius, "Life in Totalitarian Captivity, 1953-1980." Lecture 16. *The Great Courses: A History of Eastern Europe*, 2015.

[664] Jenkins, *Short History of Europe*, 2019, pg. 276

Soviet Union. A sense of general unrest spread throughout Eastern Europe, with rebellions against Soviet control breaking out during the 1950s and 1960s.[665]

Of course, Khrushchev's administration wasn't without its blunders. His modernization campaign didn't mean that the Soviet Union was releasing its hold on the Eastern Bloc. In 1956, the Hungarian Revolution temporarily established a democratic government.[666] The student-led protest ignited into a larger movement for overthrowing the Soviet regime. Revolutionaries, led by Imre Nagy, overthrew Hungary's communist government, expanding more freedoms to the general population, including democratic elections and a multi-party government structure.

This was too much for Nikita Khrushchev.[667] It was one thing to modernize and relax some of the more violent aspects of Stalinization, but this was an open rebellion against Soviet control. He launched a military occupation of Hungary; he captured Imre Nagy and restored Soviet control over the government. In 1958, Nagy was executed for his role in the Hungarian Revolution, but his efforts were not in vain. Until the fall of communism, Hungary practiced self-government more than her neighbors.[668]

The Berlin Wall

Since the end of the war, Berlin had become a four-sector city. The Allied nations—Britain, the US, the Soviet Union, and France—divided Berlin between them, each occupying a part of the

---

[665] Liulevicius, "Power of the Powerless: Revolts and Unrest." Lecture 17. *The Great Courses: A History of Eastern Europe*, 2015

[666] "Hungarian Revolution, 1956." *Encyclopedia Britannica.*
https://www.britannica.com/event/Hungarian-Revolution-1956 ; Liulevicius, "Power of the Powerless: Revolts and Unrest." Lecture 17. *The Great Courses: A History of Eastern Europe*, 2015.

[667] "Hungarian Revolution, 1956." *Encyclopedia Britannica;* Jenkins, *Short History of Europe*, 2019, pg. 276.

[668] "Hungarian Revolution, 1956." *Encyclopedia Britannica.*

city.[669] This system of control had been one of the points agreed upon at the Yalta Conference. Berlin was essentially split in half, with West Berlin under a democratic government and East Berlin under communist rule.

However, East Germany had a problem; all of its young, trained professionals flocked to Berlin, escaping the communist government into the Western side of the city. The country would soon be left with no professionals or skilled workers to keep the economy running.

The Soviets approved of a wall separating Berlin that would keep the people of Soviet-controlled East Germany from escaping to West Germany.[670] Construction began in 1961; it was so secret that almost no one knew about it until it was already up. People who tried to cross the wall were shot on sight. The Berlin Wall would come to symbolize the oppressive regime of communism and the divide between Western and Eastern Europe.

The Cuban Missile Crisis

As the Cold War continued, the relationship between the United States and the Soviet Union fractured even further. Each side was obsessively suspicious of the other and on the alert for any violation of the unsteady peace they managed to carve out after World War II. The United States was particularly alarmed by the Soviet Union's alliance with communist Cuba.[671] Having a communist nation so close to home completely went against everything for which the democratic West stood.

[669] "Four Power Status and Reconstruction of Berlins (1945-1950s)." *Visit Berlin.* https://www.visitberlin.de/en/four-power-status-and-reconstruction-berlins-1945-1950s

[670] Liulevicius, "Toppling Idols: The Communist Collapse." Lecture 19. *The Great Courses: A History of Eastern Europe,* 2015; Jenkins, *Short History of Europe,* 2019, pg.278-279; Jankowski, *Eastern Europe!,* 2015, pg. 515-516.

[671] Jenkins, *Short History of Europe,* 2019, pg.279-280; "The Cuban Missile Crisis, October 1962." The Office of the Historian, Department of State Archives. https://history.state.gov/milestones/1961-1968/cuban-missile-crisis

After President John F. Kennedy's botched invasion of Cuba to end communist rule, Nikita Khrushchev promised to protect its ally with nuclear weapons. Cuba started building sites for Soviet missiles. The United States Navy surrounded Cuba to block any Soviet deliveries of nuclear weapons. Khrushchev denounced the barricade around the island of Cuba as "an act of aggression" against the Soviet Union and promised that the US could not stop any deliveries between the Soviet Union and Cuba.

Each side dug in their heels, with no end in sight. Finally, Khrushchev backtracked. The showdown between the two powers risked nuclear war, something that neither side wanted. Kennedy and Khrushchev came to an agreement; the Soviets would withdraw their weapons from Cuba, and the United States would withdraw their weapons from Turkey. The Cuban Missile Crisis was the closest that the US and the Soviet Union came to armed conflict during the Cold War.

Prague Spring, 1968

The 1960s also brought a shift in personal politics in the Soviet Union.[672] The generation who knew nothing of war, invasion, Hitler, or Stalin came of age. They didn't adhere to party lines, only to their sense of justice between right and wrong. Rebellions spread throughout the Eastern Bloc; while some gained traction, others were immediately crushed.

Perhaps the most significant period of rebellion in the Eastern Bloc was Prague Spring, a revolution overthrowing communism in Czechoslovakia.[673] In January 1968, the new first secretary of the Communist Party, Alexander Dubček, refused to toe the party

---

[672] Liulevicius, "Life in Totalitarian Captivity, 1953-1980." Lecture 16. *The Great Courses: A History of Eastern Europe*, 2015; Liulevicius, "Power of the Powerless: Revolts and Unrest." Lecture 17. *The Great Courses: A History of Eastern Europe*, 2015;

[673] Jenkins, *Short History of Europe*, 2019, pg. 279-280; Liulevicius, "Power of the Powerless: Revolts and Unrest." Lecture 17. *The Great Courses: A History of Eastern Europe*, 2015; "Prague Spring." *Encyclopedia Britannica.* https://www.britannica.com/event/Prague-Spring

line. Among his first actions were to protect more freedom of the press and split Czechoslovakia into two nations: a Czech one and a Slovak one. This would guarantee Czechoslovakia's Slovak population independence and self-rule. These changes were dangerously close to democracy, and the Soviet Union didn't like it.

According to the Warsaw Pact of 1955, the USSR and its satellite states entered a mutual defense agreement, which stated that an attack on one member of the bloc guaranteed that the other members would defend them. Dubček's efforts were an attack on communism from the inside. In June 1968, six months after Dubček's election, the people took to the streets, clamoring for even more rights and freedoms. The head of the Soviet government, Leonid Brezhnev, reacted by calling on other members of the Warsaw Pact. He gathered thousands of troops to crush the rebellion in Czechoslovakia. By the end of August, the Soviet Union had regained control of the country. It supervised a readjustment of the political system in Czechoslovakia and reappointed communists to their governmental positions. In April the following year, the Soviet Union deposed Alexander Dubček, ending the revolution.

Nuclear Disarmament

The Cuban Missile Crisis convinced every nation that had nuclear weapons, not just the US and the Soviet Union, that an international agreement was necessary to keep the peace.[674] In 1968, over sixty nations around the world—led by the United States, Great Britain, and the Soviet Union—signed the Treaty on the Non-Proliferation of Nuclear Weapons. It states that every nation would not help any other government use their nuclear weapons or sell them to others. After nearly three decades after the treaty was first signed, it was extended indefinitely in 1995.

---

[674] "Treaty on the Non-Proliferation of Nuclear Weapons." *Encyclopedia Britannica.* https://www.britannica.com/event/Treaty-on-the-Non-proliferation-of-Nuclear-Weapons

The signing of this nuclear disarmament agreement ushered in a new diplomatic phase of the Cold War. The détente between the United States and the Soviet Union was facilitated by a change in American foreign policy.[675] Under Secretary of State Henry Kissinger, the United States sought to establish an evenly distributed international balance of power instead of focusing on its rivalry with the Soviet Union and its efforts to contain communism.

However, this détente in international relations between the United States and the Soviet Union was only temporary. By the 1980s, both the United States and Great Britain denounced communism. President Ronald Reagan publicly antagonized the Soviet Union by pumping money into developing anti-ballistic missiles that could be launched into space.[676]

In 1985, the election of Mikhail Gorbachev would soften the relationship between the United States and the Soviet Union. After less than six months in power, Gorbachev and Ronald Reagan met at the Geneva Summit of 1985 to discuss nuclear disarmament.[677] Although neither could come to an agreement on a mutual disarmament treaty, it secured Gorbachev's approach to policy.

When it came to promoting a common security policy, Gorbachev supported working with his rivals, not antagonizing them. Friendly, diplomatic relations was the real protection against attack by nuclear weapons, not the number of weapons their rival had in their possession. Reagan and Gorbachev would successfully come to an agreement the following year at the Reykjavík Summit of 1986, with both nations agreeing to reduce their nuclear arms holdings.[678]

---

[675] Jenkins, *Short History of Europe*, 2019, pg. 281-282.

[676] Jenkins, *Short History of Europe*, 2019, pg. 281-283.

[677] "Reagan and Gorbachev: The Geneva Summit." *Atomic Heritage Foundation.* July 26, 2018. https://www.atomicheritage.org/history/reagan-and-gorbachev-geneva-summit

[678] "Reagan and Gorbachev: The Reykjavik Summit." *Atomic Heritage Foundation.* August 7, 2018. https://www.atomicheritage.org/history/reagan-and-gorbachev-reykjavik-summit

The Collapse of the Soviet Union

When Mikhail Gorbachev was elected general secretary of the Communist Party of the Soviet Union, he was seen as a moderate candidate. While his reforms—perestroika and glasnost—modernized the Soviet Union, they also reduced the iron grip that the Soviet Union had over the Eastern Bloc.[679]

The key to power relied upon dominating politics and society while silencing opposition. Glasnost encouraged opposition, as it urged the people to campaign for issues important to them without the fear of the government locking them up or, worse, executing them.[680] It contributed to a more politicized society, one that stretched the boundaries of what it meant to be in the Eastern Bloc.

At the same time, perestroika upturned the Soviet economic model. For decades, the government had controlled the economy. To revitalize the economy, Gorbachev reduced government control over business and production. What resulted from the perestroika and glasnost reforms was a loosening of control over the countries in the Soviet Union, as well as a more active politicized population.

Between 1989 and 1991, the communist nations of Eastern Europe started to fall.[681] It started in November 1989 with the fall of the Berlin Wall, which had become a cultural symbol of communism and the East-West divide. It represented repression, a stalwart barrier that blocked Europe's path to healing.[682]

---

[679] Jenkins, *Short History of Europe*, 2019, pg. 283-284.

[680] Jenkins, *Short History of Europe*, 2019, pg. 283-284; "Perestroika and Glastnost." Seventeen Moments in Soviet History: An Online Archive of Primary Sources. http://soviethistory.msu.edu/1985-2/perestroika-and-glasnost/

[681] Liulevicius, "Toppling Idols: The Communist Collapse." Lecture 19. *The Great Courses: A History of Eastern Europe*, 2015.

[682] Jankowski, *Eastern Europe!*, 2015, pg. 543-544.

But how did this happen? It started with the people. A new generation arose, and they itched for more democratic power. More importantly, they turned over a new leaf. The people of Eastern Europe now used nonviolent protest.[683] There was only one violent episode: the coup against Romanian President Nicolae Ceausescu in December 1989.

Generally, the call for the fall of communism came from the need and desire to become part of Western Europe again.[684] The countries in the Eastern Bloc were tired of being cut off from the world. Part of the reason for the push to independence was the decolonization movements of the 20th century. The Eastern European push was an extension of the spirit of revolution and the desire for self-rule found in other former colonies throughout the world.

One by one, states in the Soviet Bloc called for independence. In December 1991, the leaders of Russia, Ukraine, and Belarus all met, and they decided to do away with the Soviet Union. By Christmas later that month, Soviet Prime Minister Mikhail Gorbachev had resigned.

After the Fall of Communism: The 1990s Bring an Uncertain Future

Traditional histories of Eastern Europe end with the fall of communism. Over the past three decades, the region has endured changes in borders and identity.[685] After communism, the nations of

---

[683] Liulevicius, "Toppling Idols: The Communist Collapse." Lecture 19. *The Great Courses: A History of Eastern Europe*, 2015; Jenkins, *Short History of Europe*, 2019, pg. 286.

[684] Liulevicius, "Toppling Idols: The Communist Collapse." Lecture 19. *The Great Courses: A History of Eastern Europe*, 2015; Jenkins, *Short History of Europe*, 2019, pg. 284-285.

[685] Liulevicius, "The Turn: The Post-Soviet 1990s." Lecture 20. *The Great Courses: A History of Eastern Europe*, 2015.

Eastern Europe had to learn how they fit into the larger world while accepting their own past.

Joining NATO and the EU

After the fall of communism, Eastern European countries that were free from the yoke of the Eastern Bloc knew they needed to move forward, but to what degree? Did they want to affiliate themselves with Western Europe, or did they want to carve out a region all their own?

Joining the North Atlantic Treaty Organization (NATO) and the European Union (EU) was a common goal for most Eastern European countries. Becoming part of an international community would help the countries that no longer felt secure after the fall of communism.[686]

Joining NATO and the EU was difficult, but it was worth it to some countries. They had to successfully establish market economies and democracies before they were admitted. Becoming part of the EU meant that the organization could regulate the economies of its members. However, the organization offered certain protections the countries of Eastern Europe couldn't find elsewhere. Throughout its history, Eastern Europe had been victim to the expansionist designs of both Germany and Russia. Both NATO and the EU kept their nations from impeding on each other, so Eastern European countries felt protected and could possibly become equal players in the organization.

Only four Eastern European countries had joined NATO by 1999: the Czech Republic, Hungary, Poland, and East Germany (after it had rejoined with West Germany). Within ten years, Albania, Croatia, Bulgaria, Slovakia, Slovenia, Romania, and the

---

[686] Liulevicius, "The New Europe: Joining NATO and the EU." Lecture 22. *The Great Courses: A History of Eastern Europe*, 2015.

Baltics (Estonia, Lithuania, and Latvia) were admitted.[687] Between 2004 and 2013, Croatia, the Czech Republic, Poland, Slovenia, Romania, Hungary, Bulgaria, and the Baltic states joined the EU.

Still, it wasn't a perfect fit for every country. NATO and the EU tried to maintain harmonious relations between its members a little *too* much. When it did act, it alienated someone. For example, when NATO launched airstrikes to end the conflicts in Bosnia and Kosovo, Serbia—the target of the airstrikes—refused to join.

Changing Economies and Demographics

One important question Eastern European countries had to answer was how to become self-sufficient.[688] The change from a communist economy to a capitalist economy was not an easy one. Should economic sectors receive subsidies to cushion the transition to such a drastically new economy? While the countries of Eastern Europe struggled economically, it was the workers who suffered. Some industries didn't survive the fall of communism. Others did, but they struggled to find their footing in the new reality of post-communist life. As a result, there was a new phase of mass immigration that would affect the foundations of Eastern Europe.

A country is only as good as its people, and countries rebuilding themselves needed a strong professional and business class. Opportunities were lacking, so workers started leaving their home countries[689]. This would affect Eastern Europe's development for decades all the way up to the present day. If Eastern Europeans weren't leaving their homes for better opportunities abroad, they were forced out. The Yugoslav Wars created hundreds of thousands of refugees who sought sanctuary in neighboring Eastern

---

[687] Jenkins, *Short History of Europe*, 2019, pg.294; Liulevicius, "The New Europe: Joining NATO and the EU." Lecture 22. *The Great Courses: A History of Eastern Europe*, 2015.

[688] Liulevicius, "The Turn: The Post-Soviet 1990s." Lecture 20. *The Great Courses: A History of Eastern Europe*, 2015.

[689] Liulevicius, "The New Europe: Joining NATO and the EU." Lecture 22. *The Great Courses: A History of Eastern Europe*, 2015.

European countries and abroad. They left their homes from persecution, and they encountered discrimination in their new homes.

Migration worked both ways in Eastern Europe. As more people returned home after displacement and exile, the question became what role they would play. In the year 2000, Vaclav Havel, the president of the Czech Republic, challenged Madeline Albright, who was the Czech-born American secretary of state, to immigrate back home and run for president. One imagines he was only half-serious, but she turned him down just the same.

The Baltic states repeated a pattern of exiles returning home and becoming president. After living in Canada since she was a teenager, Vaira Vike-Freiberga was elected president of Latvia twice, in 1999 and 2003. She would become the first female president of Latvia, as well as the first woman head of state in an Eastern European country.[690]

In 1998, Valdas Adamkus was narrowly elected as president.[691] He had been involved in the Lithuanian resistance movement against Nazi and Soviet forces during World War II. Since 1944, he had lived abroad in Germany and the United States. After spending nearly forty years in the US, enjoying a long career with the EPA (the Environmental Protection Agency), he returned to Lithuania. Adamkus joined the presidential race to mixed results; he won by a narrow margin in 1998. He didn't win reelection in 2003, but he was called back to the position the following year when his successor was removed from office. During his tenure, which lasted until 2009, Adamkus improved the economy and encouraged friendly diplomatic relations with other Eastern

---

[690] Liulevicius, "The New Europe: Joining NATO and the EU." Lecture 22. *The Great Courses: A History of Eastern Europe*, 2015; "Vaira Vike Freiberga." Columbia World Leaders Forum. https://worldleaders.columbia.edu/directory/vaira-vike-freiberga

[691] Liulevicius, "The New Europe: Joining NATO and the EU." Lecture 22. *The Great Courses: A History of Eastern Europe*, 2015; "Valdas Adamkus." *Encyclopedia Britannica*. https://www.britannica.com/biography/Valdas-Adamkus

European countries. He actively campaigned for Lithuania to join the international community during his first term. During the brief hiatus between his two terms, Lithuania joined NATO and the EU. More recently, Toomas Hendrik Ilves, president of Estonia from 2006 to 2016, was the son of Estonian refugees, and they spent several years living in the United States.[692]

Making Peace with the Past

The fall of communism also meant that the people finally learned the truth about their history.[693] The introduction of a free press exposed truths about Eastern European history that had been previously silenced. A perfect example is the existence of secret police that violated the privacy of those the state targeted for suspicious anti-communist behavior. While the Stasi (Ministry for State Security) in East Germany enlisted professional spies, the Securitate in Romania relied on the population to inform on their neighbors. When communism fell in East Germany, the Stasi had files on millions of people. Spouses and family members reporting on each other was a common occurrence.

Now that former state secrets were out in the open, Eastern European countries had to consider what the consequences would be. High-ranking government officials in communist regimes retained their positions after the fall of communist governments. Should these people be removed for what they did under the regime? Or could they still lead under a new political system?

---

[692] Liulevicius, "The New Europe: Joining NATO and the EU." Lecture 22. *The Great Courses: A History of Eastern Europe*, 2015; "Toomas Hendrik Ilves." *Columbia World Leaders Forum.* https://worldleaders.columbia.edu/directory/toomas-hendrik-ilves

[693] Liulevicius, "The Turn: The Post-Soviet 1990s." Lecture 20. *The Great Courses: A History of Eastern Europe*, 2015.

One example of a public figure who successfully transitioned between governments was Simeon Borisov von Saxe-Coburg-Gotha, the prime minister of Bulgaria from 2001 to 2005.[694] Simeon was the son of Tsar Boris III of Bulgaria; when Simeon was two years old, Adolf Hitler occupied Poland. Boris III was pressured into an alliance with Hitler, and the bullying started immediately. Hitler pushed Boris to send troops to the Eastern Front. He also pressured Boris to deport all Bulgarian Jews to Poland. When Boris denied Hitler's requests the final time in 1943, he was poisoned to death. Simeon became a boy king at six years old.

A team of family members and regents helped Simeon navigate rulership, but they were stuck between the dominant personalities of Hitler and Stalin. When Bulgaria tried to remain neutral in 1944, the Soviet Union invaded. The Soviet army didn't waste any time; they slaughtered the entire Bulgarian government and army generals and held the royal family hostage. In September 1946, the Soviet Union proclaimed Bulgaria to be a communist state, exiling the king, his sister, and his mother.

Simeon grew up in exile in Spain; when he was eighteen, he plotted a return to Bulgaria by forming a "government in exile," which means that he wanted to reclaim the monarchy and rule outside of the country. When he realized this wouldn't work, he settled into a life as a private citizen. He married, started a career, became a father, then a grandfather. In 1996, fifty years after his exile, Simeon returned to Bulgaria. He rejoined politics but in a much different way. He founded a new political party, running on his own ticket. In 2001, five years after his return, Simeon Borisov von Saxe-Coburg-Gotha became the prime minister of Bulgaria—

---

[694] Liulevicius, "The New Europe: Joining NATO and the EU." Lecture 22. *The Great Courses: A History of Eastern Europe*, 2015; Martina Petkova, "The Last Living Tsar and His Tango with Democracy." *History of Yesterday*. Published August 20, 2020. https://historyofyesterday.com/the-last-living-tsar-and-his-tango-with-democracy-edb7c76aa01a

the only monarch to achieve a position in a democratic government.

Emerging from Communism: Czechoslovakia and Belarus

For many Eastern Europeans, the cloak of communism was all they knew.[695] Some didn't see the fall of their governments as liberating. Many didn't know how to feel about independence from the Soviet Union or how they fit into the new state. Feelings of security were especially important to the people of Eastern Europe. Under the new system, they didn't feel as if the state would take care of them.

This anxiety presented itself in different ways. Let's look at what happened in Czechoslovakia compared to Belarus. In Czechoslovakia, as wide-scale demonstrations spread throughout Eastern Europe for the end of communist rule, the state peacefully considered more.[696] In November 1989, student protests in Prague and Bratislava started peacefully, but they quickly turned violent when the participants started criticizing the regime. Over fifty thousand protestors took to the streets, where they were beaten by the police to break up the demonstrations.[697] The violence sparked even more protests across Czechoslovakia. This period would become known as the Velvet Revolution.

---

[695] Liulevicius, "The Turn: The Post-Soviet 1990s." Lecture 20. *The Great Courses: A History of Eastern Europe*, 2015.

[696] "Czechoslovak history." *Encyclopedia Britannica.*
https://www.britannica.com/topic/Czechoslovak-history
https://www.britannica.com/topic/Czechoslovak-history

[697] Richard Nelsson. "Czechoslovakia's Velvet Revolution - archive, November 1989." *The Guardian.* https://www.theguardian.com/world/from-the-archive-blog/2019/nov/13/czechoslovakia-velvet-revolution-november-1989 ; "Czechoslovak history." *Encyclopedia Britannica.*

The protest movement against the communist regime was so strong that communist leaders heard them out.[698] An interim government was set up to transition Czechoslovakia out of communist rule in December 1989.[699] The following June, Czechoslovakia held free elections, which upheld the provisional government. As the state started to introduce democratic institutions and create a new constitution, long-standing rivalries threatened to halt the peaceful transition of power.

Both Czechs and Slovaks formed their own nationalist movements in this period.[700] Slovaks never felt like they were truly part of the state, and they pushed for their own representation. This eventually morphed into a separatist movement, creating a new state for Slovaks. On January 1st, 1993, Czechoslovakia quietly and peacefully separated into two countries—the Czech Republic and Slovakia—in what is known as the "Velvet Divorce."

While Czechoslovakia managed to pull off a relatively bloodless transition to democracy, freedom from oppressive Soviet rule would evade Belarus.[701] Over one-fifth of the country was destroyed by the Ukrainian Chernobyl disaster of 1986, leading to the mandatory and voluntary resettlement of hundreds of thousands of Belarussians.[702] In the aftermath of Chernobyl and the dissolution of the Soviet Union, Belarus remained steadfast to its former

[698] Liulevicius, "The Turn: The Post-Soviet 1990s." Lecture 20. *The Great Courses: A History of Eastern Europe*, 2015.

[699] "Czechoslovak history." *Encyclopedia Britannica.*

[700] Liulevicius, "The Turn: The Post-Soviet 1990s." Lecture 20. *The Great Courses: A History of Eastern Europe*, 2015; "Czechoslovak history." *Encyclopedia Britannica.*

[701] Liulevicius, "The Turn: The Post-Soviet 1990s." Lecture 20. *The Great Courses: A History of Eastern Europe*, 2015.

[702] Liulevicius, "The Turn: The Post-Soviet 1990s." Lecture 20. *The Great Courses: A History of Eastern Europe*, 2015; "Belarus ignoring risks of farming near Chernobyl?" *CBS News.* April 25, 2016. https://www.cbsnews.com/news/chernobyl-radiation-belarus-farm-produce-milk-high-level-radiation/

relationship with Russia.[703] In 1994, a member of parliament, Alexander Lukashenko, was elected president. He has remained in power ever since, keeping power through communist methods, such as repression, silencing opposition, and controlling the press. In 2005, Lukashenko deployed Belarussian soldiers to violently put down a rebellion against his rule. Through passing laws that allow him to seek more terms and falsifying election results, Lukashenko has been called "Europe's last dictator."[704] Since 2011, Belarussian protestors have used social media to speak out against Lukashenko's government. He keeps such a tight rein over the country that free speech doesn't exist. Protestors are arrested for any statements against him, the Belarussian government, or representatives of the state. The brutality of his regime even made headlines in the 2021 Olympics when Belarussian sprinter Krystsina Tsimanouskaya fled in exile to Poland; she feared reprisals back home after criticizing her country's Olympic coaches.[705]

[703] Liulevicius, "The New Europe: Joining NATO and the EU." Lecture 22. *The Great Courses: A History of Eastern Europe*, 2015; Cheryl Teh. "Who is Alexander Lukashenko? A closer look at the dictator who has maintained an iron grip on Belarus for over 2 decades." *INSIDER.* August 3, 2021. https://www.businessinsider.com/who-is-alexander-lukashenko-closer-look-at-the-belarusian-dictator-2021-5

[704] Liulevicius, "The Turn: The Post-Soviet 1990s." Lecture 20. *The Great Courses: A History of Eastern Europe*, 2015; Liulevicius, "The New Europe: Joining NATO and the EU." Lecture 22. *The Great Courses: A History of Eastern Europe*, 2015; Cheryl Teh. "Who is Alexander Lukashenko?" 2019.

Lecture 20, 22; https://www.businessinsider.com/who-is-alexander-lukashenko-closer-look-at-the-belarusian-dictator-2021-5

[705] Vladimir Isachenkov, Alex Schuller. "Belarus Olympic runner who feared going home lands in Poland." Associated Press/ABC News. August 4, 2021. https://abcnews.go.com/Sports/wireStory/belarus-runner-flies-europe-feud-team-managers-79259922

The Yugoslav Wars (1991–2001)

Perhaps the lowest point in post-communist Eastern Europe was the Yugoslav Wars, a series of conflicts in the former Yugoslavia that was characterized by brutal warfare, violence, and human rights violations, especially against women. Serbia dominated Yugoslavia, and its fervent nationalism made other minorities feel isolated and persecuted.[706] As Eastern Europe moved into the 21st century, the states of the former Yugoslavia seemed like they would never recover.

Yugoslavia Breaks Apart

The former Yugoslavia was made up of six nations and two territories.[707] The modern-day states of Slovenia, Croatia, Bosnia and Herzegovina, Serbia, Montenegro, and Macedonia were once Yugoslavia. The provinces of Vojvodina and Kosovo were included as provinces of Serbia. This union of states brought together several ethnicities and religions that would soon struggle to coexist.

As communism declined in the late 1980s, nationalism returned. Under Slobodan Milošević, Serbian nationalism reached its peak.[708] Every region of Yugoslavia had a Serbian population. Milošević used nationalism to target these areas and bring them all under Serbian control. In other words, he was trying to create a Serbian Yugoslavia. Parties in Yugoslavian states split into those who supported remaining in Yugoslavia (the Serbians) and others

---

[706] Liulevicius, "Yugoslav Wars: Milosovic and Balkan Strife." Lecture 21. *The Great Courses: A History of Eastern Europe*, 2015.

[707] Liulevicius, "Yugoslav Wars: Milosovic and Balkan Strife." Lecture 21. *The Great Courses: A History of Eastern Europe*, 2015; "The Conflicts." International Criminal Tribunal for the Former Yugoslavia. https://www.icty.org/en/about/what-former-yugoslavia/conflicts ; "Top 10 Facts About the Kosovo War." The Borgen Project. https://borgenproject.org/the-kosovo-war/

[708] Liulevicius, "Yugoslav Wars: Milosovic and Balkan Strife." Lecture 21. *The Great Courses: A History of Eastern Europe*, 2015.

who wanted their own independent republics.[709] This type of nationalism used fear-mongering to turn ethnic groups against each other, leading to violent conflicts in the region.

1991: Slovenia and the Ten-Day War

Slovenia quickly adjusted to post-communist life. Just six months after the fall of the Berlin Wall, it held free elections.[710] By that December, the new government supported what the people had already voted for—separation from Yugoslavia. At the time, Serbia dominated Yugoslavia, and it interfered in Slovenian politics. Serbian president Slobodan Milošević installed a blockade on Slovenia, cutting it off from supplies and trade. As a result, the state of Slovenia was the first to leave Yugoslavia, declaring independence on June 25th, 1991.[711]

On June 27th, Milošević sent the Yugoslav People's Army (the national army of the state of Yugoslavia) into Slovenia to gain control of the country. The Slovenians had their own army, one that was much better prepared than the People's Army. The Slovenian Army was trained in how to defend Slovenian borders from invasion. Over the next ten days, the Slovenian Army's skirmishes with the Yugoslav People's Army ended in victory. The Ten-Day War ended, and Slovenia remained independent from Yugoslavia.

---

[709] "The Conflicts." International Criminal Tribunal for the Former Yugoslavia.

[710] Jenkins, *Short History of Europe*, 2019, pg.291; "Slovenia." *Encyclopedia Britannica.* https://www.britannica.com/place/Slovenia

[711] Liulevicius, "Yugoslav Wars: Milosovic and Balkan Strife." Lecture 21. *The Great Courses: A History of Eastern Europe*, 2015; "Slovenia." *Encyclopedia Britannica*; "The Conflicts." International Criminal Tribunal for the Former Yugoslavia.

1991-1995: Conflict in Croatia

Croatia also separated from Yugoslavia on June 25th, 1991, but it would descend into more chaos than Slovenia.[712] There was an ethnic element to the conflict in Croatia that made the revolution more violent. Croatia's Serbian population refused to be a part of the separation of Croatia; they wanted Croatia to stay connected to Yugoslavia. The Croatian Serbs allied with the Yugoslav People's Army and the Serbian state. They separated from Croatia and occupied 30 percent of the country to create their own Serbian state. The conflict in Croatia was violent and bloody, destroying the landscape. Croatian Serbs deported anyone in their territory that was non-Serbian.

By early 1992, the United Nations stepped in and ordered an end to the hostilities in Croatia. The conflict temporarily stopped, and the Croatian state used that time to beef up its military. In the summer of 1995, the Croatian Army launched two campaigns to return the area occupied by Serbs to Croatian rule. Thousands of Serbs fled to Bosnia and Serbia to escape the violence. Although the conflict was over by the fall of 1995, it took three years for Croatia to become united again. By January 1998, UN intervention successfully returned the contested area to Croatia.

1992-1995: Ethnic Cleansing in Bosnia and Herzegovina

The war in Bosnia and Herzegovina would become the deadliest conflict of the Yugoslav Wars. Bosnia and Herzegovina is a small state between Serbia and Croatia, both of whom had tried to conquer the territory. By 1991, the two countries worked together, each planning to separate from Yugoslavia and occupy Bosnia and Herzegovina, splitting it between them. Serbia and Croatia knew they were taking on a multi-ethnic state. Bosnia's

---

[712] Liulevicius, "Yugoslav Wars: Milosovic and Balkan Strife." Lecture 21. *The Great Courses: A History of Eastern Europe*, 2015; Jenkins, *Short History of Europe*, 2019, pg. 291; "The Conflicts." International Criminal Tribunal for the Former Yugoslavia.

population was made up of mostly Serbs (about 30 percent of the population), Croatians (about 17 percent of the population), and Muslims, also known as Bosniaks (about 40 percent of the population).[713] Both Serbia and Croatia agreed to section off part of the state for the Bosniak population.

The elections of March 1992 derailed any plans for splitting up Bosnia between its neighbors. More than half the country had voted for independence from Yugoslavia; Bosnia's Serbian population was not pleased with the results. Just like in Croatia, Bosnian Serbs wanted to remain part of the Yugoslavian state.

Both the Yugoslav People's Army and the Serbian government offered their support to the Bosnian Serbs. In April 1992, they rebelled against the government, sieging the capital of Sarajevo for nearly 1,500 days.[714] As the Serbs gained control of half of Bosnia, the Croatian and Bosniak populations each rebelled. Bosnia soon became a war zone, with all three parties fighting for dominance.

The international community was anxious to end the violence. Several countries set up embargoes against Bosnia, but the war continued. By 1994, Bosniak and Croat forces joined together to battle the Serbs. At first, the United Nations would not interfere, which is surprising given its dedication to ending the war crimes used during World War II. The UN only sent food, necessities, and medical supplies to the region. Eventually, it sanctioned NATO (the North Atlantic Treaty Organization) airstrikes between 1994 and 1995.[715] This was the first time that NATO would resort

---

[713] Liulevicius, "Yugoslav Wars: Milosovic and Balkan Strife." Lecture 21. *The Great Courses: A History of Eastern Europe*, 2015; "Bosnia and Herzegovina." *Encyclopedia Britannica*. https://www.britannica.com/place/Bosnia-and-Herzegovina

[714] Liulevicius, "Yugoslav Wars: Milosovic and Balkan Strife." Lecture 21. *The Great Courses: A History of Eastern Europe*, 2015; Jenkins, *Short History of Europe*, 2019, pg. 291.

[715] Liulevicius, "Yugoslav Wars: Milosovic and Balkan Strife." Lecture 21. *The Great Courses: A History of Eastern Europe*, 2015; Jenkins, *Short History of Europe*, 2019, pg. 292.

to military intervention in international affairs, but it wouldn't be the last.

Bosnia was under external pressure to end the war.[716] The Serbian Army commanded almost three-quarters of the country, so they refused to compromise in peace talks. Finally, negotiations in Dayton, Ohio, the United States, were successful. Signed in December 1995, the Dayton Accords split Bosnia and Herzegovina into two sections of land: one for the Serbs and one for the Bosniaks and Croats. Over sixty thousand troops were pulled from several countries and sent to Bosnia to ensure the peaceful transition.

The Bosnian conflict is well known for its human rights violations and violence against women. Although each side experienced the loss of life, the Serbians enacted massive ethnic cleansing campaigns reminiscent of World War II. Homes were torched, and churches and mosques were destroyed. Serbs, Croats, and Bosniaks all languished in jail cells and detention centers as prisoners of war. To create an ethnically Serbian state, Bosnian Serbs systematically raped Bosniak and Croatian women, holding them hostage so that they couldn't abort their pregnancies.[717] At the concentration camp of Omarska, Serbian soldiers repeatedly raped women prisoners.[718]

The Serbians were not the only ones who used ethnic cleansing as a war tactic. After retaking the city in August 1995, Croatian

---

[716] "Bosnia and Herzegovina." *Encyclopedia Britannica*, Liulevicius, "Yugoslav Wars: Milosovic and Balkan Strife." Lecture 21. *The Great Courses: A History of Eastern Europe*, 2015.

[717] "The Conflicts." International Criminal Tribunal for the Former Yugoslavia; Elizabeth A. Kohn, "Rape as a Weapon of War: Women's Human Rights During the Dissolution of Yugoslavia." *Golden Gate University Law Review*. Issue 1: Women's Law Forum. Volume 24. January 1994, 199-200.

[718] Liulevicius, "Yugoslav Wars: Milosovic and Balkan Strife." Lecture 21. *The Great Courses: A History of Eastern Europe*, 2015.

forces eliminated Krajina's Serbian population through murder and exile. Over half a million Serbs were executed or displaced.

Millions fled Bosnia from April 1992 to November 1995, finding safety in other countries or in refugee camps. It is estimated that over 100,000 died in the Bosnian War, and more than two million were exiled or displaced.[719] It wasn't until the Srebrenica massacre in summer 1995 that the international community rallied to end the conflict.[720]

Due to the mass violence surrounding the town, the UN had passed a resolution protecting Srebrenica, located in eastern Bosnia and Herzegovina, from further attack.[721] In July 1995, the Bosnian Serbian army, led by General Ratko Mladić, moved into the town.[722] For the cameras, Mladić played nice, giving the children candy and assuring the population that nothing would happen to them.[723] After the cameras stopped rolling, Mladić and his men slaughtered eight thousand Bosnian Muslim men and boys, tossing their remains into mass graves.[724] After taking control of the city, he exiled the women and the rest of the children.

[719] Liulevicius, "Yugoslav Wars: Milosovic and Balkan Strife." Lecture 21. *The Great Courses: A History of Eastern Europe*, 2015; "Bosnia and Herzegovina." *Encyclopedia Britannica*; "The Conflicts." International Criminal Tribunal for the Former Yugoslavia.

[720] "Bosnia and Herzegovina." *Encyclopedia Britannica*; "Srebenica massacre." *Encyclopedia Britannica*. https://www.britannica.com/event/Srebrenica-massacre

[721] Liulevicius, "Yugoslav Wars: Milosovic and Balkan Strife." Lecture 21. *The Great Courses: A History of Eastern Europe*, 2015; "Srebenica massacre." *Encyclopedia Britannica*.

[722] Liulevicius, "Yugoslav Wars: Milosovic and Balkan Strife." Lecture 21. *The Great Courses: A History of Eastern Europe*, 2015; "Bosnia and Herzegovina." *Encyclopedia Britannica*.

[723] Julian Borger. "Ratko Mladić: Life in prison is as close to justice as his victims will get." *The Guardian*. June 8, 2021. https://www.theguardian.com/world/2021/jun/08/ratko-mladic-life-in-prison-is-as-close-to-justice-as-his-victims-will-get

[724] Liulevicius, "Yugoslav Wars: Milosovic and Balkan Strife." Lecture 21. *The Great Courses: A History of Eastern Europe*, 2015

According to a war crimes tribunal, the violence in Srebrenica amounted to genocide. After years of escaping justice, Mladić was captured and convicted of crimes against humanity and genocide.[725] He is serving a life sentence to this day. It seems little consolation to the women of Srebrenica, many of whom were only able to recover the bodies of their loved ones through DNA analysis.[726]

1998–2008: Kosovo

Many countries and territories in Eastern Europe have diverse populations. In the 1990s, the majority of the population in the Serbian territory of Kosovo were Albanian Muslims.[727] This majority supported separating from Yugoslavia as well as shaking off Serbian rule.[728] Yugoslavian president Slobodan Milošević's campaign to bring Kosovo, an area that was traditionally Serbian, under his control threatened the Albanian population. He banned the practice of Albanian religion and culture, enforcing Serbian traditions on the whole population.

Albanians who opposed Milošević's policies and Serbian rule formed the Kosovo Liberation Army to take control of the territory.[729] In 1998, this radical group launched a terror campaign against the Serbian government, targeting members of the

[725] "Bosnia and Herzegovina." *Encyclopedia Britannica*; Borger, "Ratko Mladić: Life in prison is as close to justice as his victims will get." 2021.

[726] "DNA from Srebrenica women." *The New York Times.* https://www.nytimes.com/2000/07/07/opinion/IHT-dna-from-srebrenicas-women.html

[727] "The Conflicts." International Criminal Tribunal for the Former Yugoslavia; "Top 10 Facts About the Kosovo War." The Borgen Project.

[728] "The Conflicts." International Criminal Tribunal for the Former Yugoslavia; "Top 10 Facts About the Kosovo War." The Borgen Project; Liulevicius, "The New Europe: Joining NATO and the EU." Lecture 22. *The Great Courses: A History of Eastern Europe*, 2015.

[729] "The Conflicts." International Criminal Tribunal for the Former Yugoslavia; "Top 10 Facts About the Kosovo War." The Borgen Project; Liulevicius, "Yugoslav Wars: Milosovic and Balkan Strife." Lecture 21. *The Great Courses: A History of Eastern Europe*, 2015

government and the police force.[730] Milošević sent in Yugoslavian and Serbian troops to retake Kosovo. They responded to violence with violence, and soon, the whole territory was embroiled in civil war.

Milošević's forces used ethnic cleansing to terrorize Albanian communities. They massacred whole communities and burned them to the ground. The US and other European nations, namely France, Great Britain, Germany, Italy, and Russia, forced Yugoslavia to end the violence in Kosovo. Milošević promised to pull his troops out of Kosovo and allow Albanian refugees to return, but he went back on his word.

In 1999, Serbia was hostile to peace talks with Albanian representatives. Just as it had in the Bosnia conflict, NATO sent airstrikes to break up the conflict.[731] Instead, it just killed more civilians and created more refugees. Other casualties included Albanian communities that were slaughtered by Serbian and Yugoslav forces while NATO bombed the territory. In June, NATO and Milošević came to terms. He withdrew the military and allowed Kosovo's displaced communities to return. The Kosovo conflict displaced most of the territory's population, totaling up to 1.5 million people. Over one million of them were Albanian.

The violence between Serbians and Kosovo's Albanian population would continue into the 21ˢᵗ century. Although Kosovo earned its autonomy in June 1999, there were more protests

[730] "The Conflicts." International Criminal Tribunal for the Former Yugoslavia; "Top 10 Facts About the Kosovo War." The Borgen Project; "NATO's role in relation to the conflict in Kosovo." NATO. https://www.nato.int/kosovo/history.htm; Liulevicius, "Yugoslav Wars: Milosovic and Balkan Strife." Lecture 21. *The Great Courses: A History of Eastern Europe*, 2015; Jenkins, *Short History of Europe*, 2019, pg. 291-292.

[731] "Top 10 Facts About the Kosovo War." The Borgen Project; "The Conflicts." International Criminal Tribunal for the Former Yugoslavia; Liulevicius, "Yugoslav Wars: Milosovic and Balkan Strife." Lecture 21. *The Great Courses: A History of Eastern Europe*, 2015; Jenkins, *Short History of Europe*, 2019, pg. 292.

against Serbia in March 2004. The resulting violence displaced thousands of people. Four years later, Kosovo officially separated from Serbia. Although many Western countries recognize Kosovo as its own state, its Eastern European neighbors wouldn't acknowledge Kosovo's independence. Neither would the United Nations. Serbia still maintains that Kosovo is a Serbian territory. Further investigations in 2011 and 2016 tried members of the Kosovo Liberation Army for war crimes for the violent reprisals that took place in Kosovo.

2001: Macedonia

While the conflict in Macedonia did see some violence, it was relatively tame compared to Bosnia and Kosovo.[732] Since achieving independence from Yugoslavia in 1991, the people of Macedonia—which includes Macedonians, Albanians, Turks, and Roma—lived in peace. Although the transition to self-rule was peaceful, the 21st century would bring a renewed sense of nationalism among the Albanian population.

The end of the Kosovo conflict in 1999 brought more Albanians into Macedonian borders, which may have incited the protests of 2001.[733] In January 2001, radical Albanians formed their own army, using terror tactics to demand equal treatment by the Macedonian government. This campaign didn't last long; NATO stepped in to return peace to Macedonia. Under NATO supervision, the Albanian army stood down and disbanded later that year. The Macedonian government made an important gesture and addressed the Albanian cause. It changed its constitution, naming the state's minority populations as citizens.

---

[732] "Top 10 Facts About the Kosovo War." The Borgen Project; "The Conflicts." International Criminal Tribunal for the Former Yugoslavia; Liulevicius, "Yugoslav Wars: Milosovic and Balkan Strife." Lecture 21. *The Great Courses: A History of Eastern Europe*, 2015; "North Macedonia." *Encyclopedia Britannica.* https://www.britannica.com/place/North-Macedonia

[733] Alek Vasilevski. "Macedonia 2001: Uncovering the Truth." UMD Voice. April 13, 2017. https://www.umdgenm.org/2017/04/13/macedonia-2001-uncovering-the-truth/

The Downfall of Milošević

With the bloody conflicts that broke out in the former states of Yugoslavia, Slobodan Milošević would not stay in power for long.[734] Due to the growing protests and opposition movements against his leadership, he did not win reelection as president of the Federal Republic of Yugoslavia in 2000. The following year, he was arrested and tried for war crimes for the events in Bosnia and Kosovo. The war crimes tribunal in the Hague lasted for years; he died in prison in 2006 before they were completed.

2014: Russia Annexes the Crimea

In the four decades since the fall of the Soviet Union, Russia has emerged as one of the dominant world powers. While the rest of Eastern Europe was finding their footing, with most developing into democratic states, Russia retains most of its Soviet characteristics. The country is fond of throwing its weight around, and it has resorted to modern methods to dominate its neighbors. It is especially fond of electronic attacks. Russian hackers shut down the Estonian government in 2007 after a statue of a Russian soldier was moved from a public square to a cemetery.[735] And who could forget the US election scandal of 2016?[736]

Russia Since the Fall of the USSR

After the fall of the USSR, Russia struggled to find its place in the international community. The presidency of Boris Yeltsin encouraged diplomatic relations with the United States, but neither

---

[734] Liulevicius, "Yugoslav Wars: Milosovic and Balkan Strife." Lecture 21. *The Great Courses: A History of Eastern Europe*, 2015.

[735] Liulevicius, "The New Europe: Joining NATO and the EU." Lecture 22. *The Great Courses: A History of Eastern Europe*, 2015.

[736] Justin Fishel. "Inside the Russian Hacking Scandal and Trump's Election." *ABC News.* December 12, 2016. https://abcnews.go.com/Politics/inside-russian-hacking-scandal-trumps-election/story?id=44143340

country could agree on political matters.[737] In 1999, Yeltsin resigned in favor of his prime minister, Vladimir Putin, who became president of Russia.[738] He has been in control of the country ever since and forged a new path for Russia, one with decidedly autocratic characteristics.

Formally elected in 2000, Putin served as president until 2008. While engaging in diplomacy with the US, Putin also enhanced relationships with other prominent nations in Europe, the Middle East, and Asia. He supported the campaign of his own successor, his prime minister, Dmitry Medvedev. Putin returned to his old post of prime minister when Medvedev was elected president in 2008. After a disastrous first term, Medvedev appointed Putin as *his* successor, and Medvedev returned to the prime minister post in 2012.

During his second term as president, Putin's relations with the US soured as he negotiated Russia's place as a world power. He set about crushing any opposition to his government, famously prosecuting the band Pussy Riot for speaking out against his administration in 2012. However, the defining moment of Putin's second term, which proved what type of politician he was, was the Ukrainian crisis of 2014.

The Ukrainian Revolution of 2014

When Russia annexed the Crimean Peninsula on the Black Sea, an area that belonged to Ukraine, it exposed the long-standing tensions between Ukrainians and Russians. Ukraine has a complicated history with several examples of foreign rule and domination. Remember the Mongol Horde? And the Poland-Lithuanian Commonwealth's rule over the territory?

---

737 "Russia." *Encyclopedia Britannica*, Jenkins, *Short History of Europe*, 2019, pg. 293.

738 Liulevicius, "The New Europe: Joining NATO and the EU." Lecture 22. *The Great Courses: A History of Eastern Europe*, 2015; "Russia: The Putin Presidency." *Encyclopedia Britannica*.; Jenkins, *Short History of Europe*, 2019, pg. 293.

Russia came into play during the Cossack rebellion of 1654.[739] Cossack chief Bogdan Khmelnytsky approached Russia to help with their war against the Polish-Lithuanian Commonwealth. The Russians agreed, promising self-rule when they won the conflict. After it was all over, Russia went back on their word; the Ukrainians were now under Russian rule. Originally, the commonwealth and Russia split Ukraine between them, but the fall of the commonwealth at the end of the 18th century brought Ukraine completely under Russian control.

The Ukrainians suffered under Russian rule, especially the Stalin regime. Stalin employed ethnic cleansing and deported everyone who wasn't of Ukrainian descent to create an ethnically homogenous territory. Ukrainians never forgot the Terror Famine, which lasted from 1932 to 1933, that decimated the population. Ukraine even allied with Hitler during World War II to break the Soviet hold over the territory.

In 1954, as a gesture of goodwill, Soviet leader Nikita Khrushchev gifted the Crimean Peninsula back to Ukraine on the three-hundred-year anniversary of the Cossack rebellion.[740] However, Ukraine was still under Soviet control. In 1991, when the USSR disintegrated, Ukrainians desired independence from their long-time overlords.

But even an independent Ukraine couldn't shake its connections to Russia.[741] The country suffered economically in the first years of post-communist Eastern Europe, and it depended on Russia for its energy sources. In 2004, a beleaguered population protested against its government, charging it with serving its own interests and ignoring the plight of the people. The Orange

---

[739] Liulevicius, "The Unfolding Ukraine-Russia Crisis." Lecture 23. *The Great Courses: A History of Eastern Europe*, 2015.

[740] Liulevicius, "The Unfolding Ukraine-Russia Crisis." Lecture 23. *The Great Courses: A History of Eastern Europe*, 2015; Jenkins, *Short History of Europe*, 2019, pg. 295.

[741] Liulevicius, "The Unfolding Ukraine-Russia Crisis." Lecture 23. *The Great Courses: A History of Eastern Europe*, 2015.

Revolution gained traction, and one of their leaders, Viktor Yushchenko, even ran for president. In September of that year, his enemies stopped his campaign by poisoning him.

Yushchenko was incapacitated, so he couldn't run in that election. The election was rigged, leading to a renewed round of protests in the streets over the next seventeen days. A new election was ordered, and Yushchenko won the presidency. It would seem that peace would come to Ukraine, but the members of Yushchenko's party each rallied for their own interests. There was little compromise in the Ukrainian government. In 2010, Viktor Yanukovych became president, leading Ukraine with pro-Russian policies.[742]

Further unrest in Ukraine plagued Yanukovych's presidency. In November 2013, Vladimir Putin reportedly pressured Yanukovych not to join a trade deal with the European Union.[743] Unwilling to support a Russian puppet regime, Ukrainians protested against the government in what would become the Ukrainian Revolution of 2014. Thousands of protestors lined the streets for weeks, calling for an end to Yanukovych's presidency.[744] In January 2014, Yanukovych sent in the riot police, who violently attacked demonstrators to put down the protests. Over one hundred protestors and police were killed in the violence. Fearing for his safety, Yanukovych fled Ukraine for Russia, where he maintained his control over the government from abroad.

---

[742] Jenkins, *Short History of Europe*, 2019, pg. 295.

[743] "Russia: The Putin Presidency." *Encyclopedia Britannica*; Alan Yuhas and Raya Jalabi. "Ukraine's revolution and Russia's occupation of Crimea: How we got here." *The Guardian*. March 5, 2014. https://www.theguardian.com/world/2014/mar/05/ukraine-russia-explainer

[744] "Russia: The Putin Presidency." *Encyclopedia Britannica*; Jenkins, *Short History of Europe*, 2019, pg. 295; Alan Yuhas and Raya Jalabi. "Ukraine's revolution and Russia's occupation of Crimea: How we got here," 2014.

Russia, Ukraine, and the Crimean Peninsula

After the president left Ukraine, he was impeached, and a new interim government more aligned with Western interests replaced him.[745] As for Vladimir Putin, he continued to support Yanukovych's presidency. He mobilized tens of thousands of troops near the Ukrainian border, sending soldiers into the country. Putin forbade them from wearing uniforms so that he could deny that he was staging a military occupation. He denied that he sent soldiers to Ukraine and silenced press coverage on the occupation.[746]

After the Russian military was in place, Vladimir Putin annexed Crimea. The international community was outraged. The annexation of Crimea went against the basis and protections provided by international law. In March 2014, voters approved a referendum to annex the Crimean Peninsula to Russia. Of course, the country was under military occupation, so the validity of the referendum was called into question. As for the Ukrainian government, they denied that the referendum was legal. As a result, both the United States and the European Union refused to recognize it. Protestors supporting Ukrainian policies and a pro-Russian government clashed in Ukraine, leaving over one million people dead and displaced.

Today, Russia still controls the Crimean Peninsula. Ukraine demands its return. Ukraine's allies in the EU and the international community support the Crimean Peninsula's return.

---

[745] "Russia: The Putin Presidency." *Encyclopedia Britannica*; Liulevicius, "The Unfolding Ukraine-Russia Crisis." Lecture 23. *The Great Courses: A History of Eastern Europe*, 2015.

[746] "Russia: The Putin Presidency." *Encyclopedia Britannica*; Jenkins, *Short History of Europe*, 2019, pg. 295; Liulevicius, "The Unfolding Ukraine-Russia Crisis." Lecture 23. *The Great Courses: A History of Eastern Europe*, 2015.

Conclusion – Modern Eastern Europe

With the fall of communism, the former Soviet Union broke off into independent states. The denouement of the end of communism changed how Eastern Europeans related to their government. Now, they were ruling themselves. Many of these countries had to make peace with their past, which helped them create a new sense of identity. However, most struggled to make sense of their new world, and this is a prevailing theme we can see in Eastern European politics from the fall of communism to the present day.

The last forty years of Eastern European history are the culmination of decades of repression and foreign rule. Each nation has its own experience with independent self-rule. Some achieved it peacefully, while others suffered violent bloodshed. The nations of Eastern Europe are still dealing with the repercussions of the violence of the past four decades to this day.

Over the course of Eastern European history, not one nation has remained stagnant. States led to empires, empires broke down into states, people migrated, and some left and moved somewhere else. Borders have been redrawn and redrawn again. The story of

Eastern Europe is one of the waxing and waning of territory, control, and power, but it is also a tale of resilience.

Here's another book by
Captivating History that you might like

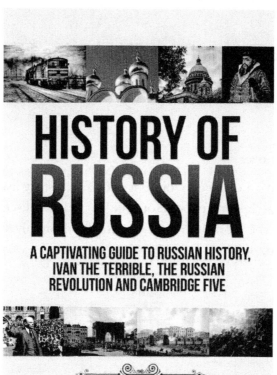

HISTORY OF
RUSSIA

A CAPTIVATING GUIDE TO RUSSIAN HISTORY,
IVAN THE TERRIBLE, THE RUSSIAN
REVOLUTION AND CAMBRIDGE FIVE

CAPTIVATING HISTORY

Free Bonus from Captivating History
(Available for a Limited time)

Hi History Lovers!

Now you have a chance to join our exclusive history list so you can get your first history ebook for free as well as discounts and a potential to get more history books for free! Simply visit the link below to join.

Captivatinghistory.com/ebook

Also, make sure to follow us on Facebook, Twitter and Youtube by searching for Captivating History.

References:

Tomek Jankowski. *Eastern Europe! Everything You Need to Know About the History (and More) of a Region that Shaped Our World and Still Does.* Kindle edition. Williamstown, Massachusetts: New Europe Books, 2013.

Elizabeth A. Kohn, "Rape as a Weapon of War: Women's Human Rights During the Dissolution of Yugoslavia." *Golden Gate University Law Review.* Issue 1: Women's Law Forum. Volume 24. January 1994, 199-200.

Vejas Gabriel Liulevicius. *The Great Courses: A History of Eastern Europe.* Chantilly, VA: The Teaching Company, 2015.

Simon Jenkins. *A Short History of Europe: From Pericles to Putin.* New York: Public Affairs, 2019

Rachel L. Bledsaw, "No Blood in the Water: The Legal and Gender Conspiracies Against Countess Elizabeth Bathory in Historical Context" (2014). Theses and Dissertations. 135.

The following list are internet sources that are a great starting point for further research. We have used them through this text, and we hope you will find even more information on the subjects that interested you in our text.

Francis Tapon. "Eastern Europe: Innovation's Hidden Hub." The Washington Post. December 28, 2011. https://www.washingtonpost.com/national/on-innovations/eastern-europe-innovations-hidden-hub/2011/12/22/gIQAe67DLP_story.html

"Andy Warhol." The Andy Warhol Museum. https://www.warhol.org/andy-warhols-life/

"Franz Liszt." BIOGRAPHY. Updated April 27, 2020. Original April 27, 2017. https://www.biography.com/musician/franz-liszt

"Archaeological Timescale." Encyclopedia Britannica. Revised and updated June 2, 2008. https://www.britannica.com/science/archaeological-timescale

National Science Foundation & University of Wisconsin-Madison, "Isotopic data show farming arrived in Europe with migrants." Proceedings of the National Academy of Sciences, Feb 11, 2013. https://news.wisc.edu/isotopic-data-show-farming-arrived-in-europe-with-migrants/

"The Peloponnesian War." National Geographic. https://www.nationalgeographic.org/encyclopedia/peloponnesian-war/

Guy Thompson Griffith. "Philip II, king of Macedonia." Encyclopedia Britannica. https://www.britannica.com/biography/Philip-II-king-of-Macedonia

Frank W. Walbank. "Alexander the Great, king of Macedonia." Encyclopedia Britannica. https://www.britannica.com/biography/Alexander-the-Great

"Macedonia." HISTORY. Published February 13, 2018. https://www.history.com/topics/ancient-rome/macedonia

Donald L. Wasson. "Wars of the Diadochi." World History Encyclopedia. Published July 14, 2016. https://www.worldhistory.org/Wars_of_the_Diadochi/

Joshua J. Mark. "Ancient Rome." World History Encyclopedia. Published September 2, 2009. https://www.worldhistory.org/Rome/

Andrews, Evan. "6 Civil Wars That Transformed Ancient Rome." HISTORY. Published August 28, 2015. https://www.history.com/news/6-civil-wars-that-transformed-ancient-rome

"Julius Caesar." HISTORY. Published November 4, 2019. https://www.history.com/topics/ancient-history/julius-caesar

Roman Empire: Julius Caesar - Master of Rome. Netflix documentary, 2019.

Donald L. Wasson. "First Triumvirate." World History Encyclopedia. Published March 20, 2016. https://www.worldhistory.org/First_Triumvirate/

Mark Cartwright. "Marcus Licinius Crassus." World History Encyclopedia. Published November 5, 2013. https://www.worldhistory.org/Marcus_Licinius_Crassus/

Patrick Scott Smith. "Parthia (Empire)." World History Encyclopedia. Published July 22, 2019. https://www.worldhistory.org/Parthia_(Empire)/

Joshua J. Mark. "Augustus." New World Encyclopedia. Published May 4, 2018. https://www.worldhistory.org/augustus/

Frederik Pohl. "Tiberius." Encyclopedia Britannica. https://www.britannica.com/biography/Tiberius

"Caligula. Encyclopedia Britannica. https://www.britannica.com/biography/Caligula-Roman-emperor

Mason Hammond. "Trajan." Encyclopedia Britannica. https://www.britannica.com/biography/Trajan

John Anthony Crook. "Marcus Aurelius." Encyclopedia Britannica. https://www.britannica.com/biography/Marcus-Aurelius-Roman-emperor

Cristian Violatti. "Slavs." World History Encyclopedia. Published September 10, 2014. https://www.worldhistory.org/Slavs/

"Lothar I." Encyclopedia Britannica.
https://www.britannica.com/biography/Lothar-I

"Wenceslas I." Encyclopedia Britannica.
https://www.britannica.com/biography/Wenceslas-I-prince-of-Bohemia

"Boleslav I." Encyclopedia Britannica.
https://www.britannica.com/biography/Boleslav-I

"Khazars." The Jewish Virtual Library.
https://www.jewishvirtuallibrary.org/khazars

Mark Cartwright. "Teutonic Knight." World History Encyclopedia.
Published July 11, 2018.
https://www.worldhistory.org/Teutonic_Knight/

John R. Lampe. "Bosnia and Herzegovina." Encyclopedia
Britannica. https://www.britannica.com/place/Bosnia-and-Herzegovina

"Wenceslas, king of Bohemia and Germany." Encyclopedia
Britannica. https://www.britannica.com/biography/Wenceslas

Milan Hauner. "Czechoslovak History: The Hussite Wars."
Encyclopedia Britannica.
https://www.britannica.com/topic/Czechoslovak-history/The-Hussite-wars

Nicholas A. Vardy. "Hungary: The Period of Partition."
Encyclopedia Britannica.
https://www.britannica.com/place/Hungary/The-period-of-partition

Hugh Seton-Watson. "Russia." Encyclopedia Britannica.
https://www.britannica.com/place/Russia

"Russia: The Putin Presidency." Encyclopedia Britannica.
https://www.britannica.com/place/Russia/The-Putin-presidency

"Ivan the Terrible." Encyclopedia Britannica.
https://www.britannica.com/biography/Ivan-the-Terrible

"Mindaugas." Encyclopedia Britannica.
https://www.britannica.com/biography/Mindaugas

"Jagiellon dynasty." Encyclopedia Britannica.
https://www.britannica.com/topic/Jagiellon-dynasty

"Sigismund II Augustus." Encyclopedia Britannica.
https://www.britannica.com/biography/Sigismund-II-Augustus

"Thirty Years' War." HISTORY. Published November 9, 2009.
Last Updated August 21, 2018.
https://www.history.com/topics/reformation/thirty-years-war

"Stephen Báthory." Encyclopedia Britannica.
https://www.britannica.com/biography/Stephen-Bathory

"John II Casimir Vasa." Encyclopedia Britannica.
https://www.britannica.com/biography/John-II-Casimir-Vasa

"John III Sobieski." Encyclopedia Britannica.
https://www.britannica.com/biography/John-III-Sobieski

"Siege of Vienna, 1683." Encyclopedia Britannica.
https://www.britannica.com/event/Siege-of-Vienna-1683

"Phanariote." Encyclopedia Britannica.
https://www.britannica.com/topic/Phanariote

"History of Montenegro." Encyclopedia Britannica.
https://www.britannica.com/place/Montenegro/History

"Janissary." Encyclopedia Britannica.
https://www.britannica.com/topic/Janissary

"Mehmed IV." Encyclopedia Britannica.
https://www.britannica.com/biography/Mehmed-IV

"Treaty of Carlowitz." Encyclopedia Britannica.
https://www.britannica.com/event/Treaty-of-Carlowitz

"Poland: Augustus II." Encyclopedia Britannica.
https://www.britannica.com/place/Poland/Augustus-II

"Battle of Zenta." Encyclopedia Britannica.
https://www.britannica.com/event/Battle-of-Zenta

"War of the Austrian Succession." Encyclopedia Britannica.
https://www.britannica.com/event/War-of-the-Austrian-Succession

"Prussia." Encyclopedia Britannica. https://www.britannica.com/place/Prussia

"Prussia.eu - The Official Site of the House of Hohenzollern." https://www.preussen.de/en/

"Second Northern War." Encyclopedia Britannica. https://www.britannica.com/event/Second-Northern-War

"Catherine I." Encyclopedia Britannica. https://www.britannica.com/biography/Catherine-I

"Anna, empress of Russia," Encyclopedia Britannica. https://www.britannica.com/biography/Anna-empress-of-Russia

"Elizabeth, empress of Russia." Encyclopedia Britannica. https://www.britannica.com/biography/Elizabeth-empress-of-Russia

"Catherine the Great." Encyclopedia Britannica. https://www.britannica.com/biography/Catherine-the-Great

"Crimean War." HISTORY. Published November 9, 2009. https://www.history.com/topics/british-history/crimean-war

"Balkan Wars." Encyclopedia Britannica. https://www.britannica.com/topic/Balkan-Wars

"November Insurrection." Encyclopedia Britannica. https://www.britannica.com/event/November-Insurrection

"January Insurrection." Encyclopedia Britannica. https://www.britannica.com/event/January-Insurrection

"Pan-Slavism." Encyclopedia Britannica. https://www.britannica.com/event/Pan-Slavism

"The German Spring Offensive: The Kaiser's Battle." Sir John Monash Centre. Australian National Memorial France. Published March 5, 2018. https://sjmc.gov.au/german-spring-offensives-kaiserschlact-kaisers-battle/

"June 4, 1916: Brusilov Offensive Begins." HISTORY. Published October 28, 2009. https://www.history.com/this-day-in-history/brusilov-offensive-begins

"Yugoslavia." World War II Database. https://ww2db.com/country/Yugoslavia

"The Siege of Leningrad." HISTORY. https://www.history.com/news/the-siege-of-leningrad

"Reinhard Heydrich." Jewish Virtual Library. https://www.jewishvirtuallibrary.org/reinhard-heydrich-bio

"Historical Background: The Jews of Hungary During the Holocaust." Yad Vashem: The World Holocaust Remembrance Center. https://www.yadvashem.org/articles/general/jews-of-hungary-during-the-holocaust.html

"Warsaw Ghetto Uprising." HISTORY. Published November 6, 2009. https://www.history.com/topics/world-war-ii/warsaw-ghetto-uprising

"Yalta Conference." HISTORY. November 4, 2019. https://www.history.com/topics/world-war-ii/yalta-conference

"Prague Spring." Encyclopedia Britannica. https://www.britannica.com/event/Prague-Spring

"Vaira Vike Freiberga." Columbia World Leaders Forum. https://worldleaders.columbia.edu/directory/vaira-vike-freiberga

"Valdas Adamkus." Encyclopedia Britannica. https://www.britannica.com/biography/Valdas-Adamkus

"Toomas Hendrik Ilves." Columbia World Leaders Forum. https://worldleaders.columbia.edu/directory/toomas-hendrik-ilves

Martina Petkova. "The Last Living Tsar and His Tango with Democracy." History of Yesterday. Published August 20, 2020. https://historyofyesterday.com/the-last-living-tsar-and-his-tango-with-democracy-edb7c76aa01a

"Czechoslovak history." Encyclopedia Britannica. https://www.britannica.com/topic/Czechoslovak-history

Richard Nelsson. "Czechoslovakia's Velvet Revolution - archive, November 1989." The Guardian.

https://www.theguardian.com/world/from-the-archive-blog/2019/nov/13/czechoslovakia-velvet-revolution-november-1989

Cheryl Teh. "Who is Alexander Lukashenko? A closer look at the dictator who has maintained an iron grip on Belarus for over 2 decades." INSIDER. August 3, 2021. https://www.businessinsider.com/who-is-alexander-lukashenko-closer-look-at-the-belarusian-dictator-2021-5

"Belarus ignoring risks of farming near Chernobyl?" CBS News. April 25, 2016. https://www.cbsnews.com/news/chernobyl-radiation-belarus-farm-produce-milk-high-level-radiation/

Vladimir Isachenkov, Alex Schuller. "Belarus Olympic runner who feared going home lands in Poland." Associated Press/ABC News. August 4, 2021. https://abcnews.go.com/Sports/wireStory/belarus-runner-flies-europe-feud-team-managers-79259922

"The Conflicts." International Criminal Tribunal for the Former Yugoslavia. https://www.icty.org/en/about/what-former-yugoslavia/conflicts

"Top 10 Facts About the Kosovo War." The Borgen Project. https://borgenproject.org/the-kosovo-war/

"Slovenia." Encyclopedia Britannica. https://www.britannica.com/place/Slovenia

"Bosnia and Herzegovina." Encyclopedia Britannica. https://www.britannica.com/place/Bosnia-and-Herzegovina

"Srebenica massacre." Encyclopedia Britannica. https://www.britannica.com/event/Srebrenica-massacre

Julian Borger. "Ratko Mladić: life in prison is as close to justice as his victims will get." The Guardian. June 8, 2021. https://www.theguardian.com/world/2021/jun/08/ratko-mladic-life-in-prison-is-as-close-to-justice-as-his-victims-will-get

"DNA from Srebrenica women." The New York Times. https://www.nytimes.com/2000/07/07/opinion/IHT-dna-from-srebrenicas-women.html

"NATO's role in relation to the conflict in Kosovo." NATO. https://www.nato.int/kosovo/history.htm

"North Macedonia." Encyclopedia Britannica. https://www.britannica.com/place/North-Macedonia

Alek Vasilevski. "Macedonia 2001: Uncovering the Truth." UMD Voice. April 13, 2017. https://www.umdgenm.org/2017/04/13/macedonia-2001-uncovering-the-truth/

Justin Fishel. "Inside the Russian Hacking Scandal and Trump's Election." ABC News. December 12, 2016. https://abcnews.go.com/Politics/inside-russian-hacking-scandal-trumps-election/story?id=44143340

Alan Yuhas and Raya Jalabi. "Ukraine's revolution and Russia's occupation of Crimea: How we got here." The Guardian. March 5, 2014. https://www.theguardian.com/world/2014/mar/05/ukraine-russia-explainer

"Ukraine: The Cossacks." Encyclopedia Britannica. https://www.britannica.com/place/Ukraine/The-Cossacks

Alex Gendler. "A Day in the Life of a Cossack Soldier." *TED-Ed.* August 2019.

"Winston Churchill's Iron Curtain Speech—March 5, 1946." *National World War II Museum.* March 5, 2021. https://www.nationalww2museum.org/war/articles/winston-churchills-iron-curtain-speech-march-5-1946

"Hungarian Revolution, 1956." *Encyclopedia Britannica.* https://www.britannica.com/event/Hungarian-Revolution-1956

"Four Power Status and Reconstruction of Berlins (1945-1950s)." *Visit Berlin.* https://www.visitberlin.de/en/four-power-status-and-reconstruction-berlins-1945-1950s

"The Cuban Missile Crisis, October 1962." The Office of the Historian, Department of State Archives. https://history.state.gov/milestones/1961-1968/cuban-missile-crisis

"Treaty on the Non-Proliferation of Nuclear Weapons."
Encyclopedia Britannica. https://www.britannica.com/event/Treaty-on-the-Non-proliferation-of-Nuclear-Weapons

"Reagan and Gorbachev: The Geneva Summit." Atomic Heritage Foundation. July 26, 2018.
https://www.atomicheritage.org/history/reagan-and-gorbachev-geneva-summit

"Reagan and Gorbachev: The Reykjavik Summit." *Atomic Heritage Foundation.* August 7, 2018.
https://www.atomicheritage.org/history/reagan-and-gorbachev-reykjavik-summit

Made in the USA
Middletown, DE
29 June 2022

68037965R00205